THE
COMPLETE
BOOK OF
MICROWAVE
COOKERY

THE COMPLETE BOOK OF MICROWAVE COOKERY

Sonia Allison

Edited by Carolyn Humphries

foulsham
LONDON • NEW YORK • TORONTO • SYDNEY

foulsham

The Publishing House
Bennetts Close, Cippenham, Berkshire SL1 5AP

ISBN 0-572-02135-6

CONTENTS

Acknowledgements and thanks to:

Anchor Dairy Products

Billingtons Sugars

Butterball Turkey Products

Button Geese

Buxted Chicken Products

Brittany Artichokes

Cadbury-Schweppes

Campbell's Soups

Central Bureau of Fruit & Vegetable Auctions in Holland

Colman's Products

Cherry Valley Duckling

Corningware/Pyrex

Dairy Crest Products

Daregal Quick Frozen Herbs

Davis Gelatine

Elsenham Foods

Iceland Foods

Kraft Foods

Lakeland Plastics

Magimix

Bernard Matthews Turkey Products

Scottish Salmon Information Service

Sharp Microwave Ovens

Suchard Chocolate

Schwarz Herbs & Spices

Tate & Lyle

INTRODUCTION

Since the mid-seventies, microwave cooking has become part and parcel of my busy everyday life and given me more flexibility and freedom in and out of the kitchen than I ever imagined possible. Speedy, cool, hygienic, reliable and undemanding, the microwave works like a charm, cooks like a dream and uses only sparing amounts of electricity, a major consideration in times of rising energy costs and the need to make savings where we can.

It is an accepted fact that microwave ovens cannot replace, in toto, conventional ovens and hobs but they do go a long way towards it. Used to full capacity, a microwave can become the most efficient, valued and respected piece of equipment in your kitchen, and my intention in writing this book is to put together a package of innovative recipes in addition to old favourites, proving that a wide range of dishes can be microwaved successfully. In some cases, I've given an alternative method of cooking some of the ingredients used in a specific recipe to save time. In others, I've suggested finishing off a dish under the grill to crisp skin or brown a topping. In these instances, your microwave will work in perfect harmony with your conventional oven.

I have to admit that some recipes are not at their best if given the microwave treatment. Yorkshire pudding collapses. Pancakes fare no better though reheat to perfection. Soufflés and eclairs fail with irritating predictability. Meringues just about work but take so long, you might just as well bake them conventionally and have done with it. And deep frying is taboo because it is impossible to control the temperature of the fat or oil.

Many people still regard the microwave as something to use strictly for defrosting and reheating. A pity, because they're missing out. Others grow to love it and soon come to understand and appreciate its seemingly magical properties ... Over to you.

GUIDE TO MICROWAVE COOKING

What are Microwaves?

Based on the principle of radar, microwaves are a form of energy which are electro-magnetic, short-length, non-ionising, high frequency radio waves at the top end of the radio band. They are close to infra-red rays but not as powerful, and the frequency is 2450MHz or megahertz which literally translates into millions of cycles or vibrations per second. The word 'hertz' comes from Heinrich Hertz, the scientist who first discovered the nature of the waves.

Inside the cavity of a microwave oven, with its extraordinary number of compulsory cut-outs and safety devices, the microwaves are completely confined and will be unable to leak out and attack you. In any event, microwaves are a different kettle of fish altogether from X-rays, Gamma-rays and ultra-violet rays which are ionising and known to cause dangerous cellular alterations to the body with minimal or no temperature change. Microwaves have none of these effects and, more importantly, are non-cumulative. Leaks, when and if they occur, will do so only if the oven is worn, damaged or mishandled and for safety reasons, it should be checked from time to time by a qualified engineer to make sure the door fits snugly, the seal around the door is secure, and the hinges are not rusty. If the door front fractures, stop using the oven at once and request a service call as soon as possible. What would happen if one were, briefly, exposed to microwaves? The answer is a burn which is never pleasant. Therefore look after the oven, keep it serviced and clean it regularly.

How Microwaves cook food

When the microwave is plugged into a socket, the door closed and the oven switched on, microwaves are emitted from a magnetron (or microwave energy generator), usually towards the top of the oven and placed to one side. The magnetron is protected by a cover, generally plastic. The microwaves are transmitted into the inside of the oven cavity down a channel called a waveguide, bounce off the sides, and 'beam' on to the food from all directions. Instantaneously, the food absorbs the microwaves which in turn

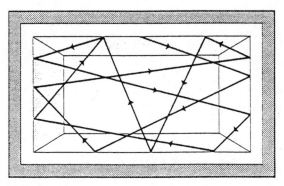

Microwaves deflecting in an oven

cause the water molecules within the food itself to vibrate frantically. The result is excessively rapid friction which creates enough heat to cook food fast and furiously, effectively and cleanly. For a simple comparison of how friction makes heat, rub your hands together vigorously and feel how warm they become. Now multiply this umpteen times and you will understand how the microwaves work. For even cooking, most models are fitted with what is called either a wave stirrer, stirrer blade or paddle (invisible and again at the top) which helps to distribute the waves. Most have a round and rotating turntable as well. Turntables do restrict the shape and size of the dishes to some extent and therefore consider a model where the turntable can be switched off or removed if necessary. (But you will have to turn dishes regularly during cooking if not using the turntable.)

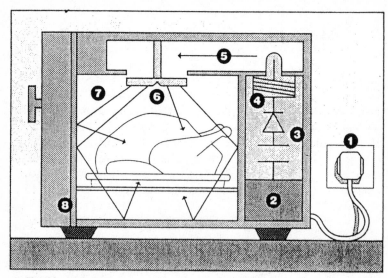

1. *Flexible cord;* 2. *Power transformer;* 3. *High voltage rectifier and capacitor;* 4. *Magnetron;* 5. *Waveguide;* 6. *Wave stirrer (paddle);* 7. *Oven cavity;* 8. *Oven door and frame with special seals.*

Successful Cooking

Because microwaves are short-length, high-frequency radio waves, they are able to penetrate only 1 inch (2.5 cm) of the food in all directions. Thus **shallow dishes** are better than deep ones, except those used for some cakes and puddings which need headroom in order rise satisfactorily. **Round dishes** give the most satisfactory results, followed by **oval**. Sometimes food in oblong or square dishes cooks unevenly, especially at the corners. The food will also cook more satisfactorily if **thick pieces** are placed towards the **outside edges of the dish** and **not** piled up. **Stirring** during the cooking cycle helps to distribute heat and, where practical, this has been recommended in the recipes. If possible, **whole potatoes** and other similar-shaped foods (apples for example) should be arranged, on a plate or in a dish, in the shape of a **hollow triangle, square or ring**. Most microwave ovens are now fitted with a turntable. If yours is an older model without one, make sure you turn dishes several times during cooking.

Resting and Standing Times

In order for heat to penetrate the food and work its way gently from the outside to the centre, it is recommended that the food be allowed to **rest or stand after or between cooking.** Individual recipes will specify. If some dishes were cooked without a rest (and this applies especially to large quantities, turkeys, etc.), the outside would become overdone and the middle remain underdone. Depending on what is more convenient, food may be left to rest or stand inside or outside the microwave. **As a further precaution,** it is advisable to undercook a dish and return it briefly to the oven if necessary, rather than add extra time for 'good measure'. The microwaves act so swiftly that even a few seconds too many could sometimes spoil the food.

Seasonings

As salt tends to toughen meat, poultry and vegetables cooked in a microwave, it should be added half way through the cooking cycle or at the very end. Other seasonings, such as herbs and spices, may be added at the beginning.

Caution

Never operate the oven while empty because without food or liquid to absorb the microwaves, they will bounce straight back to the magnetron and shorten its life span. Similarly, melting 1 or 2 teaspoons of fat, or heating a tiny amount of liquid, will have the same effect, so it is best to place a cup or tumbler of water into the oven at the same time. Just in case an empty oven gets switched on by accident, it is a wise safety measure to **keep a container of water inside until the oven is needed for cooking.**

To Clean

Suggestions for cleaning have been given in the Hints and Tips Section on page 308. As fresh food spills are so easy to remove from the cool interior of a microwave (nothing burns on in the conventional sense), a wipe over with a damp cloth immediately after use will ensure that it stays spotless and fresh.

Selection of microwave containers

Cookware

Metal containers reflect microwaves away from the food and prevent it from cooking. Therefore **never use metal containers or tins** of any sort in the oven. It is also important to note that crockery with metal trims, and manufacturers' names or pattern designs printed in gold or silver underneath, could cause arcing which resemble tiny flashes of lightning. The arcing not only damages the magnetron but also ruins the metallic decorations. The exceptions here are small amounts of foil used to cover poultry wing tips and ends of legs to prevent scorching; also metal skewers for kebabs which are well covered by the surrounding food. However, **ensure** that the skewers do not come into direct contact with any part of the oven interior.

In order for the microwaves to reach the food and subsequently cook it, the dishes chosen should be made of materials through which the microwaves can pass most readily – like sun rays through a window pane. These are listed below and although most stay cool and even cold, some kinds absorb heat from the cooked food and feel hot to the touch. For comfort, the cookware should be removed from the oven with oven gloves.

BASKETS

These may be used for **brief** reheating of rolls, etc. Prolonged spells in the microwave cause dryness and cracking.

CLING FILM (See-through plastic wrap)

Excellent for covering and lining dishes. To prevent the film from ballooning up in the oven and bursting, or being sucked back on to the food (the latter is a disaster if this happens to a pudding which is supposed to rise), I have recommended puncturing the film twice with the tip of a knife to allow steam to escape. By puncturing, I mean a small slit and not a tiny pin-prick.

GLASS

Not your best crystal but Pyrex-type glassware is ideal. Corningware, which is ceramic glass, is also excellent. Other, sturdy, glass may also be used.

Metal reflects

Ceramics transmit

Food absorbs

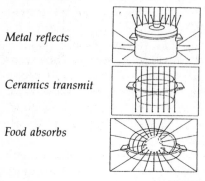

PAPER

Kitchen paper or serviettes may be used to line the oven base if food is to be cooked directly on it (it is a great absorber), and also to cover food to prevent spluttering.

PLASTIC

Use rigid plastic only to prevent collapse, and **not** empty yoghurt or cottage cheese containers. Look for special microwave utensils made by firms like Lakeland Plastics or other reliable makes stocked by specialist kitchen shops, supermarkets and departmental stores. Note that plastic spatulas are useful in that they can be left, say in a sauce while it is cooking and then used for stirring as and when required.

POTTERY AND PORCELAIN

Both may be used but not a best tea or dinner set. Avoid dark utensils and ironstone pottery as they become very hot and take heat away from the food or liquid.

ROASTING BAGS (also called Boiling Bags)

With a hundred and one uses, see-through plastic roasting bags are convenient to use and also clean. Ideal for cooking joints of meat or poultry, close the tops with elastic bands or string, **not** metal ties.

WAXED PAPER PRODUCTS

Rather like basketware, these should be used **very briefly** or the wax will begin to melt.

WOOD

Wood, like basketware, dries out in the microwave and should be used only for brief reheating.

Extras

BROWNING DISH

This is a white ceramic dish, the base of which is coated with a special tin oxide material. It becomes very hot indeed when preheated, making it possible to sear food prior to cooking in the microwave. This gives the food a brown finish associated with conventional grilling or frying. As the dish needs to be preheated, empty, for varying lengths of time (depending on the food being cooked), be guided by your own microwave oven instruction book. As a general rule, the preheating time should be around 6 minutes for steaks and chops and 2 to 3 minutes for eggs. It should **never** be preheated for longer than 8 minutes, nor used in a conventional oven. Every time a batch of food has been cooked, the browning dish will need cleaning and preheating again but for **half the length of time allowed initially.** Although it will take on a yellowy tinge when hot, the dish will return to its original colour when cool. Preheating this type of dish does not harm the oven.

TEMPERATURE PROBE and THERMOMETERS

This looks like a thick knitting needle attached to a plastic-coated lead and is generally available with the more sophisticated models of microwave ovens. One end slots into the side of the oven while the other end (the needle part) is inserted into the food to be cooked and registers the internal temperature.

The cooking cycle is therefore geared to temperature and not time and when, for example, a joint of well-done beef registers 160°F (71°C), the oven will switch off automatically. As every make of cooker varies, please refer to your own microwave book before using the probe and setting the temperature.

Thermometers for use in microwave ovens are now obtainable and they, too, must be used according to the manufacturers' instructions. Never use a conventional meat thermometer in a microwave (although it can be used to test the meat for doneness when the joint is resting **after** cooking).

TIP FOR PROBE: *The temperature given above is just one example. Pork requires a higher internal temperature; rare beef a lower one.*

Choice of Microwave Ovens

People ask me, often, which model I would recommend and I always find this a difficult question to answer. Those who are non-technically minded will be best off with a fairly basic model which does its job efficiently and is, additionally, straightforward to operate. Others, who are into electronics, will find the new models a joy in that they bear some relation to computers and can be easily programmed and manipulated to suit all purposes. The only advice I can give on the selection front is to suggest that you call in at your nearest Electricity Board or departmental store, have a thorough look at as many ovens as you can, and ask for a demonstration. You will then be in a better position to buy what suits you, not what looks fabulous, is very expensive and turns out to be more complex to cope with than you bargained for.

Power Controls

Most domestic microwave ovens vary between 500 and 850 watt output.

All recipes in this book have been prepared in a 600 watt output oven using only **two power settings:** HIGH/FULL POWER which is 100% power (600 watts), and DEFROST which is 50% (300 watts). If your oven has a different output, the guide below may prove useful and be warned: if you have a higher wattage output oven, make sure you **do** reduce cooking time and check a little before your calculated cooking time. You can always cook for a few seconds more – you can't take it away.

For a 500/550 watt output oven, **increase** cooking time by about 20%. e.g. 10 minutes becomes 12 minutes.

A 650 watt output oven will be much the same as a 600 watt one.

For a 700 watt output oven, **decrease** cooking time by about 20%. e.g. 10 minutes becomes 8 minutes.

For a 850 watt output oven, **decrease** cooking time by about 30%. e.g. 10 minutes becomes 7 minutes.

Using these figures will give a fairly accurate conversion time but for greater accuracy, refer to your own microwave oven recipe book. Note that many microwaves call defrost 30% power. Check your manual if yours does and you have a 650 watt or less output microwave, use medium (50%) power for the recipes. If you have a higher output (700-850 watts), use defrost, 30% power.

Variable power settings can range from 1 to 10 although many have settings 1-5 (see figures in brackets on page 20) and are to be found in some of the more technically advanced microwave ovens. The variable settings enable a selection of dishes to be cooked more slowly than others and some users find this advantageous, especially when making stews and casseroles. Some models have a system whereby the power comes on and off automatically. Listen and you can hear it happening. Other models have an automatic reduction in output at the lower settings and this is silent.

Summary of the Settings

Setting 1 (1) equates to 10% of power output and is also termed warm. It is used to keep cooked dishes warm or take the chill off cold ones. It is also called low.

Setting 2 equates to 20% of power output and is recommended for warming or very gentle simmering. It is called either warm or low as well.

Setting 3 (2) equates to 30% of power output and is used for defrosting and simmering. It is called either defrost, medium-low, simmer or soften.

Setting 4 equates to 40% of power output and is often chosen for defrosting, braising and stewing. It is called either slow cook, medium, low defrost, stew, simmer or braise.

Setting 5 (3) equates to 50% of power output and is used for defrosting. It can also be used for simmering and stewing. It is called either medium, defrost, simmer or stew.

Setting 6 equates to 60% of power output and is used chiefly for reheating cooked dishes, baking or simmering. It is called either reheat, bake or simmer.

Setting 7 (4) equates to 70% of power output and is used primarily for roasting. It is called either medium high, bake or roast.

Setting 8 equates to 80% of power output and is also used for reheating and baking. It is called either reheat or bake.

Setting 9 equates to 90% of power output and is used for fast cooking of vegetables in fat (i.e. when making a stew). It is called either medium high, roast, fast reheat or sometimes sautée.

Setting 10 (5) equates to 100% of power output and is used for the majority of recipes in this microwave book. It is called either full power, high, maximum or fast cook.

Even if you have a microwave with variable power settings such as listed above, **do not try** to convert my recipes which were cooked at full or 50% power.

Colour

Microwaved foods can look pale when cooked and also insipid. Hence bastes (see page 75) for roast meat and poultry, a few shakes of soy sauce or a dusting of paprika, brown gravy cubes for stews and casseroles, and icings for cakes. I have also incorporated a number of other tricks – like using Red Leicester cheese instead of Cheddar for toppings – as you will soon find out when you make up some of the recipes in the book. *None* lack colour!

Reheating

Slow reheating of meat and poultry, or keeping plates of food warm in a cool oven, can sometimes cause a build-up of bacteria, resulting in mild food poisoning.

With a microwave oven, the action is so fast that germs have no time to breed, and the food stays fresh and moist without looking frayed round the edges.

Bonuses

Freshness of flavour and colour, plus retention of nutrients, characterise most foods cooked in a microwave oven. The foods also tend to shrink less, and cooking smells do not invade the kitchen or the rest of the house.

It is a consoling thought to know that when cooking in the microwave, the electricity saved is between 50 and 70%. Also no pre-heating is necessary and there is minimal residual heat in the oven cavity. It has been estimated that using a microwave is four times as efficient as conventional cooking because **all** the energy is directed to the food with no 'over-spill'. No more steamy kitchens either!

Notes on the Recipes

1. Measures are given in metric, then Imperial followed by American where necessary. Use one set only in a recipe, do not mix.

2. All spoon measures are level: 1 tsp = 5 ml, 1 tbsp = 15 ml.

3. Wash fresh produce before preparation.

4. Adjust strong flavoured ingredients and seasonings to taste.

5. 'Chopped' or 'sprigs' of herbs refer to fresh. If you substitute dried, halve the amounts.

6. 'Preparation time' at the beginning of each recipe is approximate and includes cooking and standing time but usually not setting or chilling time.

And on a Final Note

Standard recipes are **not** convertible to microwave ovens, so please use only those which have been specifically designed for the appliance – as those in my book. NEVER pre-heat a microwave oven as it is both unnecessary and damaging to the magnetron. Where the letter (F) appears by a recipe title, this indicates the dish is suitable for freezing.

CONVENIENCE FOODS

Microwave Labels

Newer microwave ovens have a symbol on the front which ties in with the new heating instructions on small food packs like ready made meals. Matching the information on the pack with that on the oven will enable you to calculate the heating time required.

The symbol on ovens

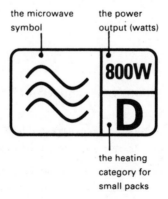

the microwave symbol

the power output (watts)

the heating category for small packs

THE HEATING CATEGORY

Heating categories range from A to E. A is for the lowest wattage ovens (500w), E for the highest (850w). If your oven displays a C, for example, on the label, it will heat more quickly than an A or B category oven, but not as fast as a D or E.

THE FOOD PACK LABEL

Most packaged food suitable for microwaving has a label similar
to the one below.

≋ T O   M I C R O W A V E

For ovens marked with a heating category, select appropriate time(s) for
your oven. For other ovens, refer to timings given for oven wattage. When
using ovens of different power, heating time must be increased or decreased accordingly. Always check that the food is piping hot before serving.

heating category		oven wattage	
B	D	650W	750W
6	5	5	4
m i n u t e s		m i n u t e s	

In the illustration, information is given for B and D category ovens
only.

* For C category ovens, you would need to choose a time midway
between B and D – in this case 5½ minutes.

* For A category ovens, you would need to heat the food for a little
longer than B – in this case 6½ minutes.

* For E category ovens, you would need to heat the food for
slightly less than D – in this case 4½ minutes.

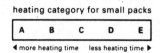

heating category for small packs

A	B	C	D	E

◀ more heating time   less heating time ▶

It also only shows 650w and 750w output. The same thing applies as above. For lower wattage ovens, you will need to add on a proportionate amount of time, for higher ones, decrease the time proportionately.

oven power rating

500W	600W	700W	800W

◀ more heating time   less heating time ▶

ALWAYS CHECK FOOD IS PIPING HOT ALL THE WAY THROUGH BEFORE SERVING.

HELPLINE

If you're at all confused or would like more information, phone the freephone foodline at the Food Safety Advisory Centre.

0800 282407

*Reproduced by permission of MAFF, based on "A Guide to the New Microwave Labels.'

Convenience Foods – Frozen

	DEFROST SETTING	COOK/HEAT FULL POWER	COMMENTS & GUIDELINES
Bacon Rashers (slices)			
225g (8oz)	3 minutes Stand 6 minutes	3 minutes, turn over, cook 2 minutes.	Separate after defrosting. Transfer to a microwave rack over a large plate, arranging rashers in single layer. Cover with kitchen or greaseproof (waxed) paper.
Beefburgers			
2 × 50g (2oz)	2 minutes Stand ½ minute	1½ minutes	Put on a microwave rack over a plate to defrost and cook. Cover with kitchen or greaseproof (waxed) paper. Turn over once during cooking.
4 × 50g (2oz)	3 minutes Stand 1 minute	2½ to 3 minutes	As above
2 × 100g (4oz)	3 minutes Stand 2 minutes	3 minutes	As above.
4 × 100g (4oz)	6 minutes Stand 3 minutes	5½ to 6 minutes	As above.
Beef, roast in gravy			
225g (8oz)	6 minutes Stand 4 minutes	4 minutes	Remove from foil container. Put into glass or pottery dish. Cover with film. Slit twice. Alternatively cover with matching lid.
350g (12oz)	8 minutes Stand 4 minutes	6 minutes	As above.
Bread			
1 slice	20 to 30 seconds Stand 1 minute		Stand on kitchen paper or plate. Time depends on thickness of slice.

	DEFROST SETTING	COOK/HEAT FULL POWER	COMMENTS & GUIDELINES
2 slices	30 to 40 seconds Stand 1 minute		As above.
4 slices	1 to 1½ minutes Stand 1½ to 2 minutes		As above.
6 slices	2 minutes Stand 2 minutes		As above.
Small loaf	4 minutes Stand 5 to 6 minutes		Wrap loaf in kitchen paper.
Large loaf	6 to 8 minutes Stand 8 to 10 minutes		As above.
Bread Rolls 2 rolls	½ to 1 minute		Put on to a plate. Cover with kitchen paper.
Burger Buns 2 buns	½ to 1 minute		Put on to a plate. Cover with kitchen paper.
4 buns	1½ to 2 minutes		As above.
Croissants 2 croissants	½ to 1 minute	½ minute	Put on kitchen paper. Cover with more paper.
4 croissants	1½ to 2 minutes	¾ to 1 minute	As above.
Butter 100g (4oz)	15 seconds Stand 15 seconds 10 seconds Stand 15 seconds		Remove from foil. Put on to plate. Repeat the 10 seconds defrost and 15 seconds standing until thawed. Check often to be sure the butter does not become too soft.
225g (8oz)	30 seconds Stand 30 seconds 15 seconds Stand 30 seconds		As above.

	DEFROST SETTING	COOK/HEAT FULL POWER	COMMENTS & GUIDELINES
Cakes and Puddings			
Cake 1 slice	¾ minute to 1¼ minutes		Put on kitchen paper or plate. Time to defrost will depend on size of slice.
Cream cake/Pastry Individual	¾ minute Stand 3 minutes		Put on kitchen paper or plate.
Cream sponge 275g (10oz)	1 to 1½ minutes Stand 20 to 25 minutes		Put on kitchen paper or plate. Stand until cream thaws through.
3 Layer cake 475g (17oz)	1 to 1½ minutes Stand 2 to 3 minutes		Put on to a plate.
Cheesecake 275g (10 oz)	1½ to 2½ minutes Stand 10 minutes		Remove from foil container. Place on kitchen paper or plate.
475-525g (17-19oz)	2 to 4 minutes Stand 10 to 15 minutes		As above.
Doughnut, cream 1 doughnut	30 seconds Stand 4 minutes		Put on kitchen paper or plate. Check that cream is not melting too fast.
2 doughnuts	45 seconds Stand 5 minutes		As above.
4 doughnuts	¾ to 1 minute Stand 8 minutes		As above.
Doughnut, jam 1 doughnut	½ to 1 minute Stand 3 minutes		Put on kitchen paper or plate.
2 doughnuts	1 minute Stand 5 minutes		As above.
4 doughnuts	1 to 1½ minutes Stand 8 minutes		As above.
Cannelloni			
400g (14oz)	7 minutes Stand 4 minutes	5 to 6 minutes	Remove from foil container and place in a similar-sized dish. Cover with film and slit twice.

	DEFROST SETTING	COOK/HEAT FULL POWER	COMMENTS & GUIDELINES
Chicken, coated and fried (pre-cooked)			
2 to 3 pieces 200-250g (7-9oz)	4 minutes Stand 4 minutes	2 to 3 minutes Stand 2 to 3 minutes	Separate and arrange on plate or dish with thickest pieces round edge. Cover with kitchen paper. Halfway through cooking time, re-arrange the pieces and re-cover.
4 pieces 350g (12oz)	6 minutes Stand 4 minutes	3 to 4 minutes Stand 2 to 3 minutes	As above.
5-7 pieces 450g (1lb)	8 minutes Stand 6 minutes	6 to 8 minutes Stand 3 to 4 minutes	As above.
Chicken Cordon Bleu 350g (12oz)	4 minutes Stand 4 minutes	6 minutes	Remove wrapping and put on to plate. Cover with kitchen paper.
Chicken Kiev 350g (12oz)	As above	As above	As above. **Note:** all crumb-coated portions can be crisped under a hot grill after cooking.
Chipolatas			
225g (8oz)	3 minutes Stand 2 minutes	3 minutes	Stand on kitchen paper or a microwave rack on a plate. Cover with greaseproof (waxed) or kitchen paper.
450g/1lb	5 minutes Stand 3 minutes	4½ minutes	As above.
Cottage/Shepherd's Pie			
Individual	3 minutes Stand 2 minutes	3 minutes	If in foil, remove to plate or dish and cover with lid or kitchen paper.
450g (1lb)	8 minutes Stand 4 minutes	7 minutes	Remove from foil and place in a similar-sized dish. Cover with film and slit twice. Alternatively, cover with matching lid.

	DEFROST SETTING	COOK/HEAT FULL POWER	COMMENTS & GUIDELINES
Cream 300 ml (1/2 pt/1 1/4 cups)	1 1/2 minutes Stand 5 minutes 1/2 minute Stand 2 minutes Repeat until almost thawed		Place in a bowl and break up with fork while thawing. If in carton, remove lid. Transfer to bowl as soon as cream can be removed easily. Don't overheat! Best to let last ice crystals melt naturally.
Eclairs – Chocolate 4	1 to 1 1/2 minutes Stand 15 to 20 minutes		Stand on kitchen paper on a plate. Check to make sure cream does not melt too quickly or it will run.
Faggots in sauce 4, total weight 375 g (13 oz)	3 minutes Stand 3 minutes	4 1/2 to 5 minutes	Remove from foil container and put into dish. Cover with film and slit twice. Alternatively, cover with matching lid. When faggots have defrosted, uncover and arrange round edge of dish to cook. Re-cover as above.
6, total weight 500 g (18 oz)	5 minutes Stand 5 minutes	7 to 9 minutes	As above.
Fish Cakes 4	3 minutes Stand 2 minutes	1 1/2 to 2 minutes	Put on to plate. Cover with kitchen paper. Turn over at half time during defrosting.
Fish Fingers 4	2 minutes Stand 1 minute	2 minutes	Put on to plate. Cover with kitchen paper. Turn over half way through cooking time.
8	4 minutes Stand 2 minutes	2 minutes	As above.

	DEFROST SETTING	COOK/HEAT FULL POWER	COMMENTS & GUIDELINES
Fish in Sauce, cod, plaice, etc (boil-in-bag)			
1 × 175g (6oz)	4 to 4½ minutes Stand 2 minutes	2½ to 3 minutes	Put on to a plate. Make a slit with scissors in a
2 × 175g (12oz)		4½ to 5 minutes	corner of each bag. This is necessary as the bag might
	6 to 6½ minutes Stand 2 minutes		balloon up and burst. Do not cook more than one bag at a time because the sauce heats up faster than the fish and may seep out, on the longer time, before the fish is cooked. After cooking, the sauce will be hot, so carefully cut along slit end of bag and slide fish and sauce on to same plate.
Fruit Juice, to soften			
175ml/6floz/¾cup	3 minutes		Remove lid. Stand upright on kitchen paper. If metal top and bottom, or if container has a metallic lining, soften block of juice by running under warm water then transfer to jug or bowl to defrost. Break up as soon as possible and stir frequently to thaw fast.
Haddock, buttered, smoked			
200g (7oz)	4 minutes Stand 4 minutes	4 minutes	Put on to plate. Make a slit with scissors in a corner of the bag so that the bag will not balloon up and burst. After cooking the butter will be hot, so carefully cut along slit end of bag and slide fish and butter gently on to same plate.

	DEFROST SETTING	COOK/HEAT FULL POWER	COMMENTS & GUIDELINES
Ice Cream, to soften			
1 litre (1¾ pt · 4½ cups)	30 to 45 seconds		Leave, covered, in original container. Check every 10 seconds that not melting.
Kippers, fillets with butter in bag			
175-225 g (6-8 oz)	4 minutes Stand 2 minutes	2 to 3 minutes	Put on to a plate. Make a slit with scissors in a corner of the bag so that the bag will not balloon up and burst. After cooking, the butter will be hot so carefully cut along the slit end of the bag and slide fish and butter gently on to same plate.
275 g (10 oz)	6 minutes Stand 2 minutes	5 minutes	As above.
Lasagne			
450 g (1 lb)	8 minutes Stand 4 minutes	6 minutes	Remove from foil container and place in a similar-sized dish. Cover with matching lid or cling film and slit twice.
Mackerel, smoked fillets (2)			
to serve cold 225 g (8 oz)	2 to 2½ minutes Stand 2 to 3 minutes		Put on to plate and cover with kitchen paper.
to serve hot 225 g (8 oz)	2 to 2½ minutes Stand 2 to 3 minutes	2 to 3 minutes	As above.
Mackerel, buttered smoked fillets (boil-in-bag)			
175 g (6 oz)	4 minutes Stand 2 minutes	3 minutes	Put on to a plate. Make a slit with scissors in a corner of the bag so that the bag will not balloon up and burst. After cooking, the butter will be hot, so carefully cut along the slit end of the bag and slide fish and butter gently on to same plate.

	DEFROST SETTING	COOK/HEAT FULL POWER	COMMENTS & GUIDELINES
Moussaka 400g (14oz)	7 minutes Stand 4 minutes	5 to 6 minutes	Remove from foil container and place in a similar-sized dish. Cover with film and slit twice. Alternatively, cover with matching lid.
Mousse, individual	30 seconds Stand 15 minutes		Remove lid.
Oven Chips 225g (8oz)		2½ minutes and rearrange. 2½ minutes Stand 3 minutes	Arrange in a single layer on 10inch (25cm) plate. Cover with kitchen paper. Flash briefly under a hot grill, turning once, to crisp if liked instead of standing time. First remove paper.
Pancakes 4 filled	5 minutes	1½ to 2 minutes	Put on to plate. Cover with kitchen paper.
Pastry (pie crust) – raw 397g (14oz)	2 minutes		Stand 5-10 minutes until soft enough to roll out.
Pâté 1 portion	2 to 2½ minutes Stand 5 to 10 minutes		Transfer to plate and cover with kitchen paper. Take care not to heat.
Pizza 12.5cm (5inch) 200g (7oz)	2 minutes Stand 2 minutes	2 minutes	Snip wrapping after defrosting and before cooking/heating or remove completely according to packet instructions.
18cm (7inch) 250-275g (9-10oz)	3 minutes Stand 2 minutes	2½ minutes	As above.
Pizza, French Bread 2 pieces	2 minutes Stand 2 minutes	2 minutes	As above.

	DEFROST SETTING	COOK/HEAT FULL POWER	COMMENTS & GUIDELINES
Pizza Buns, 2 buns	1 minute Stand 1½ minutes	2 minutes	As above. NOTE: If any of the above are not wrapped top and bottom, stand on a plate and cover with kitchen paper while defrosting and cooking/heating.
Plate Meal home-prepared and frozen	1 minute Stand 5 minutes	4½-5 minutes	If covered with cling film, slit twice before defrosting and cooking. If not, cover with kitchen paper.
Pork Pies individual	2 minutes Stand 15 minutes		Place paper on a plate. Do not overheat or jelly will melt.
Prepared Meals (Shop bought) e.g. Sweet and Sour Chicken			
175 to 225g (6 to 8oz)	3 to 4 minutes Stand 3 minutes	3 to 4 minutes	Remove from container and put into suitable dish. Cover with film and slit twice. Alternatively, cover with matching lid. Stir before serving.
Salmon smoked in a pack 200g (7oz), sliced	45 seconds Stand 25 to 30 minutes		Turn over after 20 seconds defrosting. Take care not to heat.
Sausage Rolls, cooked			
1	45 seconds Stand 2 minutes	15 seconds	Stand on kitchen paper on a plate. Cover with more paper.
4	1½ to 2 minutes Stand 3 minutes	45 seconds	As above.
Sausages, large (6 to 450g (1lb))			
2 sausages	1½ minutes Stand 2 minutes	3½ minutes	Stand on kitchen paper or a microwave rack on plate. Brush with a baste (page 75). Cover with grease-proof or microwave dome. Alternatively use a browning dish for best results.

	DEFROST SETTING	COOK/HEAT FULL POWER	COMMENTS & GUIDELINES
4 sausages	2 minutes Stand 2 minutes	5 minutes	As above.
medium, (8 to 450g (1lb))			
2 sausages	1½ minutes Stand 1 minute	2½ minutes	As above.
4 sausages	2 minutes Stand 2 minutes	3½ minutes	As above.
Sausages, cocktail or chipolatas			
225g (8oz)	3 minutes Stand 2 minutes	3 minutes	As for large sausages above.
450g (1lb)	5 minutes Stand 3 minutes	4½ minutes	As above.
TRIFLES, individual			
(Shop-bought)	1 to 2 minutes Stand 5 minutes		Remove lid.
Waffles			
2		1 to 2 minutes Stand 2 minutes	Place on kitchen paper, cover with more paper. Flash under a hot grill to crisp if liked.
Yoghurt			
individual	2 to 3 minutes Stand 5 minutes		Remove lid. Stir before serving.

Convenience Foods – Canned

	COOK/HEAT FULL POWER	COMMENTS & GUIDELINES
Casserole, soya-type chunks or meat		
439g (15½oz)	4 minutes Stand 2 minutes	Place in a bowl. Cover with plate. Stir after 2 minutes cooking.
Corn		
350g (12oz)	4 to 4½ minutes	Place in a bowl. Cover with cling film and slit twice. Or cover with plate or lid.
Custard		
to warm 425g (15oz) can	1½ to 2 minutes	Pour custard into jug or bowl. Cover with plate. Stir once or twice. Do not boil.
to heat until hot 425g (15oz) can	3½ minutes	As above.
to heat until hot 500ml (17floz/2¼cups) container	4 to 4½ minutes	As above.
Pasta, spaghetti hoops, etc.		
439g (15½oz)	3 minutes Stand 2 minutes	Place in a bowl. Cover with plate. Stir once or twice.
Rice Pudding		
439g (15½oz)	3 minutes	Place in a bowl. Cover with plate. Stir once or twice.
Soup, condensed		
about 295g (10oz)	6 to 6½ minutes	Empty soup from can into bowl. Add 1 can cold water. Mix in well. Cover with plate. Stir every minute while cooking Do not allow to boil. Time will vary depending on consistency of soup.
Soup, ready-to-serve		
425g (15oz)	4 to 5 minutes	Place in mugs or bowls. Cover with plate. Stir every minute. Time will depend on personal taste in hot soup but **DO NOT** allow to boil vigorously.
Sponge Pudding		
225-275g (8-10oz)	1½ to 2 minutes	Remove from tin and place in bowl. Cover with cling film and slit twice. Alternatively, cover with plate.

	COOK/HEAT FULL POWER	COMMENTS & GUIDELINES
Steak and Kidney Pudding 439g (15½oz)	4 to 5 minutes Stand 5 minutes	Remove from tin and place in bowl. Cover with cling film and slit twice. Alternatively, cover with plate.
Vegetables Small (peas, beans, etc) 225-275g (8-10oz)	2 to 3½ minutes Stand 2 minutes	Pour 2 tablespoons of liquid from can into serving dish or bowl. Drain off rest of liquid and discard. Put vegetables into dish. Cover with cling film. Slit twice. If vegetable is in sauce, e.g. baked beans, **do not drain.** If preferred, cover dish or bowl with plate. Stir vegetables at least once during cooking/heating. Drain before serving.
400-439g (14-15½oz)	3 to 4 minutes Stand 3 minutes	As above.
Large (artichoke, asparagus, etc.) 425-439g (15-15½oz)	4 to 5 minutes Stand 3 minutes	As above but do not stir.

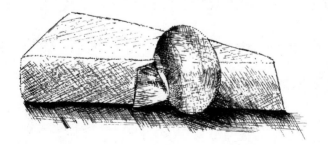

Convenience Foods – Miscellaneous

	DEFROST SETTING	COOK/HEAT FULL POWER	COMMENTS & GUIDELINES
Butter			
to soften from refrigerator			
225g (8oz)	40 to 50 seconds		Remove from foil wrapping. Stand on plate.
to melt, from room temperature			
15g (½oz/1tbsp)	40 to 50 seconds		Put into cup or jug. Cover with saucer or plate to prevent spluttering.
25g (1oz/2tbsp)	1 to 1½ minutes		As above.
50g (2oz/¼cup)	1½ to 2 minutes		As above.
75g (3oz/6tbsp)	2 to 2½ minutes		As above.
100g (4oz/½cup)	2½ to 3 minutes		As above.
225g (8oz/1cup)	3 to 3½ minutes		As above.
If from refrigerator, allow a little extra time			
Christmas Pudding (at room temperature)			
1 portion to heat		45 seconds Stand 1 minute	Stand on plate. Cover with kitchen paper.
450g (1lb) to heat		3 to 4 minutes Stand 2 minutes	In bowl. Cover with kitchen paper or plate.
900g (2lb) to heat		5 minutes Stand 5 minutes 5 minutes Stand 5 minutes	In bowl. Cover with kitchen paper or plate.
Cheese, to bring back to serving temperature if taken directly from refrigerator			
Firm cheese 225g (8oz)	30 to 45 seconds		Put uncovered on plate.
Soft cheese 225g (8oz)	15 to 45 seconds		As above.
Chocolate, to melt from room temperature			
1 bar 100g (4oz)	3 to 3½ minutes		Put into bowl in pieces. Stir once and watch carefully as soon as it starts to melt. If over-heated, chocolate may become granular or burn.

	DEFROST SETTING	COOK/HEAT FULL POWER	COMMENTS & GUIDELINES
1 bar 200g (7oz)	4 to 5 minutes Allow an extra ½ to 1 minute if taken straight from refrigerator.		As above.
Gelatine, to dissolve 1 packet/envelope.			
11g (0.4oz)	1½ to 1¾ minutes		Add 2 tablespoons cold liquid to granules in jug or bowl. Cover with plate. Swirl round after 1 minute. Stir thoroughly after removing from microwave to ensure gelatine has dissolved. Do not allow to boil.
Jelly, to melt 1 packet			
135g (4¾oz)	2 to 2½ minutes		Break into cubes and put into jug. Cover with plate.
Meat Pie Individual		45 seconds to 1¼ minutes	Remove from foil tray. Stand on kitchen paper. Cover with more paper.
Family size 450g (1lb)		3 minutes Stand 4 minutes 3 minutes Stand 4 minutes	As above.
Mince Pies, cooked 1 pie		15 seconds Stand 1 to 2 minutes	Stand on paper. Leave uncovered.
4 pies		1 minute Stand 2 to 3 minutes	As above.
Plate Meal 1 serving, from refrigerator		4-4½ minutes Stand 30 to 40 seconds	Cover with cling film if not already done. Slit twice. Alternatively, cover with inverted plate.

SNACKS AND BREAKFASTS

With the busy lifestyle we lead today, snacks and breakfasts need to be quick to prepare. Well your microwave can be a real boon when time is of the essence. You can be fortified and ready to get on with your day in next to no time. *And* you'll have no impossible pans to wash up.

Granola

One of America's most popular breakfast cereal mixes and fast catching on over here, my version contains bran for added fibre and a sprinkling of plump raisins. It is very sweet and needs toning down with milk. You can reduce the sugar but you won't get quite such a crisp result.

Preparation time: about 16 minutes

Makes about 675 g (1½ lb), allowing for evaporation

100 g (4 oz/½ cup) butter or margarine
100 g (4 oz/6 tbsp) golden (lightcorn) syrup
250 g (9 oz/2¼ cups) rolled oats
40 g (1½ oz/3 tbsp) coarse bran
100 g (4 oz/½ cup) soft dark brown (coffee) sugar
75 g (3 oz/¾ cup) walnuts, finely chopped
100 g (4 oz/⅔ cup) Californian seedless raisins

1 Put butter or margarine into a 25 cm (10 inch) round glass or pottery dish. Add syrup. Leave uncovered and melt 4 minutes at defrost setting.

2 Mix in all remaining ingredients except raisins. Leave uncovered and cook 9 to 9½ minutes at full power, stirring 4 or 5 times so that Granola browns evenly and becomes the colour of brown bread crust.

3 Remove from the oven, add raisins and mix in well. Leave to stand until crispy and cold, stirring from time to time until crumbly. Store in an airtight container.

Honey Granola

Use honey instead of golden (light corn) syrup.

Hazelnut Granola

Use chopped hazelnuts instead of walnuts.

Porridge

For 1 portion
Put 25 g/1 oz/¼ cup rolled oats into a bowl. Add 150 ml/¼ pint/⅔ cup water or milk and a pinch of salt. Leave uncovered and cook 1¾ to 2 minutes at full power, stirring twice. Stand 1½ minutes. Serve with milk or cream and either sugar or salt.

For 2 portions in 2 bowls
Cook 3 to 3½ minutes at full power.

For 3 portions in 3 bowls
Cook 3½ to 4 minutes at full power.

For 4 portions in 4 bowls
Cook 4 to 4½ minutes at full power.

Bacon

Bacon cooks extremely well in the microwave and shrinks less than if grilled or fried conventionally. To prevent sticking, do not, as some books suggest, line the dish or plate with kitchen paper. However, the bacon should be loosely covered with kitchen or greaseproof paper while cooking to prevent spluttering and dirtying the oven. Drain at the end by wiping with more paper. For best results cook on a microwave rack over a plate.

1 rasher (slice)
Cook ¾ to 1 minute at full power.

2 rashers (slices)
Cook 1½ to 1¾ minutes at full power.

3 rashers (slices)
Cook 2 to 2¼ minutes at full power.

4 rashers (slices)
Cook 2½ to 2¾ minutes at full power.

5 rashers (slices)
Cook 3 to 3½ minutes at full power.

6 rashers (slices)
Cook 4 to 4½ minutes at full power.

NOTE: Timing is a guide only and depending on the type of bacon and size of rashers (slices) you may need to allow a little less or more time.

Welsh Rarebit

A favourite snack which adapts beautifully – and fast – to microwave cooking. The topping is enriched with egg yolk and has a warm, round flavour.

Preparation time: about 8 minutes

Serves 3

100g (4oz/1cup) Cheddar cheese, finely grated
5ml (1tsp) mustard powder
5ml (1tsp) cornflour (cornstarch)
1egg yolk
10ml (2tsp) milk
salt and pepper to taste
3 large slices freshly made brown or white toast
paprika

1 Mix cheese with mustard, cornflour, egg yolk and milk. Season to taste.

2 Spread over 3 slices of toast. Put on to individual plates.

3 Leave uncovered and cook 1 minute each at full power. Dust lightly with paprika and serve straight away.

Buck Rarebit

Serves 3

Make as above. Pop a poached or fried egg (pages 100, 103) on top of each. Sprinkle very lightly with paprika.

Bacon Rarebit

Serves 3

Make as Welsh Rarebit then top with one or two bacon rashers, cooked as given in either the Convenience Food Chart (page 38) or page 43.

Baked Beans on Toast

For 1

Stand a large slice of fresh toast on a plate and spread with butter
or margarine. Top with 80 ml/4 rounded tablespoons canned
baked beans in tomato sauce. Leave uncovered and heat 1½ to 2
minutes at full power.

For 2

Make as above but allow 3 to 3½ minutes for 2 plates.

Rarebit Beans

For 1 or 2

Make as above, sprinkling each with 25 g/1 oz/¼ cup grated
cheese. Allow ¼ minute extra cooking time.

Canned Spaghetti (or any of its variations) on Toast

Follow directions for Baked Beans on Toast, using any of the
canned pastas in sauce.

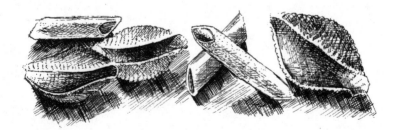

STARTERS

Starters, more appropriately appetisers, should be just that and set the taste buds tingling for the culinary pleasures still to come. Thus, keep to smallish portions, garnish attractively, and thank your lucky stars that some of the dishes can be made in the microwave while you are relaxing over a pre-meal drink.

Although the selection is relatively short, there are also soups to choose from, while some of the fish, vegetarian, egg and vegetable dishes are also appropriate to serve as hors d'oeuvres.

Please bear in mind that the number of servings is a guide only. You may wish to offer less if the main course is robust, more if it is light.

Stuffed Tomatoes

A light starter and just right for spring and summer evenings.

Preparation time: about 15 minutes

Serves 6

6 medium tomatoes
25g (1oz/2tbsp) butter or margarine
100g (4oz/1cup) onion, peeled and chopped
50g (2oz/1cup) fresh white breadcrumbs
5ml (1tsp) prepared mustard
5ml (1tsp) salt
5ml (1tsp) dried basil or mixed herbs
50g (2oz/½cup) cooked chopped meat, poultry, tongue,
prawns (shrimp) or grated Cheddar cheese

1   Cut tops off tomatoes, reserve for lids and scoop centres into bowl. Discard hard cores. Stand tomato cups upside down to drain on kitchen paper.

2   Put butter or margarine into a dish and melt 1 to 1½ minutes at defrost setting. Add onion and cook 2 minutes at full power, leaving uncovered.

3   Stir in crumbs, tomato pulp, mustard, salt, basil or herbs and the meat, fish or cheese.

4   Pile into tomato cups and top with lids. Arrange in a ring round the edge of a dinner plate.

5   Cover with kitchen paper and heat 6 to 7 minutes at full power. Serve straight away while hot.

Artichokes in Red Wine with Gribiche Dressing

A powerful blend of flavours, slightly exotic and with plenty of French flair. Make the sauce and leave to cool while preparing artichokes.

Preparation time: about 1¼ hours

Serves 4

Gribiche Dressing

4 (size 3) eggs
7.5 ml (1½ tsp) French mustard
5 ml (1 tsp) salt
300 ml (½ pt/1¼ cup) sunflower oil
45 ml (3 tbsp) light coloured malt vinegar
20 ml (4 tsp) chopped parsley
20 ml (4 tsp) fresh chopped herbs
to include chives, tarragon, savoury and thyme (leaves only)
45 ml (3 tbsp) mixture of drained
chopped capers and gherkins
pepper to taste

Artichokes in Red Wine

4 large globe artichokes
salted water
150 ml (¼ pt/⅔ cup) dry red wine
1 garlic clove, peeled and crushed
7.5 ml (1½ tsp) salt

1   For sauce, break 3 of the eggs carefully into a medium-sized greased dish. Pierce each yolk in 2 places with tip of pointed knife to stop them bursting and spluttering while cooking.

2   Cover with a plate then 'hardboil' (hardcook) by microwaving for 8 minutes at defrost setting. Stand 3 minutes. Carefully remove yolks with a spoon and put into blender goblet or food processor. Reserve whites.

3 Add whole egg, mustard and salt to yolks. Blend until very smooth. With machine still running, add oil in a thin, continuous stream. The mixture will gradually thicken to mayonnaise consistency.

4 Blend in vinegar then spoon out into a bowl. Cut egg whites into strips then add to sauce with remaining ingredients. Cover and leave in the cool.

5 To cook artichokes, cut away stalks, leaving bases flat. With a sharp and non-serrated knife, cut tops off upper leaves as though you were slicing a loaf of bread. You will find the easiest way to do this is to place each artichoke on its side.

6 Soak for 20 minutes in cold, salted water. Lift out and shake to remove surplus liquid.

7 Pour wine into a large dish about 25 cm square by 5 cm deep. Add garlic and salt. Add artichokes, placing them upright with leaves facing.

8 Cover with cling film, then puncture twice with the tip of a knife. Alternatively, cover with a matching lid.

9 Cook 25 minutes at full power. Leave to stand 10 minutes. Uncover and put on to serving plates. Accompany with Gribiche Dressing.

TIP: To eat, pull off leaves one at a time and dip fleshy part nearest the stalk end in dressing. Pass through the teeth. Continue until you come to a cone of inedible leaves. Lift these off and underneath you will find the 'choke', a mass of very fine spikes which look like silken threads or fine bristles. Lift off by pulling with the fingers then eat the heart, the luxury portion, with a knife and fork plus extra dressing.

To prepare artichokes for guests or for stuffing, cook as above then gently ease leaves apart until you come to the centre. Remove core of inedible leaves and the spiky choke, then either fill with dressing or stuff and reheat. Water, white wine or cider can be used instead of red wine, and garlic omitted completely if preferred.

Veal Stuffed Peppers

Stuffed Peppers may be made from the vivid red variety, through yellow to the more subdued green. They are colourful and tasty and can be served hot or cold, basted with juices from the dish for added succulence. Use minced (ground) beef or pork sausagemeat if liked.

Preparation time: about 40 minutes

Serves 4, allowing 1 per person (F)

4 medium red, yellow or green (bell) peppers
25 g (1 oz/2 tbsp) butter or margarine, at room temperature
150 g (5 oz/1¼ cup) onions, peeled and chopped
225 g (8 oz/1 cup) minced (ground) veal
50 g (2 oz/¼ cup) easy-cook, long grain rice
5 ml (1 tsp) salt
75 ml (5 tbsp) tomato juice, chicken stock or water
2.5 ml (½ tsp) dried thyme

Cooking liquid
60 ml (4 tbsp) tomato juice or chicken stock

1 Cut tops off peppers and set aside for lids. Remove inside seeds and fibres. Cut a sliver off the base of each so that it stands upright without falling.

2 Put butter or margarine into a dish and heat, uncovered, for ¾ to 1 minute at full power. Stir in onions. Continue to cook, still uncovered, for 3 minutes. Mash in veal, cook 3 minutes more.

3 Remove from oven and add all remaining ingredients. Spoon equal amounts into peppers. Top with lids.

4 Stand upright in a 1.75 litre/3 pt/7½ cup deep dish. Add cooking liquid. Cover with cling film, then puncture twice with the tip of a knife. Alternatively, cover with a matching lid.

5 Cook 15 minutes at full power. Leave to stand 10 minutes. Serve hot or cold, coated with juices from dish.

Liver Paste

Luxury personified. A glorious paste which is, I think, as top class as any-thing gastronomes of France could produce. It cooks in 10 minutes but does depend on a food processor or blender for its ultra-smooth texture.

Preparation time: about 15 minutes

Serves about 10 to 12 (F)

175g (6oz/¾ cup) salted butter
1 garlic clove, peeled and sliced
450g (1lb/2 cups) chicken livers, washed and dried
good pinch nutmeg
seasoning to taste
50-75g (2-3oz/¼-⅓ cup) extra butter for the top

1   Put butter into a 1.75 litre/3 pt/7½ cup dish and heat 2 minutes uncovered, at full power.

2   Add garlic and chicken livers. Cover with cling film, then puncture twice with the tip of a knife.

3   Cook 8 minutes at full power.

4   Remove from microwave then add nutmeg and seasoning to taste. Spoon butter and cooked liver together into a food pro-cessor or blender goblet. Do this in 2 batches and run machine each time until mixture is very smooth.

5   Spread evenly into a smallish, soufflé-type dish. For an airtight seal (the best there is) melt extra butter and pour over the top. leave, without moving, until butter sets then 'store' covered, in the refrigerator.

6   To serve, spoon out on to plates and serve with hot toast.

TIP: Best eaten within 2 days, but undisturbed will keep longer.

Aubergine (Eggplant) Dip

Characterfully Middle Eastern, this is a simply made dip to mop up with pieces of Greek-style bread – either Pitta or the crustier sesame seed. It responds best to being mixed in a blender or food processor and I have the State of Louisiana to thank for teaching me how to cook aubergines; boiling and not frying which renders them delicate, non-greasy and better able to harmonise with other foods and absorb their flavours.

Preparation time: about 12 minutes plus chilling time

Serves 4 to 6

450g (1lb) aubergines (eggplant), peeled and cut into
5cm (2in) pieces
60ml (4tbsp) water
2.5-5ml (½ to 1 tsp) salt
15ml (1tbsp) lemon juice
15ml (1tbsp) corn or sunflower oil
(for a typically South European taste, use olive oil instead)
1 small garlic clove, peeled and sliced

1   Tip aubergines into a dish and add the water. Cover with cling film, then puncture twice with the tip of a knife. Alternatively, cover with a matching lid.

2   Cook for 6 minutes at full power, stirring once. Remove from oven, stand 2 minutes and drain.

3   Transfer aubergines to a blender goblet or food processor. Add salt, lemon juice, oil and garlic. Run machine until mixture forms a smooth purée.

4   Spoon into a small serving bowl, cover securely and chill before eating.

Mushrooms a la Grècque

Supposedly Hellenic, this is a popular restaurant starter, quite simple to emulate at home and refreshingly piquant.

Preparation time: about 7 minutes plus chilling time

Serves 2

2 bouquet garni bags
1 garlic clove, peeled and crushed
1 large bay leaf, broken into 4 pieces
30 ml (2 tbsp) water
15 ml (1 tbsp) lemon juice
15 ml (1 tbsp) malt vinegar
15 ml (1 tbsp) corn oil
2.5 ml (½ tsp) salt
225 g (8 oz) button mushrooms
15 ml (1 tbsp) chopped parsley

1 Put all ingredients, except mushrooms and parsley, into a medium glass or pottery bowl.

2 Cover with a plate and cook 2½ minutes at full power.

3 Gently toss in mushrooms. Cover as above. Cook 3 minutes at full power.

4 Remove from oven and leave until cold. Lift mushrooms into a dish. Coat with juices, strained through a fine sieve.

5 Chill several hours before serving. Transfer mushrooms and juices to 2 dishes and sprinkle with parsley.

Potted Prawns (Shrimp)

In the old days, it used to be tiny pink shrimps that were potted but, coastal regions apart, where are they to be found other than in cans from far away places? On the assumption that shrimps are not readily available, I have substituted prawns with equal success. In the USA prawns are known as shrimp.

Preparation time: about 5 minutes plus chilling time

Serves 6 (F)

225 g (8 oz/1 cup) unsalted butter
275 g (10 oz) peeled prawns (shrimps), thawed if frozen
15 ml (1 tbsp) lemon juice
good pinch nutmeg
2.5 ml (½ tsp) paprika

GARNISH
6 unpeeled prawns (shrimp) or 6 watercress sprigs

1   Melt 175 g (6 oz/¾ cup) butter in a dish for 3 minutes at defrost setting. Leave uncovered.

2   Coarsley chop prawns and add to butter with the lemon juice, nutmeg and paprika. Leave in a cool place until the mixture just begins to firm up.

3   Spread neatly and smoothly into 6 baby pots or dishes. Chill until firm in the refrigerator.

4   Melt rest of butter and spoon over each. Chill again until butter has set in an even layer.

5   To serve, run a knife dipped in hot water round inside of each pot, and invert on to a plate. Garnish with prawns or watercress and eat with hot toast.

Smoked Salmon Quiche

Why not luxuriate in a stylish quiche, filled with Pacific smoked salmon, notable for its own character and interesting flavour? Not in the same league as the much costlier Scottish salmon, it is nevertheless well suited for quiche and also makes a fine pâté to go with fingers of toast.

Preparation time: about 25 minutes

Serves 8

Shortcrust pastry (basic pie crust) made with 175g (6oz/1½ cups) plain (all-purpose) flour and 75g (3oz/6tbsp) fat, etc
1 egg yolk

FILLING
175g (6oz/1½ cups) Pacific smoked salmon, finely chopped
3 (size 3) eggs
300ml (½pt/1¼ cups) single (light) cream
2.5ml (½tsp) salt
2.5ml (½tsp) finely grated lemon rind

1 Roll out pastry fairly thinly and use to line a lightly-greased, 20cm (8inch) round glass or pottery fluted flan dish.

2 Prick well all over with a fork, especially where sides of pastry meet base. Leave uncovered and cook 6 minutes at full power.

3 Remove from oven, brush all over with egg yolk to seal holes and cook a further minute at full power.

4 Remove from oven and cover base with the chopped salmon.

5 Beat all remaining ingredients well together. Pour into flan over salmon. Cook 10 to 12 minutes at full power or until bubbles just begin to break in the middle.

6 Remove from oven, cut into wedges and serve hot, warm or cold.

Asparagus Quiche

Serves 8

Make exactly as the Smoked Salmon Quiche (page 55) but use a 350 g (12 oz) can of green asparagus spears which, when drained, will yield about 175 g (6 oz). Reserve 6 spears for decoration, coarsely chop remainer and use to cover base of pastry.

Quiche Lorraine

Serves 8

Make as Smoked Salmon Quiche (page 55), but cover base of pastry with 175 g (6 oz/9 slices) microwaved bacon, finely chopped and used cold. Sprinkle filling with a little nutmeg before cooking.

Cheese and Bacon Quiche

Serves 8

Make as Smoked Salmon Quiche (page 55), but cover base of pastry with 100 g (4 oz/6 slices) microwaved bacon, finely chopped and used cold. Sprinkle filling with 50 g (2 oz/½ cup) grated Red Leicester or Cheshire cheese before cooking.

Spinach Quiche

Serves 8

Make as Smoked Salmon Quiche (page 55), but cover base of pastry with 175 g (6 oz/¾ cup) cooked spinach, *very well drained.* Sprinkle filling with a little nutmeg before cooking.

Soups

The warmth and comfort of homemade soup is undeniable, so is its flavour, and this short selection offers some vintage favourites in addition to what I call 'modern' soups, concocted from cans and other fast-cooking ingredients.

Curry Rice Soup

More like a broth than a soup, this is a blissfully heart-warming brew to come home to on chilly days and takes only 20 minutes to cook.

Preparation time: about 25 minutes

Serves 6 (F)

50g (2oz/¼ cup) butter or margarine
100g (4oz/1cup) onions, peeled and chopped or grated
175g (6oz) well-scrubbed celery, cut into thin strips
15ml (1tbsp) curry powder
30ml (2tbsp) medium sherry
1 litre (1¾pt/4¼cups) chicken stock
(use cubes and water in the absence of the real thing)
100g (4oz/½cup) easy-cook, long-grain rice
5ml (1tsp) salt
15ml (1tbsp) Soy sauce
175g (6oz) cooked cold chicken, cut into strips
thick yoghurt or soured (dairy sour) cream for serving

1   Put butter or margarine in a 2.25 litre (4pt/10cup) dish and melt, uncovered, 1½ to 2 minutes at defrost setting.

2   Add onions and celery. Leave uncovered and cook 5 minutes at full power, stirring once.

3   Mix in curry powder, sherry, stock, rice, salt and Soy sauce. Cover with a plate and cook 10 minutes at full power, stirring twice.

4   Add chicken and continue to cook for a further 5 miutes at full power. Stir round, ladle into soup plates or bowls and top each with 1 tablespoon of yoghurt or soured cream.

Cream of Carrot Soup

Perhaps one of my favourite soups with its rich texture, subtle flavour and delicate orange colour. It is also incredibly convenient and inexpensive, based on nothing more demanding than cornflour (cornstarch), a can of carrots, milk, water and seasoning.

Preparation time: about 15 minutes

Serves 6 (F)

30 ml (2 tbsp) cornflour (cornstarch)
1 large can (about 550 g/1¼ lb) carrots
450 ml (¾ pt/2 cups) milk (skimmed if liked)
5 ml (1 tsp) onion salt
5 ml (1 tsp) salt
150-300 ml (¼-½ pt/⅔-1¼ cups) extra boiling water

1   Put cornflour into a 2.25 litre (4 pt/10 cup) glass or pottery dish. Mix smoothly with liquid from can of carrots.

2   Blend carrots to a purée in a food processor, blender goblet or by rubbing through a fine sieve. Add to dish with milk and both the salts.

3   Leave uncovered and cook 12 minutes at full power, stirring 4 times. By this time, the soup should have come to the boil and thickened.

4   Remove from oven and thin down to taste with the boiling water. Adjust seasoning to taste and serve straight away.

Cream of Vegetable Soups

Serves 6 (F)

Pea, broad bean, celery soup and so forth may be made in exactly the same way as the Carrot Soup, using appropriate cans of vegetables.

Avocado Soup

Totally uncomplicated, comfortably warming and pleasingly light; a change from chilled avocado soups and perfect for entertaining. Add 2 teaspoons of cooked grated beetroot to each and get a fascinating colour combination but for conservative eating, sprinkle with chopped parsley, a few croûtons or a dusting of paprika.

Preparation time: about 8 minutes

Serves 6

900 ml (1½ pt/3¾ cups) hot chicken stock
2 medium sized ripe avocados
15 ml (1 tbsp) lemon juice
5 ml (1 tsp) onion powder
2.5-5 ml (½-1 tsp) salt

1   Pour chicken stock into a bowl and cover with a plate. Heat for 4½ minutes at full power.

2   Meanwhile halve avocados, remove flesh and mash *very finely* with lemon juice and onion powder. Alternatively, work to a purée in a blender or food processor.

3   Whisk into soup with salt. Cover as above. Reheat for 3 minutes at full power.

4   Ladle into warm bowls or plates and serve straight away.

TIP: *Do not reheat leftovers as flavour and colour will spoil.*

Rustic Tomato Soup

A wealth of flavour and rugged texture characterise this vivid red soup based on summer-ripe tomatoes. Serve it with crusty brown bread or rolls spread with either butter or peanut butter.

Preparation time: about 25 minutes

Serves 6 to 8 (F)

900 g (2 lb) blanched tomatoes, skinned and quartered
50 g (2 oz/¼ cup) butter or margarine
100 g (4 oz/1 cup) celery, finely chopped
100 g (4 oz/1 cup) onions, peeled and finely chopped
30 ml (2 tbsp) dark brown (coffee) sugar
7.5 ml (1½ tsp) salt
300 ml (½ pt/1¼ cups) hot water
30 ml (2 tbsp) cornflour (cornstarch)
120 ml (4 fl oz/½ cup) cold water

1   Blend tomatoes to a purée in a blender or food processor. Leave aside temporarily.

2   Put butter or margarine into a 1.75 litre (3 pt/7½ cup) glass or pottery dish and heat 1 minute at full power.

3   Mix in celery and onions. Cover dish with plate or lid and cook 3 minutes at full power.

4   Add sugar, salt, hot water and the tomato purée (made under point one). Cover as above or use cling film, puncturing twice with the tip of a knife. Cook 8 minutes at full power.

5   Uncover. Blend in cornflour, mixed smoothly with water.

6   Leave uncovered and cook a further 8 minutes at full power, stirring 4 times. Ladle into bowls and serve while still very hot.

Lettuce Soup

Delicately balanced in colour and flavour, creamy Lettuce Soup is unusual and well-recommended for summer eating. Serve plain, or top each portion with a tablespoon of soured (dairy sour) cream and a hint of chopped parsley. The soup may also be served chilled, garnished with lemon slices and mint. Substitute spinach for lettuce if preferred.

Preparation time: about 25 minutes

Serves 6

50 g (2 oz/¼ cup) butter or margarine
175 g (6 oz/1½ cups) onions, peeled and grated
225 g (8 oz/4 cups) green lettuces (round variety), shredded
600 ml (1 pt/2½ cups) cold milk
30 ml (2 tbsp) cornflour (cornstarch)
300 ml (½ pt/1¼ cups) boiling water or chicken stock
5-10 ml (1-2 tsp) salt

1 Put butter or margarine into a 1.75 litre (3 pt/7½ cup) deepish casserole (Dutch oven). Melt 1½ to 2 minutes at defrosting setting.

2 Mix in onions and lettuces. Cover with plate or matching lid and cook 3 minutes at full power.

3 Transfer to blender goblet with one third of the milk. Run machine until ingredients are mixed to a purée.

4 Return to dish. Mix in cornflour, remaining milk, boiling water or stock and the salt.

5 Cover as before then cook soup for 15 minutes at full power, whisking gently at the end of every 3 minutes.

Belgian-Style Lettuce Soup

Serves 6

Use single (light) cream instead of milk and add 5 ml (1 tsp) butter to each portion.

Chilled Cream of Cheshire Soup

Rich and quite different from the usual run-of-the-mill soups, this one is based on the two famous Cheshire cheeses – blue and white.

Preparation time: about 25 minutes plus chilling time

Serves 6 to 8

25g (1oz/2 tbsp) butter or margarine
175g (6oz/1½ cups) onions, peeled and chopped
75g (3oz/¾ cup) celery, chopped
25g (1oz/¼ cup) plain (all-purpose) flour
900ml (1½ pt/3¾ cups) warm chicken stock
45ml (3 tbsp) dry white wine
seasoning to taste
100g (4oz/1 cup) blue Cheshire cheese, crumbled
100g (4oz/1 cup) white Cheshire cheese, crumbled
150ml (¼ pt/⅔ cup) double (heavy) cream
finely chopped parsley for garnishing

1 Put butter or margarine into a 2.25 litre (4 pt/10 cup) glass or pottery dish. Melt, uncovered, 1 to 1½ minutes at defrost setting.

2 Add onions and celery. Mix in well. Cover with a plate and cook 8 minutes at full power.

3 Remove from oven. Stir in flour then gradually blend in the stock and wine. Cover as above and return to oven. Cook 10 to 12 minutes at full power, whisking every 2 to 3 minutes to keep mixture smooth.

4 Remove from oven and season to taste. Add cheeses and stir until melted. Leave soup until cold. Blend to a smooth purée in blender goblet. Pour into large bowl and whisk in two-thirds of the cream.

5 Cover and chill several hours or overnight. Before serving, stir round gently to mix then pour into bowls. Swirl in rest of cream and sprinkle each with parsley.

TIP: *If soup is too thick, thin with a little cold milk before serving.*

Tomato Soup with Avocado Mayonnaise

A bright and breezy soup, on the sophisticated side and well-suited to an intimate dinner party.

Preparation time: about 15 minutes

Serves 8

2 medium, ripe avocados
15 ml (1 tbsp) lemon juice
1 garlic clove, peeled and sliced (optional)
60 ml (4 tbsp) mayonnaise
2.5-5 ml (½-1 tsp) salt
2 cans condensed cream of tomato soup
600 ml (1 pt/2½ cups) warm water
350 g (12 oz) blanched and skinned tomatoes, cut into strips
seasoning to taste

1   Make the Avocado Mayonnaise first and leave aside temporarily while preparing the soup. Scoop avocado flesh into food processor bowl or blender goblet.

2   Add lemon juice, garlic, mayonnaise and salt. Run machine until smooth. Spoon out into a dish.

3   Tip both cans of soup into a 2.25 litre (4 pt/10 cup) dish. Mix in water and tomatoes.

4   Cover with a plate and cook 8 to 10 minutes at full power or until soup is hot but not boiling. Stir 4 times.

5   Adjust seasoning to taste then ladle into warm soup bowls or plates. Add a tablespoon of the avocado mixture to each and serve straight away.

Minestrone

An old treasure we have adopted with love and heartfelt thanks from Italy. It cooks excellently in the microwave, retaining its full flavour.

Preparation time: about 50 minutes

Serves 8 to 10 (F)

350g (12oz/3cups) courgettes (zucchini), thinly sliced
225g (8oz/2cups) carrots, peeled and thinly sliced
225g (8oz/2cups) onions, peeled and coarsely chopped
100g (4oz/1cup) green cabbage, shredded
100g (4oz/1cup) white cabbage, shredded
50g (2oz/½cup) celery, scrubbed and very thinly sliced
175g (6oz/1cup) potatoes, peeled and diced
100g (4oz/1cup) fresh or frozen sliced green beans
100g (4oz/1cup) fresh or frozen peas
400g (14oz) can tomatoes
45ml (2tbsp) tomato purée (paste)
50g (2oz/¼cup) small pasta or long-grain rice
1litre (1¾pt/4¼cups) boiling water
15-20ml (3-4tsp) salt

1   Put all the fresh and frozen vegetables into a 3.5litre (6pt/ 15cup) bowl. Mix in canned tomatoes, purée and either pasta or rice.

2   Cover with a large plate. Cook 15 minutes at full power, stirring 3 times. Pour in two-thirds of the boiling water. Cover as above.

3   Cook 20 to 25 minutes at full power, stirring 4 times. Remove from cooker and stir in rest of water with salt. If soup is too thick for personal taste, add an extra 150ml (¼pt/⅔cup) boiling water.

4   Ladle into dishes and pass grated Parmesan cheese separately.

Packet Soups (Dried Ingredients)

Serves 4 to 5

Tip packet of soup into a deepish glass or pottery dish. Gradually add cold water as directed on the packet, stirring continuously. Cover with a plate and leave to stand 15 minutes so that vegetables have time to soften slightly. Cook 6 to 8 minutes at full power when soup should come to the boil and thicken. Stir 2 or 3 times. Remove from cooker. Leave to stand 5 minutes then stir round and serve.

SAUCES AND DRESSINGS

I admit where basic white sauces are concerned, there is no saving in time when made in the microwave, measured, that is, against conventional cooking. But on the plus side there is less likelihood of the sauce 'lumping', hardly a chance of it boiling over, and no tacky pan to clean up afterwards. Also all the sauces seem to be more flavoursome, extra glossy and superbly smooth.

Hollandaise and Béarnaise sauces, the pièces de résistance of aspiring and great chefs, work miraculously in seconds with no tantrums. Bread sauce turns out deliciously creamy and pale as ivory. Egg Custard sauce is a labour of speed and Cranberry sauce, poultry's best friend, tastes as though the berries had just been gathered.

Even Apple sauce is more aromatic than usual, and the Bolognese and Neapolitan sauces have a distinctive, fresh and pungent taste, reminiscent of true Mediterranean cooking.

When I first embarked on microwave cooking all those years ago, I had certain reservations about making sauces in the oven but time and success have changed my mind completely. If any of *you* still have reservations, just try out a selection and judge the results for yourselves.

White Sauce

The coating variety and multi-purpose, this is everybody's favourite sauce with its glossy appearance and velvety smooth texture. A selection of popular variations follow.

Preparation time: about 8 minutes

Serves 4 (F)

300 ml (½ pt/1¼ cups) milk, taken from the refrigerator
25 g (1 oz/2 tbsp) butter or margarine
25 g (1 oz/¼ cup) plain (all-purpose) flour
seasoning to taste

1 Pour milk into a large glass or pottery jug. Leave uncovered and heat 1½ minutes at full power until fairly hot. Remove from oven.

2 Put butter or margarine into a bowl. Leave uncovered and melt 1 to 1½ minutes at defrost setting.

3 Stir in flour to form a roux and cook ½ minute at full power. Remove from oven and gradually blend in the warm milk.

4 Return to oven and cook, uncovered, until sauce comes to the boil and thickens. Allow about 3 to 4 minutes at full power and beat at the end of every minute to ensure sauce stays smooth.

5 Season to taste, stir well and use as desired.

NOTE: *For quickness you can make an all-in-one sauce: simply whisk flour into milk in a bowl. Add butter. Cook on full power for 6 to 6½ minutes, whisking at least 4 times until thick and smooth. Season.*

Caper Sauce

Serves 4 (F)

Make as White Sauce, adding 20 ml (4 tsp) drained and chopped capers half way through cooking time. Serve with herrings, mackerel, skate and boiled or roast lamb or mutton.

Cheese Sauce

Serves 4 (F)

Make as White Sauce, adding 50-75 g (2-3 oz/½-¾ cup) any grated cheese and 5 ml (1 tsp) prepared mustard half way through cooking. Serve with bacon, fish, poultry and vegetables.

Hard-boiled (hard-cooked) Egg Sauce

Serves 4 to 5

Make as White Sauce, adding 2 (size 3) hardboiled (hard-cooked) and chopped eggs at the end with the seasoning. Do not reheat as eggs may become rubbery. Serve with fish and poultry.

Mushroom Sauce

Serves 4 to 5

Make as White Sauce, adding 50 g (2 oz/½ cup) chopped mushrooms half way through cooking time. The mushrooms should first be cooked in a little butter or margarine for about 1 to 1½ minutes at full power. Add a light shake of nutmeg with the seasoning. Serve with fish, poultry and light meat dishes.

Mustard Sauce

Serves 4 (F)

Make as White Sauce, adding 10 ml (2 tsp) prepared English mustard and 10 ml (2 tsp) of lemon juice at the end with the seasoning. Serve with pork, bacon, offal and fish.

Onion Sauce

Serves 4 to 5 (F)

Put 100 g (4 oz/1 cup) chopped onions into a small dish. Add 15 ml (1 tbsp) water and 2.5 ml (½ tsp) salt. Cover with cling film, slit twice. Cook 4 to 5 minutes until very soft. Make White Sauce. Add onions half way through cooking. Serve with lamb.

Parsley Sauce

Serves 4 (F)

Make as White Sauce, adding 60 ml (4 tbsp) chopped parsley about 1 minute before sauce is ready. Serve with fish, vegetables, poultry and boiled bacon.

Watercress Sauce

Serves 4

Make as White Sauce, adding 60 ml (4 tbsp) chopped watercress leaves at the same time as the seasoning. Serve with fish or poultry.

Béchamel Sauce

Serves 4 (F)

This is the more aristocratic version of White Sauce, and is simply the result of adding flavourings to the milk.

Pour 300 ml (½ pt/1¼ cups) milk into a glass or pottery jug. Add 1 bouquet garni bag, 1 bay leaf, 1 small peeled and quartered onion, 2 parsley sprigs and a pinch of nutmeg. Cover with a saucer and bring just up to the boil, allowing 5 to 6 minutes at defrost setting. Cool to lukewarm outside the cooker. Strain and use as directed for White Sauce and its variations.

Pouring Sauce

Serves 4 to 6 (F)

Make White Sauce or Béchamel Sauce but reduce the flour to 15 g (½ oz/2 tbsp) only. The sauce is useful if food is dry and moisture is needed – rather like gravy but made with milk. If sweet, it makes a pleasing substitute for custard over steamed puddings.

TIP: *Any of the White Sauce variations may be made into a pouring consistency by reducing the flour as given above.*

Cornflour (Cornstarch) Sauce

The most simple of all sauces which takes well to sweet or savoury additions. It is easy to digest and perfectly suitable for convalescents and the elderly.

Preparation time: about 6 minutes

Serves 4 to 6 (F)

30 ml (2 tbsp) cornflour (cornstarch)
300 ml (½ pt/1¼ cups) cold milk (skimmed if preferred)
salt or sugar to taste

1   Tip cornflour into a 600 ml (1 pt/2½ cup) dish and blend smoothly with some of the cold milk.

2   Carefully blend in the remainder. Leave uncovered and cook 4 to 5 minutes at full power until thickened, beating at the end of every minute. The sauce *must* come to the boil and may need an extra ½ to 1 minute, depending on the temperature of the milk.

3   Remove from microwave and season to taste with salt. Alternatively, add 25 g (1 oz/2 tbsp) caster (superfine) sugar and stir until dissolved. Use as desired.

Jam or Honey Sauce

Serves 4 to 6 (F)

Instead of sugar, sweeten sauce with about 15-30 ml (1-2 tbsp) jam or honey.

Bread Sauce

A vintage tradition – Bread Sauce with poultry and the Christmas turkey in particular. It works like a charm in the microwave.

Preparation time: about 16 minutes

Serves 6 to 8 (F)

**300 ml (½ pt/1¼ cups) milk, heated with the same additions
as given for the Béchamel sauce, then strained
65 g (2½ oz/a good cup) fresh white breadcrumbs (crusts removed)
15 g (½ oz/1 tbsp) butter or margarine
pinch of nutmeg
salt and pepper to taste**

1 Pour warm milk into a clean bowl. Add crumbs. Leave uncovered and cook until thickened, allowing about 4 to 6 minutes at defrost setting and stirring at the end of every minute.

2 Mix in butter or margarine, nutmeg and salt and pepper to taste. Leave uncovered. Reheat about 1 minute at defrost setting. Serve as suggested.

Brown Bread Sauce

Serves 6 to 8 (F)

A good choice for game, make exactly as the Bread Sauce above, using brown breadcrumbs instead of white, and no crusts.

Bolognese Sauce

A long time favourite, this is a fulfilling and glowing sauce for 'Spag Bol' or any other pasta dish. It cooks in about 20 minutes and is best made one day and reheated the next to allow flavours to develop.

Preparation time: about 25 minutes

Serves 6 generously (F)

450g (1lb/2cups) minced (ground) beef
1 garlic clove, peeled and crushed
100g (4oz/1cup) onions, peeled and grated
100g (4oz/1cup) green (bell) pepper, deseeded and finely chopped
5ml (1tsp) Italian seasoning or dried mixed herbs
400g (14oz) can chopped tomatoes
45ml (3tbsp) tomato purée (paste)
1 brown gravy cube
75ml (5tbsp) red wine or water
15ml (1tbsp) soft brown (coffee) sugar
5ml (1tsp) salt

1 Put beef and garlic into a 1.75 litre (3pt/7½cup) glass or pottery dish. Thoroughly mix in onions and pepper. Leave uncovered and cook 5 minutes at full power.

2 Stir in Italian seasoning or mixed herbs, the chopped tomatoes, tomato purée, crumbled gravy cube, wine or water and the sugar.

3 Cover with cling film, then puncture twice with the tip of a knife. Cook 15 minutes at full power, stirring twice. Uncover, season with salt, stir round and serve or use as required.

TIP: *If for serving the next day, uncover and stir round as soon as sauce is ready. Re-cover as above. Refrigerate when cold. Reheat at full power until hot through, stirring twice.*

Neapolitan Sauce

Delicious, whether spooned over pasta or cooked steaks.

Preparation time: about 14 minutes

Serves 6 to 8 (F)

*675 g (1½ lb) blanched tomatoes, skinned and cut into eighths
1 garlic clove, peeled and sliced
30 ml (2 tbsp) tomato purée (paste)
15 ml (1 tbsp) caster (superfine) or
soft light brown (coffee) sugar
2.5 ml (½ tsp) salt
5 ml (1 tsp) dried basil
30 ml (2 tbsp) chopped parsley
15 ml (1 tbsp) cornflour (cornstarch)
15 ml (1 tbsp) water*

1 Put tomatoes, garlic and purée into food processor or blender goblet and run machine until smooth.

2 Pour into a 1.75 litre (3 pt/7½ cup) glass or pottery dish. Mix in sugar, salt, basil and parsley.

3 Blend cornflour smoothly with water. Add to tomato mixture and stir in well.

4 Cover with a plate and cook 6 minutes at full power, stirring 4 times. Leave to stand 4 minutes before serving.

Basting Sauces

Bastes are brushed over meat joints and poultry to increase browning and make them look more appetising. They also add to the flavour and can be used as a basis for traditional gravy or sauce.

Butter Baste

25g (1oz/2tbsp) butter or margarine, at room temperature
15ml (1tbsp) tomato ketchup (catsup) or purée (paste)
5ml (1tsp) paprika
5ml (1tsp) Worcestershire sauce

1   Melt butter or margarine, uncovered, for 1 to 1½ minutes, at defrost setting.

2   Stir in rest of ingredients. Use as required.

Spicy Curry Baste

Butter Baste as above
5ml (1tsp) mild curry powder (or to taste)
5ml (1tsp) mustard powder
1.25ml (¼tsp) garlic granules

1   Make as butter baste and add remaining ingredients.

Tomato Baste

This is completely non-fat and therefore useful for dieters and those who are on a limited fat intake for health reasons. It is also the baste to choose for fatty meats like lamb, duck and self-basting poultry.

15ml (1tbsp) tomato purée (paste)
5ml (1tsp) prepared English mustard
5ml (1tsp) malt vinegar
5ml (1tsp) Worcestershire sauce

1   Mix all ingredients well together.

Hollandaise Sauce

*Magic, or so it seems, to be able to create a perfect Hollandaise sauce, one of the trickiest of all sauces, in a matter of seconds with no complicated mixing techniques. It is **the** classic sauce to serve with microwaved salmon and salmon trout, with broccoli and cauliflower, with oven-hot globe artichokes and asparagus, in avocado pear halves (a very rich combination) or spooned over freshly cooked fennel.*

Preparation time: about 3 minutes

Serves 6 to 8

100 g (4 oz/½ cup) slightly salted butter
15 ml (1 tbsp) fresh lemon juice
2 (size 3) egg yolks
salt and pepper to taste
pinch of caster (superfine) sugar

1 Put butter into a smallish jug or dish and leave uncovered. Melt until hot and bubbly for 1 to 1½ minutes at full power.

2 Add lemon juice and egg yolks. Whisk well. Return to oven and cook 30 seconds at full power.

3 Remove from oven and stir briskly. The sauce is ready if it is thick as cold custard and clings to whisk, fork or spoon – whichever implement you have used. If not, cook a further 15 seconds.

4 Season with salt and pepper to taste, then add sugar to counteract sharpness coming from the lemon. Serve warm.

NOTE: *If Hollandaise refused to thicken and looks curdled, it means it has been overcooked. One remedy is to beat in 2 tablespoons double cream: another to blend the sauce smoothly in blender goblet and reheat about 5 seconds at full power in the microwave. A third is to gradually beat mixture into a fresh egg yolk and return to microwave for a few seconds.*

Béarnaise Sauce (Short-cut)

Serves 6 to 8

Perfect with grilled steaks and slices of rare roast beef. Make exactly as Hollandaise (page 76), substituting mild vinegar for lemon. Add 2.5 ml (½ tsp) dried tarragon with seasonings and sugar.

Maltaise Sauce

Serves 6 to 8

For freshwater fish, veal and poultry, make as Hollandaise (page 76) then add 10 ml (2 tsp) finely grated orange rind.

Short-Cut Curry Sauce

Serve this speedy sauce spooned over hard-boiled (hard-cooked) eggs, portions of microwaved chicken, slices of roast lamb or even sausages. And for using up leftovers, it is the best yet. Just add diced meat or poultry to the sauce, cover with a plate and microwave until piping hot.

Preparation time: about 7 minutes

Serves 6 to 8 (F)

1 can condensed cream of celery soup
150 ml (¼ pt/⅔ cup) boiling water
30 ml (2 tbsp) tomato purée (paste)
15 ml (1 tbsp) curry powder
1 garlic clove, peeled and crushed
5 ml (1 tsp) turmeric
30 ml (2 tbsp) mango chutney
15 ml (1 tbsp) peanut butter
20 ml (4 tsp) desiccated (shredded) coconut

1 Put soup into a 1.2 litre (2 pt/5 cup) glass or pottery dish and add half the water. Stir in rest of ingredients except coconut.

2 Cover with a plate and heat 4 minutes at full power, stirring twice. Stand 2 minutes. Whisk in rest of water and coconut.

Balalaika Sauce

Flavours of Eastern Europe merge together splendidly in this original sauce, especially designed for any fish you can think of, from sole to plaice, salmon to prawns (shrimp) even fish fingers to fish cakes.

Preparation time: about 10 minutes

Serves 6 to 8

25 g (1 oz/2 tbsp) butter or margarine
30 ml (2 tbsp) cornflour (cornstarch)
60 ml (4 tbsp) dry white wine
150 ml (¼ pt/⅔ cup) water
1 carton (150 ml/5 fl oz) soured (dairy sour) cream
30 ml (2 tbsp) lumpfish 'caviar', red or black and available from supermarket chains and delicatessens
7.5 ml (1½ tsp) salt
15 ml (1 tbsp) scissor-snipped chives or dill
*225 g (8 oz/1½ cups) blanched tomatoes,
skinned and finely chopped*

1 Put butter or margarine into a 1.2 litre (2 pt/5 cup) glass or pottery dish. Cover with a plate and heat for 2 minutes at full power.

2 Mix cornflour smoothly with wine then stir in water. Blend soured cream into mixture. Add to butter. Leave uncovered and cook at full power for 4 to 5 minutes or until sauce bubbles gently and thickens. Beat hard at the end of every minute.

3 Stir in the lumpfish 'caviar', salt, chives or dill and the tomatoes. Cook, uncovered, a further 1½ to 2 minutes at full power, stirring twice.

Gravy

This can be made very easily in the microwave, using fat-skimmed pan juices left over from roasting poultry or meat. If there is insufficient juice, it may be topped up with water, wine or cider.

Thin Gravy for Poultry

Preparation time: about 6 minutes

Serves 6 (F)

Tip 15 ml (1 level tbsp) cornflour (cornstarch) into a 1 litre (1¾ pt/4¼ cup) glass or pottery bowl or basin. Mix smoothly with 25 ml (1½ tbsp) cold water. Crumble in 1 brown gravy cube or blend in 7.5 ml (1½ tsp) brown gravy powder. Stir in 300 ml (½ pt/1¼ cups) pan juices with, if necessary, extra water, wine or cider to make up the full amount. Leave uncovered and cook 4 to 5 minutes at full power, beating at the end of every minute. Gravy is ready when it has thickened slightly and therefore may need an extra ½ to 1 minute; much will depend on the temperature of the pan juices to begin with. Season to suit personal taste and serve.

Thick Gravy for Meat

Serves 6

Make exactly as above, using 30 ml (2 tbsp) cornflour (cornstarch), smoothly mixed with 45 ml (3 tbsp) cold water.

Apple Sauce

The traditional sauce for pork, it also goes well with duck, goose and, surprisingly, roast lamb.

Preparation time: about 10 minutes

Serves 8-9

Cook 450 g (1 lb) peeled, cored and sliced cooking (tart) apples to a pulp as directed in Cooking Fresh Fruit Chart on page 224. Beat to a purée then stir in 15 ml (1 tbsp) caster (superfine) sugar and a little salt to taste. Reheat, uncovered, ½ to ¾ minute at full power to dissolve sugar. Stir round. Serve cold.

Cranberry Sauce

Bright, glistening, sweet-sour. A most stylish accompaniment to serve at any festive occasion with turkey, goose, gammon and pork, and a delight to make in the microwave. Though the sauce tends to be runny when hot, it thickens up on cooling to a jelly-like consistency.

Preparation time: about 9 minutes plus cooling time

Serves 6 to 8 (F)

225 g (8 oz/2 cups) cranberries, thawed if frozen
150 ml (¼ pt/⅔ cup) water
175 g (6 oz/¾ cup) caster (superfine) sugar
5 ml (1 tsp) finely grated lemon rind

1   Put all the ingredients into a 1.2 litre (2 pt/5 cup) dish. Cover with a plate.

2   Cook 8½ minutes at full power, stirring sauce twice and crushing fruit against sides of bowl as you do so.

3   Remove from oven, keep covered and serve when cold. Store leftovers in an airtight container in the refrigerator.

Cranberry Wine Sauce

Serves 6 to 8 (F)

Make as Cranberry Sauce, but use red wine instead of water.

Cranberry Orange Sauce

Serves 6 to 8 (F)

Make as Cranberry Sauce, adding the finely grated rind of 1 medium washed and dried orange with all remaining ingredients.

Egg Custard Sauce

This is a true, old-fashioned and authentic custard sauce which, with the aid of a microwave, can be made in under 10 minutes with minimal beating and no curdling. It keeps well, can be served hot or cold and is a dream in trifles, spooned over stewed fruits and steamed puddings, or used as a topping for strawberries and raspberries instead of cream.

Preparation time: about 8 minutes

Makes about 600 ml (1 pt/2½ cups)

*600 ml (1 pt/2½ cups) milk (long life gives an enriched flavour),
or use half milk and half single (light) cream
15 ml (1 tbsp) cornflour (cornstarch)
(prevents curdling as it acts as a stabiliser)
15 ml (1 tbsp) cold water
4 (size 2) eggs
45 ml (3 tbsp) caster (superfine) sugar
5 ml (1 tsp) vanilla essence (extract)*

1   Heat milk, uncovered in jug, for 2 minutes at full power.

2   Meanwhile, tip cornflour into a 1.2 litre (2 pt/5 cup) bowl, add water and stir until smooth. Break in eggs then add sugar.

3   Whisk until smooth then gradually blend in the hot milk. Leave uncovered. Cook 5 to 5½ minutes at full power, whisking at the end of every minute. When ready, custard should cling to the wooden fork or spatula used for whisking or, in the case of a wooden spoon, coat the back of it. Mix in vanilla.

Different Flavours

Omit vanilla and use rum, sherry, almond or rose essence (extract).

Lemon or Orange Custard

Make as above, then stir in 10 ml (2 tsp) finely grated lemon or orange rind instead of vanilla.

Hot Chocolate Sauce

The ultimate luxury for ice cream and banana splits. If allowed to cool, it may also be spooned over a dish of Profiteroles.

Preparation time: about 7 minutes

Serves 6

25g (1oz/2tbsp) butter
50g (2oz/¼ cup) soft dark brown (coffee) sugar
30ml (2tbsp) cocoa (unsweetened chocolate) powder
15ml (1tbsp) golden syrup (light corn syrup)
30ml (2tbsp) cold milk
5ml (1tsp) vanilla essence (extract)

1   Put butter into a basin and melt uncovered for 1 to 1½ minutes at defrost setting.

2   Add brown sugar then sift in cocoa powder. Stir in rest of ingredients thoroughly.

3   Leave uncovered and heat for 5 minutes at defrost setting, stirring twice. Serve hot or cold over ice cream and ice cream sundaes.

Hot Mocha Sauce

Serves 6

Make exactly as above, adding 7.5ml (1½tsp) instant coffee powder or granules with the syrup, milk and essence.

VEGETARIAN DISHES

These dishes are primarily for main courses and accompaniments and I am sure will be well accepted by all cooks, of any persuasion, who enjoy appetising food without meat or fish.

Nut Burgers

Nothing especially original about these – vegetarians have been enjoying nut cutlets for years – but the blend of mixed nuts gives the Burgers an outstanding flavour and crunchy texture. Serve them hot with one of the sauces from the Sauce Section and two or three different vegetables. Or try them cold with salad. Or slice them in half and use as a sandwich filling with lettuce, pickle and mayonnaise. Or eat as they are for a snack.

Preparation time: about 8 minutes

Makes 10 (F)

100 g (4 oz/1 cup) shelled but unskinned whole almonds
100 g (4 oz/1 cup) walnut pieces
100 g (4 oz/1 cup) cashew pieces, lightly toasted (see page 303)
100 g (4 oz/2 cups) fresh brown breadcrumbs (soft)
75 g (3 oz/¾ cup) onion, peeled and grated
2.5 ml (½ tsp) salt
5 ml (1 tsp) prepared mustard
25 g (1 oz/2 tbsp) butter or margarine,
melted 1 to 1½ minutes in microwave
30 ml (2 tbsp) milk

1   Grind nuts finely in blender or food processor. Mix with rest of ingredients.

2   Shape into 10 even-sized ovals. Arrange round edge of large greased plate. Leave uncovered and cook 4 minutes at full power, turning over once. Serve as suggested.

Nut 'Cake'

Serves 6 to 8 (F)

Make as above, using 175 g (6 oz/1½ cups) brazils, 50 g (2 oz/½ cup) toasted but unsalted peanuts and 100 g (4 oz/1 cup) unskinned but shelled almonds. Shape into a round of 17 to 20 cm (7 to 8 inches) on a greased plate. Leave uncovered. Cook 3 minutes at full power, stand 5 minutes, cook a further 2½ minutes at full power. Cut into wedges and serve hot or cold.

Paprika Mushrooms

Reminiscent of the glories of the Austro-Hungarian Empire when the food was rich, lavish and very much to Queen Marie Theresa's taste, these paprika mushrooms are enveloped in lightly seasoned soured (dairy sour) cream and attractively coloured with tomato purée (paste). They make a regal meal with baby boiled potatoes or small pasta.

Preparation time: about 20 minutes

Serves 6

900 g (2 lbs) button mushrooms
50 g (2 oz/¼ cup) butter or margarine
1 garlic clove, peeled and crushed
1 large carton (300 ml/10 fl oz) soured (dairy sour) cream
15 ml (1 tbsp) paprika
15 ml (1 tbsp) tomato purée (paste)
7.5 ml (1½ tsp) salt

1   Trim mushrooms then wash and dry.

2   Put butter or margarine into a 2.25 litre (4 pt/10 cup) glass or pottery dish and melt 1½ to 2 minutes at defrost setting. Leave uncovered.

3   Add mushrooms and garlic. Cover with a plate and cook 10 minutes at full power, stirring 3 times.

4   Mix in remaining ingredients, tossing over and over gently with a spoon. Cover as above. Cook 5 minutes at full power, stirring once.

5   Remove from oven and uncover. Stir once more then serve with suggested accompaniments.

Curried Mushrooms

Splendidly tempting, what better meal than these softly curried mushrooms? They make a sustaining lunch or supper dish, and are predictably at their finest accompanied by rice or bulgar with side dishes of chutney, sliced hard-boiled (hard-cooked) eggs showered with chopped walnuts, yoghurt mixed with 5 or 10 ml (1 or 2 tsp) chopped mint, and a salad of chopped tomatoes and cucumber.

Preparation time: about 16 minutes

Serves 6

900 g (2 lb) button mushrooms
50 g (2 oz/¼ cup) butter or margarine
15 ml (1 tbsp) curry powder
5 ml (1 tsp) salt
150 ml (¼ pt/⅔ cup) buttermilk
5 ml (1 tsp) caster (superfine) sugar
1.25 ml (¼ tsp) garlic powder
15 ml (1 tbsp) cornflour (cornstarch)
30 ml (2 tbsp) cold water

1 Trim mushrooms then wash and dry. Leave aside temporarily.

2 Put butter or margarine into a 2.25 litre (4 pt/10 cup) glass or pottery dish and melt 1½ to 2 minutes at defrost setting. Leave uncovered.

3 Add curry powder, salt, buttermilk, caster sugar and garlic powder. Cover with a plate and cook 2 minutes at full power.

4 Toss in mushrooms. Add cornflour, smoothly mixed with water. Cover as above and cook 7 minutes at full power, stirring twice.

5 Uncover, stir again and serve as suggested.

Leek and Chestnut Casserole

A tempting arrangement, remarkably easy and a hearty meal with micro-waved jacket potatoes and tomatoes. Prepare chestnuts in advance.

Preparation time: about 13 minutes plus cooking time of chestnuts

Serves 4 (F)

2 large leeks
25 g (1 oz/2 tbsp) butter or margarine
225 g (8 oz/2 cups) dried chestnuts,
cooked as described on page 305
2.5-5 ml (½-1 tsp) salt

1 Trim leeks, leaving on 5 cm (2 inches) of green 'skirt'. Slit and wash very thoroughly to remove earth and grit, then cut into 1 cm (½ inch) slices.

2 Put butter or margarine into a 18 cm (7 inch) round glass or pottery casserole and melt 1 to 1½ minutes at defrost setting.

3 Mix in leeks, cover with a plate and cook for 6 minutes at full power, stirring twice.

4 Break up chestnuts and combine with leeks. Sprinkle with salt. Cover as above and cook a further 3 minutes at full power. Stir and serve.

Cauliflower Cheese

Serves 4 (F)

Cook cauliflower as directed in Vegetable Chart on page 181. Drain. Put into dish. Coat with freshly made Cheese sauce and sprinkle with paprika.

Leave uncovered and reheat 5 to 6 minutes at defrost setting or brown under a pre-heated grill if preferred.

Kibbled Wheat Salad

Full of that slightly firm and 'al dente' texture so beloved by the Italians, kibbled wheat makes a sturdy salad indeed, and a very tasty one at that enhanced with onions, parsley, oil and fresh lemon juice. Nutritious enough for anyone into the 'naturals', the salad partners amicably with eggs and cheese.

Preparation time: about 25 minutes plus cooling time

Serves 4

225 g (8 oz/scant 2 cups) kibbled wheat
900 ml (1½ pt/3¾ cups) hot water
7.5 ml (1½ tsp) salt
15 ml (1 tbsp) sunflower oil
juice of a small lemon
75 g (3 oz/¾ cup) onion, peeled and finely grated
45 ml (3 tbsp) finely chopped parsley

1 Rinse kibbled wheat and put into a 2.25 litre (4 pt/10 cup) glass or pottery dish. Add hot water and salt.

2 Cover with cling film. Slit three times with a knife. Cook 10 minutes at full power. Uncover.

3 Return to oven and cook at full power for a further 15 minutes, stirring 3 times.

4 Remove from oven, cover with a plate and leave until completely cold. Drain if necessary but wheat should have absorbed all the moisture.

5 Fork in the rest of ingredients, transfer to a dish or bowl and serve as suggested above when cold.

Kibbled Wheat Breakfast

Serves 6

Spoon freshly cooked plain kibbled wheat into bowls. Add milk and brown sugar or honey to each.

Bulgar

Bulgar, also known as burghal or cracked wheat, is widely eaten in the Middle East and North Africa as a change from rice or potatoes, and is available over here from health food shops and oriental grocers. It is delicious served hot with main courses or cold in salads.

Preparation time: about 9 minutes

Serves 4 to 6

225 g (8 oz/1¾ cups) bulgar
600 ml (1 pt/2½ cups) boiling water
5-7.5 ml (1-1½ tsp) salt

1 Put bulgar into a 20 cm (8 inch) round and fairly deep glass or pottery dish. Leave uncovered and toast, with no water, for 3 minutes at full power, stirring at the end of every minute.

2 Mix in boiling water. Cook, uncovered, for 5 minutes at full power, stirring 3 times. Season to taste then fluff up with a fork.

Onion Bulgar

Serves 4 to 6 (F)

Put 25 g (1 oz) butter or margarine, or 15 ml (1 tbsp) sunflower oil into a 20 cm (8 inch) round and fairly deep glass or pottery dish. Heat 1 to 1½ minutes at defrost setting. Add 100 g (4 oz/1 cup) grated onion. Cook, uncovered, for 3 minutes at full power. Remove from oven. Toast bulgar as above. Stir in onions with boiling water. Continue as above. Serve with vegetable dishes or eggs.

Sultan's Salad

Serves 4

Cook bulgar as directed in first recipe then leave until lukewarm. Stir in 1 peeled and crushed garlic clove, 50 g (2 oz/½ cup) grated carrots, 15 ml (1 tbsp) chopped mint, 75 ml (4 tbsp) chopped parsley, the strained juice of 1 lemon and 45-60 ml (3-4 tbsp) corn or sunflower oil. Adjust seasoning to taste. Stud with black and green olives. Serve with Pitta bread.

Blue Cheese and Walnut Flan

Quiche-related, this makes a superb lunch dish with a crunchy chicory and orange salad, tossed in a zesty French dressing.

Preparation time: about 30 minutes

Serves 4

PASTRY (PASTE)
175 g (6 oz/1½ cups) plain (all-purpose) flour
pinch of salt
75 g (3 oz/⅓ cup) butter or margarine, at room temperature
25 g (1 oz/¼ cup) walnuts, finely chopped
about 35 ml (7 tsp) cold water to mix
1 egg yolk

FILLING
200 g (7 oz/scant cup) full fat cream cheese
30 ml (2 tbsp) snipped chives or the light green part of leek, finely chopped
100 g (4 oz) soft blue cheese such as Gorgonzola,
5 ml (1 tsp) paprika
2 (size 3) eggs, at room temperature and well beaten
60 ml (4 tbsp) cold milk

1 For pastry, sift flour and salt into a bowl. Rub in fat finely, toss in walnuts then mix to a firm dough with cold water.

2 Turn out on to floured surface, knead lightly until smooth then roll out fairly thinly into a circle. Use to a line a lightly greased 20 cm (8 inch) glass or pottery pie plate. Pinch top edge into flutes between forefinger and thumb then prick all over with a fork. Cook 6 minutes, uncovered, at full power. If pastry has bulged in places, press down very gently with an oven-gloved hand.

3 Brush all over with egg yolk. Cook a further minute at full power to seal holes. Leave to stand while preparing filling.

4 Beat cream cheese until light and very soft. Add chives. Mash in blue cheese then add rest of ingredients. Beat well until completely smooth. Pour into pastry case. Cook, uncovered, 14 minutes at defrost setting. Serve warm or cold.

Stuffed Aubergines (Eggplants)

With a mellow egg filling and golden brown pine nuts (kernels), these stuffed aubergines may be served hot or cold and team especially well with jacket potatoes and salad. I like them for lunch, but they also make a pleasing light supper dish accompanied by an assortment of cooked vegetables and perhaps homemade soup for starters.

Preparation time: about 15 minutes

Serves 2

2 medium aubergines (eggplants) (about 550g/1¼ lb)
10 ml (2 tsp) lemon juice
75 g (3 oz/1½ cups) fresh brown breadcrumbs
25 g (1 oz/¼ cup) toasted pine nuts (kernels) (see page 303)
7.5 ml (1½ tsp) salt
5 ml (1 tsp) garlic or onion powder
3 hard-boiled (hard-cooked) eggs (see page 99), chopped
60 ml (4 tbsp) milk
5 ml (1 tsp) dried mixed herbs
20 ml (4 tsp) sunflower or olive oil

1   Slit skin of aubergines all the way round lengthwise with a sharp knife, as though you were going to cut each aubergine in half.

2   Put on to a plate, cover with a piece of kitchen paper and cook 6 minutes at full power when aubergines should be tender.

3   Remove from oven and cut each in half along slit lines. Scoop pulp into blender or food processor, leaving skin intact. Add lemon juice. Run machine until mixture is smooth and purée-like.

4   Mix in crumbs, nuts, salt, garlic or onion powder, chopped eggs, milk and herbs.

5   Return to aubergine halves then stand on a plate, narrow ends towards centre. Trickle oil over tops, cover with kitchen paper and reheat 4 minutes at full power.

Tomato Upside Down Cheese Pudding

Nutrition-packed and colourful, this is an easy savoury dish to make and is ready for the table in no time at all. Serve with a green vegetable.

Preparation time: about 15 minutes

Serves 4

225 g (8 oz/2 cups) self-raising flour
5 ml (1 tsp) mustard powder
2.5 ml (½ tsp) salt
100 g (4 oz/½ cup) butter or margarine
100 g (4 oz/1 cup) Cheddar cheese, finely grated
2 (size 3) eggs, beaten
150 ml (¼ pt/⅔ cup) cold milk
450 g (1 lb) tomatoes, blanched and skinned
2.5 ml (½ tsp) salt
15 ml (1 tbsp) chopped parsley

1 Well-grease a 1.75 litre (3 pt/7½ cup) deep round dish.

2 Sift flour, mustard and salt into a bowl. Rub in butter or margarine finely. Toss in cheese.

3 Using a fork, mix to a soft consistency with eggs and milk. Spoon into a dish and spread evenly with a knife.

4 Cook, uncovered, for 6 minutes at full power.

5 Meanwhile skin tomatoes and chop. Mix with salt. Put into a shallow bowl and cover with a plate.

6 Remove pudding from oven and turn out into a dish. Return to oven and cook a further 2 minutes at full power.

7 Remove from oven, cover with kitchen paper and leave aside temporarily. Heat tomatoes for 3 minutes at full power. Spoon over pudding, sprinkle with parsley and serve while still hot.

Lentil Dhal

Distinctly oriental with origins in India, this Lentil Dahl is an elegantly-flavoured and nutritious dish which makes a fine meal with freshly cooked long grain rice and side dishes of yoghurt, chutney and sliced onions.

Preparation time: about 20 minutes

Serves 6 generously (F)

225 g (8 oz/1⅓ cups) red lentils
50 g (2 oz/¼ cup) butter or margarine
or 45 ml (3 tbsp) sunflower oil
350 g (12 oz/3 cups) onions, peeled and chopped
1 garlic clove, peeled and crushed
7.5 ml (1 tsp) turmeric
7.5 ml (1 tsp) paprika
2.5 ml (½ tsp) ground ginger
20 ml (4 tsp) garam masala
good pinch cayenne pepper
4 cardamom pods, broken open to release seeds
15 ml (1 tbsp) tomato purée (paste)
750 ml (1¼ pt/3 cups) boiling water
7.5 ml (1½ tsp) salt
coriander (cilantro) leaves, chopped

1 Rinse lentils under cold, running water. Leave on one side temporarily.

2 Put butter, margarine or oil into a 1.75 litre (3 pt/7½ cup) dish and heat, uncovered, for 1 minute at full power. Mix in onions and garlic. Cover with a plate. Cook 3 minutes at full power.

3 Stir in remaining ingredients except coriander. Cover with cling film, puncturing twice with the tip of a knife. Cook 15 minutes at full power.

4 Fluff up with a fork before serving and, if too thick for personal taste, add a little extra boiling water until the right consistency is achieved. Garnish by sprinkling with chopped coriander.

Way Down Yonder Aubergine (Eggplant) Casserole

Another hand-picked special, discovered during my travels to Louisiana. It is blissful for vegetarians, pertly-flavoured, and with just the right amount of crunch to add interest to the fairly soft texture of the aubergines. It may be 'hotted-up' by the addition of a few drops of Tabasco after the salt.

Preparation time: about 20 minutes

Serves 4

25 g (1 oz/2 tbsp) butter or magarine
50 g (2 oz/½ cup) celery, scrubbed and finely chopped
175 g (6 oz/1½ cups) onions, peeled and finely chopped
50 g (2 oz/½ cup) red or green (bell) pepper,
de-seeded and finely chopped
450 g (1 lb) cooked and puréed aubergines (eggplants)
(for method, see recipe for Aubergine Dip on page 52)
175 g (6 oz/1 cup) blanched tomatoes, skinned and chopped
75 g (3 oz/1½ cups) fresh white breadcrumbs
2.5-5 ml (½-1 tsp) salt
50 g (2 oz/½ cup) Double Gloucester cheese, grated

1 Heat butter or margarine, in 1.2 litre (2 pt/5 cup) dish, for 1 minute at full power. Leave uncovered.

2 Stir in celery, onions and pepper. Cover with plate or matching lid and cook 3 minutes at full power. Mix in aubergine purée, tomatoes, crumbs and salt.

3 Cover with plate or lid as above and cook another 3 minutes at full power.

4 Uncover, sprinkle with cheese and cook 2 minutes at full power. Stand 2 to 3 minutes and serve.

Avocado Farci

Perfect for vegetarians, this avocado dish is both unusual and delicious and may also be served as a meal starter for 4 people – vegetarian or not. In either case, the best accompaniment is crisp toast.

Preparation time: about 9 minutes

Serves 2

2 good-sized ripe avocados
juice of ½ lemon
50g (2oz/1 cup) soft brown breadcrumbs
40g (1½oz/5 tbsp) onion, peeled and finely grated
100g (4oz/⅔ cup) blanched tomatoes, skinned and chopped
50g (2oz/½ cup) Lancashire cheese, crumbled or grated
paprika
8 toasted hazelnuts

1 Halve avocados and carefully spoon flesh into a bowl. Add lemon juice and mash very finely with a fork.

2 Stir in crumbs, onion and tomatoes. Return to avocado shells and sprinkle with cheese and paprika. Top each with 2 hazelnuts.

3 Arrange on a plate with pointed ends towards centre. Cook, uncovered, for 5 to 5½ minutes at full power. Serve straight away.

Macaroni Pepperoni

An uncomplicated macaroni accompaniment, flavoured with peppers and coloured with tomato juice. If you heap grated cheese on to each serving and sprinkle with chopped parsley, you have a main meal of some substance.

Preparation time: about 20 minutes

Serves 4 as a side dish or 2 as a main course

300 ml (½ pt/1¼ cups) tomato juice
100 g (4 oz/1 cup) elbow macaroni
5 ml (1 tsp) salt
30 ml (2 tbsp) hot white wine or water
50 g (2 oz/½ cup) frozen diced green and red (bell) peppers
(used from frozen)
40 g (1½ oz/3 tbsp) butter or margarine

FOR MAIN COURSE
75 g (3 oz/¾ cup) Cheddar cheese, finely grated
30 ml (2 tbsp) chopped parsley

1   Pour tomato juice into a 1.2 litre (2 pt/5 cup) glass or pottery dish. Cover with a plate. Heat until boiling, allowing 3 to 4 minutes at full power.

2   Take out of oven and stir in macaroni, salt, wine or water, the frozen vegetables and butter or margarine. Mix well. Cover with cling film, then puncture twice with the tip of a knife. Alternatively, cover with matching lid.

3   Cook 10 minutes at full power, stirring once or twice. Leave to stand 5 minutes before serving.

EGGS

'I can't even boil an egg' is a cry from the heart I hear very often. And although dab and experienced hands may find this hard to understand, egg cookery can be problematic. I, too, have eaten my way through tough and rubbery omelets, watery scrambled eggs, leathery fried ones, runny or overcooked boiled eggs and unfortunate poached ones with floppy whites and overcooked yolks. Why a microwave oven has such a superb effect on eggs is beyond my limited scientific scope but whichever way one cooks eggs the results are always perfect – or near perfect – and the speed of operation is a joy. There is just one important factor to bear in mind: the yolks of eggs destined for poaching, frying and baking should be punctured twice, gently, with the tip of a knife or skewer to break the fine skin or membrane enveloping each. This will subsequently stop the yolks from bursting, spluttering and make a mess all over the oven.

Eggs – Warming

For those of you who decide to make a cake at the last minute, whether in the microwave or conventionally, and the recipe requires eggs at room temperature while yours are still in the refrigerator, I have overcome the problem completely by warming the eggs in a dish in the microwave.

For 1 Egg
Break into a small dish or cup. Puncture yolk twice with a metal skewer or tip of a knife to prevent bursting. Cover with plate or saucer. Warm ½ minute at defrost setting.

For 2 Eggs
Break into a small dish or cup. Puncture yolks twice with a metal skewer or tip of a knife to prevent bursting. Cover with plate or saucer. Warm ½ to ¾ minute at defrost setting.

For 3 Eggs
Follow directions for 2 eggs but warm 1 to 1¼ minutes at defrost setting.

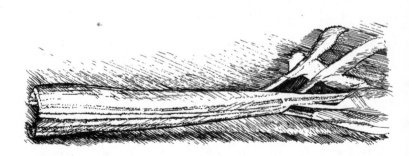

Eggs – Boiling

You can buy special microwave egg boilers now, but my way works well. It is based on 'egg in the cup'; a way of serving boiled eggs in many parts of Germany, usually for breakfast. Pursuing the same idea, I have worked out the following timings for boiled eggs with excellent results. For more tips on egg boiling see next page.

Soft Boiled (softcooked) Egg
Use 1 egg only. Break into a greased cup or one lined with cling film. Puncture yolk twice with a thin metal skewer or tip of a knife to prevent bursting. Cover with a saucer. Cook 1 minute at defrost setting. Swirl gently around. Re-cover. Continue to cook a further ½ minute at defrost. Stand ½ minute. Either eat from the cup or invert on to a slice of toast.

Medium Soft Boiled (softcooked) Egg
Follow directions for Soft Boiled Egg, but allow 2 minutes at defrost setting. Stand ½ minute.

Hardboiled (hardcooked) Egg
Follow directions for Soft Boiled Egg, but allow 2½ minutes at defrost setting, depending on size. Stand ¾ minute. Tip out of the cup and use as required. Because the egg holds its shape so well, it can be used as a basis for egg mayonnaise. For garnishing purposes, the white can be separated from the yolk and either chopped or cut into thin strips. The yolk may be rubbed through a mesh sieve and sprinkled over other foods for a bright touch of yellow.

Hardboiled (hardcooked) Eggs – cooking 2 at once
Follow directions for Soft Boiled Egg, but put into a greased dish and allow 4 minutes at defrost setting. Stand 1 minute.

Hardboiled (hardcooked) Eggs – cooking 3 at once
Follow directions for Soft Boiled Egg, but put into a greased dish and allow 5½ minutes at defrost setting. Stand 1 minute.

TIPS:

1. *Eggs taken from the refrigerator, or those larger than size 3, may need a few seconds longer than times given above.*

2. *For soft and medium boiled, it is best to cook eggs individually. Hardboiled (hardcooked) eggs are less critical and you can microwave more than one at a time.*

3. *Wash the cup* immediately after use *as any leftover white has a tendency to congeal when cold.*

4. *It is important to keep eggs covered while cooking to prevent them from drying out.*

5. *The advantages of cooking eggs in this way is cleanliness, a saving in fuel costs, ease of eating and no shells to cope with after the meal.*

Poached Eggs

Appreciated by slimmers and others who are partial to poached eggs on toast, or on cooked spinach with a coating of cheese sauce for Eggs Florentine, the egg or eggs should be cooked individually in small dishes or cups.

For 1 Egg
Pour 90 ml (6 tbsp) hot water into a small glass or pottery dish. Add 2.5 ml (½ tsp) of mild vinegar to prevent the white from spreading. Carefully break in 1 (size 3) egg. Puncture yolk twice with the tip of a knife. Cover dish with a plate. Cook from ¾ to 1¼ minutes at full power, depending on how firm you like the white to be. Leave to stand 1 minute. Remove from dish with perforated draining spoon.

For 2 Eggs in 2 Dishes (cooked simultaneously)
Cook 1½ to 2 minutes at full power. Stand 1¼ minutes. If whites are too runny, cook an extra 15 to 20 seconds.

For 3 Eggs in 3 Dishes (cooked simultaneously)
Cook 2 to 2½ minutes at full power. Stand 2 minutes. If whites are too runny, cook an extra 20 to 30 seconds.

Scrambled Eggs

Popular for all meals of the day, eggs scrambled in the microwave are light and soft in texture, almost non-fail and best made in a glass cup, bowl, dish or measuring jug so that one can monitor the action through the oven door. I offer 2 versions: one basic with a little milk, and the other enriched and softened with 1 tablespoon of milk per egg, which is slightly above the average amount usually recommended.

Basic Scrambled Eggs

For 1 Egg
Break 1 (size 3) egg into a lightly buttered glass container. Add 10 ml (2 tsp) milk, seasoning to taste and a small knob of butter or margarine. Beat well. Cover with a saucer or plate. Cook 30 seconds at full power. Stir briskly. Re-cover and continue to cook a further 10 to 15 seconds when egg should be lightly set and start rising in the container. Remove from oven, again stir briskly, leave to stand 2 minutes and serve straight away. Do not overcook or egg will become leathery and liquid will seep out.

For 2 Eggs
Add 20 ml (4 tsp) milk to eggs. Season and add a knob of butter or margarine. Cook 45 seconds. Stir briskly. Cook a further 20 to 30 seconds. Stir briskly, leave to stand 2 minutes and serve.

For 3 Eggs
Add 30 ml (6 tsp) milk to eggs. Season and add a knob of butter or margarine. Cook 1 minute. Stir briskly. Cook a further 35 to 50 seconds. Stir briskly, leave to stand 2 minutes and serve.

For 4 Eggs
Add 40 ml (8 tsp) milk to eggs. Season and add a knob of butter or margarine. Cook 1½ minutes. Stir briskly. Cook a further 1 to 1½ minutes. Stir briskly, leave to stand for 2 minutes then serve.

Extra Creamy Scrambled Eggs

For 1 Egg

Make as previously directed but add 15 ml (1 tbsp) cold milk, seasoning and butter. Cook 3 minutes at defrost setting, stirring briskly twice.

For 2 Eggs

Make as previously directed but add 30 ml (2 tbsp) cold milk, seasoning and butter. Cook 4¾ to 5 minutes at defrost setting, stirring briskly 3 times.

For 3 Eggs

Make as previously directed but add 45 ml (3 tbsp) cold milk, seasoning and butter. Cook 6½ minutes at defrost setting, stirring briskly 4 times.

For 4 Eggs

Make as previously directed but add 60 ml (4 tbsp) cold milk, seasoning and butter. Cook 8½ minutes at defrost setting, stirring briskly 5 times.

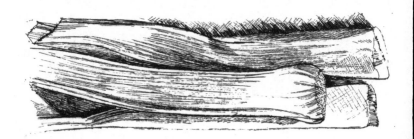

Fried Eggs

These turn out soft and tender, as only the best fried eggs should, brightly 'sunny side up', as the Americans say, and with a surround of white which never becomes frizzled and indigestible.

For 1 Egg
Brush a small dish lightly with melted butter, margarine or oil. Gently break in 1 (size 3) egg. Puncture yolk twice with the tip of a knife. Sprinkle lightly with salt and pepper to taste and, if liked, some finely chopped fresh herbs. Cover with a plate. Cook 30 seconds at full power. Stand 1 minute. Cook an extra 15 to 20 seconds when white should be set. If not, allow an extra 5 to 7 seconds.

For 2 Eggs
Break 2 eggs into greased dish. Puncture yolks twice with the tip of a knife. Season. Cover. Cook 1 minute at full power. Stand 1 minute. Cook an extra 20 to 40 seconds when whites should be set. If not, allow an extra 6 to 8 seconds.

NOTE: *Frying more than 2 eggs at a time is not recommended as the yolks would cook more quickly than the whites and become hard. This is due to the longer cooking time needed to set the whites.*

Classic Omelet

A fine-textured and light omelet which is delicous both plain and filled. For a substantial meal, allow 1 omelet per person but for a lightish snack or breakfast, half an omelet should be adequate.

Preparation time about 5 minutes

Serves 1 to 2

melted butter or margarine
3 (size 2 or 3) eggs
1.25 ml (¼ level tsp) salt
30 ml (2 tbsp) cold water
pepper to taste
parsley or watercress to garnish

1 Brush a fairly shallow 20 cm (8 inch) round glass or pottery dish with melted butter or margarine.

2 Beat eggs *very thoroughly* with all remaining ingredients (breaking them up lightly, as for traditional omelets, is not enough).

3 Pour into dish and put into microwave. Cover with plate. Cook 1½ minutes at full power.

4 Uncover then stir egg mixture gently with a wooden spoon or fork, bringing the partially set edges to the centre. Return to microwave and cover as before. Cook another 1½ minutes at full power.

5 Uncover and cook ½ to 1 minute or until top is just set. Fold into 3 like an envelope and carefully slide out on to a warm plate. Garnish with parsley or watercress and serve straight away.

Ham Omelet

Sprinkle the half cooked omelet with 25 g (1 oz) coarsely chopped ham.

Avocado Omelet

Cover half the cooked omelet with 15 ml (1 tbsp) mashed avocado, seasoned well to taste with salt and pepper and mixed with 5 ml (1 tsp) lemon juice to prevent browning.

Parsley Omelet

Shower omelet mixture with 30 ml (2 tbsp) chopped parsley after it has cooked for the first 1½ minutes.

Chive Omelet

Make exactly as Parsley Omelet.

Omelette aux Fines Herbs

This is a herb omelet flavoured with a mixture of 2 or 3 fresh herbs such as parsley, chives and basil. They should be very finely chopped and 30 ml (2 tbsp), added as directed for the Parsley Omelet above, is enough for the quantity of eggs used.

Brunch Omelet

This is an American-style omelet, very often served for Sunday brunch when people combine a relaxed late breakfast and early lunch.

Make exactly as the Classic Omelet but use 45 ml (3 tbsp) cold milk instead of water. After uncovering, cook for 1 to 1½ minutes. Fold in 3 and carefully slide out on to a plate. Garnish as suggested above.

Filled Omelets

*Either the Classic Omelet or Brunch Omelet may be filled, but then it should be folded in half and **not** into three.*

Serves 1 to 2

Tomato Omelet

Cover one half of the cooked omelet with 1 blanched tomato, skinned and chopped. Fold and serve.

Mushroom Omelet

In a small dish, melt 15 g (½ oz/1 tbsp) butter or margarine, uncovered, for ¾ minute at defrost setting. Add 50 g (2 oz/½ cup) trimmed and coarsely chopped mushrooms. Stir well to mix and return to microwave. Cover and cook until soft, allowing ½ to ¾ minute at full power. Use to cover one half of omelet. Fold and serve.

Cheese Omelet

Sprinkle half the cooked omelet with 25 g (1 oz/¼ cup) grated hard cheese (type according to individual preference) or with crumbled blue cheese. Fold and serve.

Omelet Arnold Bennett

This is a rich and luxurious omelet, said to have been masterminded by a chef at London's Savoy Hotel in honour of the famous writer. My adaptation follows.

Flake 100 g (4 oz) freshly cooked smoked haddock fillet or smoked cod fillet and transfer to a small dish. Mix in 1 carton (150 ml/5 oz) soured (dairy sour) cream. Cover with a saucer or plate and cook for 1½ minutes at full power. Remove from microwave and leave to stand while making the Brunch Omelet. Give it its full 3 minutes at full power (see directions above) then uncover and cook a further ½ minute at full power. Spread all over with smoked fish and cream mixture and sprinkle with 25-40 g (1-1½ oz) grated Red Leicester cheese. Leave uncovered and cook for a futher 1½ to 2 minutes at full power when omelet should be hot and cheese melted. Cut into 2 or 3 portions and serve with a crisp salad.

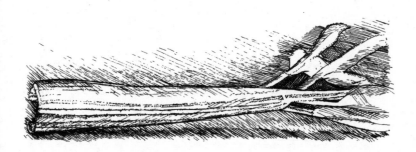

Tortilla

The famous Spanish Omelet is a flat and pancake-like egg dish containing onions and potatoes. Like the Omelet Arnold Bennett, and the Chinese one which follows, it is never folded but cut into portions and served flat. Accompany with rolls and butter. Also a crisp salad.

Preparation time: about 9 minutes

Serves 2

15 g (½ oz/1 tbsp) butter or margarine
100 g (4 oz/1 cup) onion, peeled and finely chopped
175 g (6 oz/1 cup) cold cooked potatoes, cubed
3 (size 2) eggs
3.75-5 ml (¾-1 tsp) salt
30 ml (2 tbsp) cold water

1 Melt butter or margarine, uncovered, in a 20 cm (8 inch) shallow round dish. Allow ¾ minute at defrost setting.

2 Mix in onion. Cover dish with plate then cook 2 minutes at full power. Uncover and stir in potatoes. Cover again with a plate and cook a further minute at full power. Remove from oven.

3 Beat eggs very thoroughly with salt and cold water. Pour evenly over onions and potatoes in dish. Cook, uncovered, for 4½ minutes at full power.

4 Stand 1 minute, cut into 2 portions and transfer to warm plates. Serve straight away.

Omelet Fu Yung

A personal adaptation of a Chinese egg dish. It teams well with rice or noodles and microwaved tomato halves.

Preparation time: about 12 minutes

Serves 2

15 g (½ oz/1 tbsp) butter or margarine
75 g (3 oz/¾ cup) onion, peeled and finely chopped
30 ml (2 tbsp) cooked peas
30 ml (2 tbsp) canned bean sprouts, well drained
50 g (4 oz/½ cup) trimmed mushrooms, thinly sliced
3 (size 2) eggs
3.75 ml (¾ tsp) salt
30 ml (2 tbsp) cold water
5 ml (1 tsp) Soy sauce
4 spring onions (scallions) to garnish

1 Melt butter or margarine, uncovered, in a 20 cm (8 inch) shallow round dish. Allow ¾ minute at defrost setting.

2 Mix in onion. Cover dish with plate then cook 2 minutes at full power. Uncover and stir in peas, bean sprouts and mushrooms.

3 Cover as above and cook 1½ minutes. Remove from oven. Beat eggs very thoroughly with salt, water and Soy sauce.

4 Pour evenly over ingredients in dish. Cook 5 minutes, uncovered, at full power.

5 Stand 1 minute, cut into 2 portions and transfer to warm plates. Garnish with spring onions. Serve straight away.

Omelet in Pizza Style

Marvellous for slimmers and when one fancies something a bit Pizzaish but has neither time nor inclination to make a dough.

Preparation time: about 10 minutes

Serves 2

15g (½oz/1tbsp) butter or margarine
3 (size 2) eggs
45ml (3tbsp) milk
2.5ml (½tsp) salt
350g (12oz/2cups) blanched and skinned tomatoes, sliced
100g (4oz) Mozzarella cheese, sliced
8 canned anchovies in oil
8 black olives

1 Melt butter or margarine, uncovered, in a 20cm (8inch) shallow round dish. Allow ¾ minute at defrost setting.

2 Beat eggs very thoroughly with milk and salt. Pour into dish. Cover with plate. Cook 1½ minutes at full power.

3 Uncover then stir mixture gently with a wooden spoon or fork, bringing the partially set edges to the centre. Return to microwave and cover as before. Cook another 1½ minutes at full power.

4 Uncover and cook a further ½ minute. Spread with tomatoes and cheese then garnish with anchovies and olives. Leave uncovered and cook 4 minutes at full power. Cut into 2 portions and serve while piping hot.

Soufflé Omelet

*Dreamy and soft, filled with jam and showered with icing (confectioners')
sugar – a perfect sweet to end a light meal.*

Preparation time: about 8 minutes

Serves 2

*50g (2oz/3 tbsp) jam, flavour to taste
icing (confectioners') sugar
melted butter
3 (size 1 or 2) eggs
3 drops lemon juice
15 ml (1 tbsp) caster (superfine) sugar*

1   Spoon jam into a small dish or cup. Cover with a saucer and
heat for 1½ minutes at defrost setting. Remove from oven (it
retains heat well) and leave to stand while preparing omelet.
Cover a large piece of greaseproof paper with a thickish layer of
sifted icing sugar.

2   Brush a 25 cm (10 inch) round and fairly shallow dish all over
with melted butter.

3   Separate eggs, putting yolks into one bowl and whites into
another. Add lemon juice to whites and beat until stiff.

4   Add sugar to egg yolks and whip to a thick cream. Gently
whisk in egg whites. When thoroughly combined, spoon into
prepared dish.

5   Cook, uncovered, for 3½ minutes at full power.

6   Invert on to the sugared paper, make a cut down the centre
and spread one half with the warmed jam.

7   Fold in half and cut into 2 portions. Eat straight away.

Baked Eggs

Also called Oeufs en Cocotte, this way of preparing eggs is highly esteemed in France and certainly makes a classy starter for dinner parties. It also works well for lunch, delicious with toast or crackers and highly acceptable with a crunchy green salad. It is advisable to cook 1 egg at a time in an individual dish.

Neapolitan Baked Egg

Serves 1

Brush a small ramekin dish (custard cup) or baby soufflé dish with melted butter or margarine. Add a good 15 ml (1 tbsp) of Neapolitan sauce (page 74). Gently break 1 (size 3) egg on top. Puncture yolk twice with the tip of a knife. Season to taste. Cover with a saucer. Cook 3 minutes at defrost setting. Stand 1 minute and serve.

Baked Egg with Cream

Serves 1

Brush a small ramekin dish (custard cup) or baby soufflé dish with melted butter or margarine. Gently break in 1 (size 3) egg. Puncture yolk twice with the tip of a knife. Season to taste. Coat with 15 ml (1 tbsp) double (heavy) cream and sprinkle with 5 ml (1 tsp) finely chopped parsley. Cover with a saucer. Cook 3 minutes at defrost setting. Stand 1 minute and serve.

FISH

Fish and a microwave oven are great team-mates, work harmoniously together to bring out the best qualities in each other. The microwave acts fast but sympathetically; the fish responds by turning out moist, tender and full of flavour. The colour is delicate, the texture superb. There is nothing to better this close relationship and anyone who has cooked fish in the microwave will agree what a success story it is.

Cooking Fish: Generally speaking, cutlets, steaks and fillets should be cooked for approximately 5 to 6 minutes per 450 g (1 lb) if at room temperature, 6 to 7 minutes if taken straight from the refrigerator, and 10 to 12 minutes if cooked from frozen. Obviously the times will varying depending on the type and thickness of the fish and therefore it should be watched carefully and removed from the microwave when creamy-looking and slightly flaky. Overcooking will toughen the edges and must be avoided to prevent dryness.

Basic Method

Arrange cod, haddock, coley, plaice, halibut, turbot and so on in a shallow dish. Brush with melted butter or margarine then sprinkle lightly with paprika, plain or seasoning salt and white pepper to taste. Cover with cling film, then puncture twice with the tip of a knife. Cook for times given above. Uncover, transfer to plates and serve straight away.

Amounts

Allow 175 to 225 g (6 to 8 oz) per person and cook in no more than 450 g (1 lb) batches at a time unless recipe states otherwise.

Poached Salmon Steaks

Classic in its simplicity, salmon cooked in the microwave retains its exquisite flavour and delicate pale pink colour, remaining succulent, well-shaped and tender. Serve it in a sauce of your choice taken from the Sauce Section on page 67, then garnish each with a slice of lemon and either a frond of dill or sprig of parsley.

Preparation time: about 14 minutes

Serves 4

**4 salmon steaks weighing 675 g (1½ lb) in all, thawed if frozen
150 ml (¼ pt/⅔ cup) water or dry white wine
2.5 ml (½ tsp) salt**

1 Arrange steaks round the edge of a 20 cm (8 inch) round and shallow glass or pottery dish.

2 Pour water into centre then sprinkle fish with salt. Cover with cling film, then puncture twice with the tip of a knife. Alternatively, cover with matching lid.

3 Cook for 14–16 minutes at defrost.

4 Remove from microwave and leave to stand 5 minutes. Lift out of dish with slatted fish slice and transfer to warm plates. Garnish as described above.

Salmon Mayonnaise

Serves 4

Cook fish as described above. Leave until cold then remove skin. Stand on lettuce-lined plates and garnish with other salad ingredients. Pass mayonnaise separately.

Tarragon Poached Salmon Steaks

Serves 4

Cook fish as described above but use 90 ml (6 tbsp) water and 30 ml (2 tbsp) tarragon vinegar. Sprinkle with 2.5 ml (½ tsp) *each* of salt and dried tarragon.

Sole on the Plate

For those indulgent times when one can afford to buy Dover soles, nothing treats them quite as kindly or as gently as a microwave cooker.

Allow 1 per person

Choose as many soles as are required, each about 350 g (12 oz) in weight, and cook each one individually. Wash and wipe dry. Put into a shallow, oblong glass or pottery dish. Add 15 ml (1 tbsp) hot water. Cover with cling film, then puncture twice with the tip of a knife. Cook 4 minutes at full power. Leave to stand 2 minutes. Continue to cook 5½ to 6 minutes. Using 2 fish slices or spatulas, carefully lift sole on to a large warm dinner plate. Coat with melted butter. Garnish with lemon wedges and parsley.

TIP: *Instead of melted butter, coat with one of the sauces from the Sauce Section (page 67).*

Sole Veronique

Allow 1 per person

Coat sole/soles with Béchamel sauce (page 70) and garnish with peeled, halved and de-seeded green grapes.

Fillets Veronique

Allow 175-225 g (6-8 oz) fish fillets per person and cook as directed under Cooking Fish, Basic Method. Coat with Béchamel sauce (page 70) to which has been added 75 g (3 oz) peeled, halved and de-seeded green grapes. Garnish with clusters of extra fresh grapes, either washed and dried or peeled.

Monk Fish with Egg and Lemon Sauce

By virtue of demand and price, monk fish has risen from the ranks of the mundane to a very classy and highly acclaimed fish, justifiably esteemed for its creamy-white flesh and scampi-like texture. I am confident this recipe does it full justice.

Preparation time: about 20 minutes

Serves 6

675 g (1½ lb) monk fish
25 g (1 oz/2 tbsp) butter, at room temperature
45 ml (3 tbsp) plain (all-purpose) flour
300 ml (½ pt/1¼ cups) milk, warmed for 2 minutes at full power
2 (size 2) egg yolks
juice of 1 large lemon
2.5-5 ml (½-1 tsp) salt
30 ml (2 tbsp) chopped chives, green part of leek or parsley

1 Cut monk fish away from bone then divide flesh into scampi-sized pieces with a sharp and non-serrated knife. Wash and dry.

2 Put butter into a 20 × 5 cm (8 × 2 inch) round glass or pottery dish. Leave uncovered and melt 1 to 1½ minutes at defrost setting.

3 Coat pieces of monk fish with flour then add to dish of butter. Toss round until well-coated. Mix in milk.

4 Cover with cling film, then puncture twice with the tip of a knife.

5 Cook 7 minutes at full power.

6 Meanwhile, beat egg yolks and lemon juice well together. Season with salt. Add to fish at the end of its cooking time. Stir in well.

7 Cook a further 2 minutes at full power then leave to stand 5 minutes. Stir round, sprinkle with greenery and serve with plain boiled rice or new potatoes and French beans.

'Poached' Sea Bream

Expert anglers may be able to catch sea bream with relative ease and perhaps take it for granted, but to me, living inland, it's certainly a rare luxury. Available occasionally from our local fish market, the flesh of sea bream is slightly beige before and after cooking, but it is also creamy and light in texture with a mild and delicate flavour. It takes very well to microwaving and is especially good with Hollandaise sauce speckled with grated orange peel (called Maltaise and on page 77), and with vegetable accompaniments of broccoli and creamed potatoes.

Preparation time: about 20 minutes

Serves 4 generously

1 × 1.5 kg (3¼ lb) sea bream, cleaned and scaled then cut in half by fishmonger across the middle (head and tail left on)
1 lemon, sliced
75 g (3 oz/¾ cup) onion, peeled and sliced
2 bouquet garni bags
5 ml (1 tsp) salt

1   Wash both pieces of fish under cold running water then place side by side in a large oval or oblong dish, head and tail at opposite ends.

2   Top with lemon and onion slices then add bouquet garni bags. Sprinkle with salt.

3   Cover dish completely with cling film, then puncture twice with the tip of a knife. Alternatively, cover with matching lid.

4   Remove turntable (if oven has one), or place turntable upside down, if model permits, to prevent it from rotating. This will stop the dish banging against the sides of the oven and causing damage.

5   Cook fish 14 minutes at full power, turning dish twice. Leave to stand 5 minutes.

6   Uncover. Peel away fish skin, gently remove fillets from bones and transfer to warm plates. Serve as suggested above.

Plaice with Celery Cream Sauce

Light and pleasing, this is an easy dish to put together with the novelty element being a sprinkling of toasted coconut over the top – unusual with fish but surprisingly tasty. Serve the plaice with brown rice or brown pasta, and a fresh green salad tingling with French dressing.

Preparation time: about 25 minutes

Serves 4

8 plaice fillets (about 900 g/2 lb), washed and dried
1 can condensed cream of celery soup
150 ml (1 pt/⅔ cup) boiling water
1.25 ml (¼ tsp) dried marjoram
30 ml (2 tbsp) desiccated (shredded) coconut,
toasted conventionally

1   Wash and dry fish then roll up each fillet from head end to tail, flesh sides outside.

2   Arrange in 25 cm (10 inch) round shallow dish, first brushed with butter or margarine.

3   Whisk soup and water well together. Stir in marjoram then spoon over fish.

4   Sprinkle with coconut. Cover with cling film, then puncture twice with the tip of a knife.

5   Cook 12 minutes at full power. Leave to stand 5 minutes.

6   Continue to cook a further 6 minutes at full power as above. Spoon out onto warm plates to serve.

Plaice with Mushroom Cream Sauce

Make exactly as above, using cream of mushroom soup instead of celery.

Trout 'Rollmops'

An ingenious way with trout, very appetising, typically British in concept and, served chilled with salad and brown bread and butter, a summer joy. All one needs is an obliging fishmonger who will scale and fillet the fish.

Preparation time: about 20 minutes plus chilling time

Serves 4 as a main course or 8 as a starter

4 large trout, each 450g (1lb), filleted
2 medium bay leaves, each broken into 4 pieces
175g (6oz/1½ cups) onions, peeled and cut into thin slices
15ml (1tbsp) mixed pickling spice
150ml (½pt/⅔cup) boiling water
15ml (1tbsp) granulated sugar
10ml (2tsp) salt
90ml (6tbsp) wine or cider vinegar

1   Roll up each trout fillet from head end to tail, skin side out. Arrange round edge of 25cm (10inch) round glass or pottery dish, 5-7.5cm (2-3inches) deep.

2   Stud here and there with bay leaves and onion slices separated into rings. Sprinkle with pickling spice.

3   Mix boiling water with sugar, salt and vinegar. Stir well then spoon over fish.

4   Cover with cling film, then puncture twice with the tip of a knife. Cook 18 minutes at full power.

5   Cool, refrigerate until cold then uncover and serve.

Soused Herrings

Serves 4 as a main course or 8 as a starter

Make as above, substituting filleted herrings for trout. (They will probably be slightly smaller, so will take a little less time to cook.) For half quantity, halve all ingredients and cook for 10 to 12 minutes at full power.

Trout with Almonds

One of our classic trout specialities, greatly enhanced by microwave cooking and totally unproblematic. Serve with any of the potato dishes given in the Vegetable Section on page 202 and accompany with a mixed salad or spinach.

Preparation time: about 20 minutes

Serves 4

50g (2oz/¼ cup) butter
15ml (1tbsp) lemon juice
4 trout, each weighing 175-225g (6-8oz), cleaned and well-washed
50g (2oz/½ cup) flaked and toasted almonds (page 303)
salt and pepper to taste
4 lemon wedges
parsley sprigs for garnish

1 Put butter into a small dish and melt for 1½ to 2 minutes at defrost setting. Stir in lemon juice.

2 Arrange trout, head to tail, in a buttered dish measuring about 25 × 20 cm (10 × 8 inches). Remove turntable if necessary, referring to 'Poached' Sea Bream, points 4 and 5 of method (page 117).

3 Coat with melted butter and lemon juice then sprinkle with almonds and seasoning.

4 Cover with cling film, then puncture twice with the tip of a knife.

5 Cook 9 to 12 minutes, turning dish twice if you have removed turntable. Leave to stand 5 minutes then transfer to 4 warm plates.

6 Coat with juices from dish and garnish with lemon wedges and parsley.

Hashed Fish

A nostalgic taste of the past, based on a Victorian recipe.

Preparation time: about 25 minutes

Serves 4

50 g (2 oz/¼ cup) butter or margarine
2 medium leeks, trimmed, slit then well-washed and sliced
675 g (1½ lb) fresh haddock or cod fillet, cooked and flaked
(see directions under Cooking Fish, Basic Method on page 113)
350 g (12 oz/2 cups) cold cooked potatoes, diced
150 ml (¼ pt/⅔ cup) single (light) cream
5 ml (1 tsp) salt
4 poached or fried eggs (see pages 100, 103)

1 Put butter or margarine in to a 20 cm (8 inch) round glass or pottery dish and melt 1½ to 2 minutes at defrost setting. Leave uncovered.

2 Add leeks and mix in well. Cover with a plate and cook 5 minutes at full power.

3 Stir in fish, potatoes, cream and salt. Cover as above and reheat until very hot, 5 to 7 minutes at full power. Stir once or twice.

4 Leave to stand while poaching or frying eggs. Put hash on to 4 plates and top each with an egg.

Provençale Prawns (Shrimp)

One of the most popular prawn (shrimp) dishes of all, the whole thing takes about 15 minutes to cook and is impressive served wtih freshly boiled rice fluffed with butter and a generous quantity of chopped parsley, watercress leaves or fresh basil – at least enough to give the rice a bold green colour.

Preparation time: about 20 minutes

Serves 4 to 6

*25 g (1 oz/2 tbsp) butter or margarine
(or 15 ml/1 tbsp olive oil, if preferred)
50 g (2 oz/½ cup) onion, peeled and grated
1 garlic clove, peeled and crushed
400 g (14 oz) canned tomatoes, drained
5 ml (1 tsp) Italian seasoning or dried basil
5 ml (1 tsp) soft dark brown (coffee) sugar
450 g (1 lb) frozen peeled prawns (shrimp), used from frozen
seasoning to taste
chopped parsley*

1 Put butter, margarine or oil into a 1.75 litre (3 pt/7½ cup) glass or pottery serving dish and heat 1½ minutes at defrost setting. Leave uncovered.

2 Stir in onion and garlic. Leave uncovered and cook 3 minutes at full power. Stir round.

3 Add tomatoes, Italian seasoning or basil and sugar. Cover with a plate and cook 5 minutes at full power, stirring twice.

4 Add prawns and cover as above. Cook 4 minutes then carefully separate. Re-cover and cook a further 3 to 4 minutes. Adjust seasoning to taste and sprinkle with parsley.

Mermaid Pie

Like Shepherd's Pie, but made with fish. A worthwhile midweek special.

Preparation time: about 25 minutes

Serves 4

Make up 300 ml (½ pt/1¼ cups) Cheese, Onion or Mushroom sauce (see Sauce Section on page 67). Stir in 450 g (1 lb) cooked and flaked cod or haddock fillet, all skin and bones removed. Put into a 1.75 litre (3 pint/7½ cup) serving dish and top with 675 g (1½ lb) creamed potatoes. Sprinkle lightly with nutmeg or paprika and 40 g (1½ oz/6 tbsp) grated Red Leicester cheese. Leave uncovered and reheat for 6 to 7 minutes at full power. Serve with vegetables to taste.

Crab Mornay

Another fish classic to suit connoisseurs, it is speedy to make in the microwave and excellent served on freshly made toast or a bed of rice.

Preparation time: about 20 minutes

Serves 4

Make up Béchamel sauce as directed on page 70, then mix in 75 g (3 oz/¾ cup) grated Gruyère cheese or Cheddar if preferred. Season to taste with continental mustard. Stir in 225 g (8 oz) light and dark crab meat, either fresh or defrosted if using frozen. Cover with a plate. Reheat until hot, allowing 2 to 4 minutes at full power. Arrange on 4 slices of hot buttered toast and sprinkle each with paprika. Alternatively, arrange some hot cooked rice in a border around a large plate. Pile hot crab mixture into the centre and sprinkle with paprika. Garnish with watercress.

Flan Arnold Bennett

Why not turn a successful and popular omelet into a flan, so well-suited to a light lunch, supper or even a buffet? This one has a charmed life and is best accompanied by a crisp, crunchy salad of firm lettuce, celery, cucumber, grated carrot and some coarsely chopped toasted hazelnuts tossed together with a piquant French dressing.

Preparation time: about 18 minutes

Serves 6

shortcrust pastry (basic pie dough), made with
175 g (6 oz/1½ cups) flour and 75 g (3 oz/⅓ cup) fat, etc.
1 egg yolk
100 g (4 oz) cooked and flaked smoked haddock or cod fillet
3 (size 2) eggs
1 carton 150 ml (5 oz/⅔ cup) soured (dairy sour) cream
1.25-2.5 ml (¼-½ tsp) salt
15 ml (1 tbsp) mayonnaise
75 g (3 oz/¾ cup) Cheshire or Red Leicester cheese, grated

1 Roll out pastry and use to line a 20 cm (8 inch) fluted flan dish. Prick well all over, especially where sides join the base.

2 Cook for 6 minutes at full power. If pastry has bulged in places, press down very gently with fingers protected by oven gloves.

3 Brush all over with egg yolk then cook a further 1 minute at full power to seal holes. Remove from oven and cover base with the fish.

4 Beat eggs well together with cream, salt and mayonnaise. Pour evenly over fish. Sprinkle with cheese and cook, uncovered, for 8 minutes at full power. Serve warm or cold.

Kedgeree

A souvenir from the days of the Raj, along with the light snacks called Tiffin and Mulligatawny soup. Kedgeree used to be a breakfast dish but is now eaten for lunch or supper with cooked vegetables to taste. It is a mish-mash of smoked fish, rice, eggs and seasonings. Zip it up by adding up to 15 ml (1 tbsp) mild curry powder with the rice and serve with chutney.

Preparation time: about 30 minutes

Serves 4

350 g (12 oz) smoked haddock fillet
60 ml (4 tbsp) cold water
50 g (2 oz/¼ cup) butter or margarine
225 g (8 oz/1 cup) easy-cook, long grain rice
600 ml (1 pt/2½ cups) boiling water
3 (size 3) hardboiled (hardcooked) eggs, shelled and 2 chopped
150 ml (¼ pt/⅔ cup) single (light) cream
seasoning to taste
chopped parsley for garnishing

1 Put fish into a shallow glass or pottery dish and add the cold water. Cover with cling film, then puncture twice with the tip of a knife.

2 Cook 5 minutes at full power. Drain fish and flake with 2 forks, discarding skin and bones.

3 Put butter or margarine in a 1.75 litre (3 pt/7½ cup) glass or pottery dish and melt, uncovered, 1½ to 2 minutes at defrost setting. Stir in rice and boiling water.

4 Cover with film as above and cook 15 minutes at full power. Uncover then stir in flaked fish, 2 chopped eggs and the cream. Season to taste.

5 Fluff up with a fork, cover with a plate and reheat 5 minutes at full power. Remove from cooker then garnish with the third egg, cut into slices or wedges. Add a heavy dusting of parsley.

MEAT AND POULTRY

Most meat and poultry responds well to microwave cooking but, where possible, prime cuts should be chosen as they tenderise more readily than the less expensive and muscular parts of the animal traditionally recommended for braises, stews and hot-pots. This may sound extravagant but 450 g (1 lb) rump steak, with additions, will make a generous and richly-flavoured meal for 4 to 6 people, lengthy cooking time is not called for, and the saving in fuel is substantial.

More Plus Points

Meat stewed or braised in the microwave can be cooked in its own serving dish which saves on washing up, the whole process is clean and fast, no sticking or burning occurs, and strong smells rarely filter through the house. But I have to stress that there are still a few provisos. All meat should be cut into smaller than usual pieces, such as 1 cm (½ inch) cubes instead of larger ones sugges-ted for braising or stewing; it is advisable to 'dry' cook meat or poultry, and sometimes vegetables, for a given length of time *before* liquid is added as this technique helps to soften the meat; seasonings, and salt in particular, have a toughening effect and are therefore best added half way through cooking or, alternatively, at the very end. It is also useful to know that mince behaves per-fectly in the microwave because it is virtually shredded into tiny pieces which tenderise easily. And another tip to note is that kosher meat, eaten by the Orthodox Jewish community, is salted by the butcher and reacts unfavourably to microwave cooking, the only exceptions being mince, poultry and offal such as liver.

Understanding the Charts

Many microwave cookery writers don't recommend cooking large joints in the microwave – I disagree. The meat remains moist, succulent and often more tender than a joint cooked conventionally. It isn't easy to achieve but for skilled microwave users it's worth persevering. Other, more cautious converts, may prefer to partially cook the joint in the microwave then finish off conventionally in a hot oven to give the crisp, brown appearance we traditionally associate with a roast. Obviously, as with all meat, it *must* be completely defrosted before cooking (please refer to the Defrosting Charts on page 131) and if you are at all uncertain about the cooking and standing times given in the Cooking Charts on page 133, let me explain in more detail. Large joints, as the chart says, require 7 minutes cooking time on full power for every 450 g (1 lb) and 5 minutes standing time. Thus you should cook a 3 kg (6 lb) joint for 21 minutes, leave it to stand for 15 minutes (inside or outside the microwave, depending on which is the most convenient), cook it for a further 21 minutes then leave it to stand another 15 minutes, completing the cooking and standing cycle as given in the charts. To hold in heat and moisture, the joint should be drained and then wrapped in foil for the last part of the standing time or left in its roasting bag. (More information on roasting bags follows.) Standing time is necessary to allow heat from the outside to transfer through to the centre, particularly when dealing with large joints. If no standing times were allowed or carried out only at the end, the outside of the meat would become dry and hard, leaving the centre area raw, cold or both. Joints of up to 1 kg (2 lb) can be cooked for 14 minutes, with no standing time between, and then left to stand as above for 10 minutes at the end.

Times

The times given in the charts for cooking and standing are fairly general. Pork and veal should have 2 minutes per 450g (1lb) added to the cooking time given, as should meat taken straight from the refrigerator. Medium to rare beef may be cooked 1 to 1½ minutes *less* per 450g (1lb), but standing time remains the same. If your microwave oven has a temperature probe, denoting the degree of doneness of the joint, use it according to the instructions given in *your own* microwave oven guide book. Alternatively, buy a microwave meat thermometer and use according to the instructions.

Shape of Joint

The more regular the shape the better and more evenly it will cook. As this is not always a viable proposition, wrap the narrow end of the joint (the bony part of a leg of lamb for example) with foil during the first half of cooking time to prevent frizzle and overcooking. The foil will have no detrimental effect on the workings of the oven, in that there will be much more meat in proportion to foil. If choice is possible, settle for the fillet end of pork or lamb, and a boned and rolled piece of beef or veal.

Roasting Bags

These are perfect for microwaved lamb, beef and veal and seem to encourage browning. Simply season and/or baste the joint, slide into a roasting bag and close the top by tying with an elastic band, a piece of string or any non-metallic tie twist. Cook and stand as directed in the charts on page 133.

Tips on Roasting

1 If not using a roasting bag, stand the joint in dish, cover with film and puncture twice with the tip of a knife. If the cooking time recommended is 15 minutes or over at full power, the joint will brown slightly of its own accord so you do not have to brush with baste prior to cooking, if you prefer not to.

2 For very fat joints, stand a plastic trivet or 2 inverted saucers into a dish and place meat on top. Cover as in point 1.

3 When joints have fat on one side only, place into a bag or dish with the fat side down. Turn over half way through cooking.

4 For crisp crackling on pork, rub salad oil and salt well into the scored rind. 'Open' roast by standing in a dish and covering closely with paper to prevent spluttering and soiling the oven interior with splashes of grease. Do not turn at half time but keep crackling-side uppermost all the time. Be warned, the crackling can become very hard and crisp – so watch your teeth!

Poultry tips

1 The same defrosting and cooking rules apply to poultry as well as to meat but for a golden brown effect, a chicken or turkey should be brushed with baste (see page 75) prior to cooking. If the bird is of the self-basting variety, a light brush of Soy sauce or sprinkling of paprika is all that is necessary.

2 Stuff the crop end *only* and leave the body cavity empty. Wing tips and ends of legs should be foil-wrapped to prevent over-cooking. Prepared stuffings may be heated up separately in a greased dish. Times will vary from 3 to 6 minutes at full power, depending on whether the mixture is hot, warm, cold or taken from the refrigerator. And obviously quantity also determines the length of cooking time necessary.

3 Most microwaves can only accommodate up to a 4.5 kg (10 lb) bird.

Defrosting Hints

1   To prevent slight cooking on the outside, large joints or birds are best left to defrost naturally, either overnight in a refrigerator or for several hours in the kitchen. Alternatively, partially defrost in the microwave, then finish off at room temperature.

2   When defrosting fairly large joints and birds, refer to the Defrosting Chart on page 131 and add up the number of minutes standing time required. If it works out at about 40 minutes, rest for 20 minutes at half time then rest a further 20 minutes at the end of the defrosting period. If the joint or bird is still partially frozen, leave to thaw at room temperature or in a sink of *cold* water.

3   As soon as chops, steaks and poultry joints have defrosted enough to be movable, arrange in a single layer in a ring round edge of plate or in a dish. *Never* heap up.

4   Cover meat or poultry with cling film, kitchen paper or a roaster bag as this speeds up defrosting and helps keep in the moisture.

Browning Dish

For a grilled or fried effect, use a browning dish for steaks, chops, etc., following the directions in your own microwave oven guide book or any that may come with the dish itself. In general the dish should be heated for 5 to 6 minutes at full power if small, and 7 to 8 minutes if large. It should be brushed with melted fat or oil (unless it's non-stick), then the food added.

1   For steaks weighing up to 225 g (8 oz), allow 3 to 5 minutes at full power, according to doneness preferred, turning over once.

2   For 2 pork chops, each weighing (200-225 g) (7-8 oz) allow a total of 15 minutes cooking time at full power, turning over after 3 minutes then once again after 10 minutes.

3   For 450 g (1 lb) chicken joints, allow a total of 9 to 10 minutes, placing them skin sides down. Turn over after 3 minutes then once again after 7 minutes.

4   Clean the dish thoroughly after every batch of cooking. It should then be re-greased and reheated for half the original time.

Defrosting Meat and Poultry

	DEFROST SETTING	COMMENTS
Joints for Roasting on bone, per 450g (1lb)	9 minutes per 450g (1lb), allowing same length of standing time at end. Thus 450g (1lb) joint should stand 9 minutes after defrosting, a 900g (2lb) joint, 18 minutes, and so on.	Stand joint on upturned plate or trivet in shallow dish. Turn over half way through defrosting. Wrap in foil before standing.
Joints for Roasting off bone, per 450g (1lb)	10 minutes Stand 10 minutes. Procedure as above.	As above.
Chops 100g (4oz)	3 minutes Stand 3 minutes	On plate, loosely covered with kitchen paper.
175g (6oz)	4 minutes Stand 4 minutes	As above.
225g (8oz)	5 minutes Stand 5 minutes	As above.
Minced Beef per 450g (1lb)	10 minutes Stand 10 minutes	Remove mince from wrapper and stand on plate. Cover with second inverted plate or pudding basin. As the outside edges thaw, scrape away the soft mince and transfer to another plate. This prevents the outside meat from starting to cook before the inside has thawed. Free-flow mince can be cooked from frozen.
Stewing Cubes per 450g (1lb)	8 minutes Stand 8 minutes	Stand in shallow dish. Cover with plate. Turn cubes over half way through defrosting.
Steaks 225g (8oz)	6 minutes Stand 6 minutes	On plate, loosely covered with kitchen paper. For smaller steaks, reduce time.

	DEFROST SETTING	COMMENTS
Liver		
225g (8oz)	2½ minutes Stand 8 minutes	In a covered dish. Separate before standing.
4506 (1lb)	4 minutes Stand 12 minutes	As above.
Chicken		
whole, per 450g (1lb)	8 minutes Stand 8 minutes following pattern for roasting joints on bone.	Stand in shallow dish or leave in polythene bag, having first removed metal tab and snipped off end of bag. Turn over half way through defrosting and remove giblets as soon as possible.
Chicken Portions		
225g (8oz)	6 minutes Stand 6 minutes	Stand in shallow dish. Cover loosely with kitchen paper. Turn over half way through defrosting.
350g (12oz)	8 minutes Stand 8 minutes	As above.
Duck		
whole, per 450g (1lb)	7 minutes Stand 7 minutes following pattern for roasting joints on bone.	Stand in shallow dish or as for chicken. Turn over half way through defrosting.
Duck Portions		
225g (8oz)	5 minutes Stand 5 minutes	Stand in shallow dish. Cover loosely with kitchen paper. Turn over half way through defrosting.
350g (12oz)	7 minutes Stand 7 minutes	As above.
Goose		
(about 4.5kg/10lb max) per 450g (1lb)	4 minutes	Stand in large shallow dish. Cover loosely with kitchen paper. Turn over once during defrosting. Remove giblets as soon as possible. Wrap goose in aluminium foil and stand overnight at room temperature until completely defrosted.
Turkey	See full instructions on page 170.	

Cooking Meat and Poultry

	COOK/HEAT FULL POWER	COMMENTS
Joints for Roasting on bone, per 450g (1lb)	7 minutes per 450g (1lb), allowing 5 minutes per 450g (1lb) standing time. This should take place half way through cooking time for large joints with further standing time at end. Small joints may be left to stand just at end.	Put into shallow dish. Cover with film and slit twice. Turn dish several times during cooking. When standing at the end, wrap joint in foil. Alternatively, cook and leave to stand in roasting bag.
Joints for Roasting off bone, per 450g (1lb)	8 minutes per 450g (1lb) Stand 5 minutes per 450g (1lb). For technique, see above.	As above.

Note: For pork or veal allow an extra 2 minutes per 450g (1lb). For pink lamb or beef, reduce cooking time by 1-1½ minutes per 450g (1lb).

	COOK/HEAT FULL POWER	COMMENTS
Chops 100g (4oz)	3 minutes Stand 3 minutes	Wash and dry chops and trim off surplus fat. Put on to plate or into shallow dish. Cover with film and slit twice. Turn plate or dish half way through cooking. Drain off melted fat before serving. Alternatively, cook in browning dish, following instructions given with the dish or in your own microwave oven guide book.
175g (6oz)	4 minutes Stand 4 minutes	As above.
225g (8oz)	5 minutes Stand 5 minutes	As above.
Steaks 200g (8oz)	3-5 minutes Stand 5 minutes	Wash and dry steaks. Put on to plate and cover with kitchen paper. Turn over half way through cooking. Alternatively, cook in browning dish, following instructions given with the dish or in your own microwave oven guide book. For smaller steaks cook as chops.

	COOK/HEAT FULL POWER	COMMENTS
Liver		
225 g (8 oz)	3 minutes	Wash and dry liver. Put into greased shallow dish and cover with plate or matching lid. Stir and turn liver over half way through cooking. Season at end.
450 g (1 lb)	6 minutes	As above.
Chicken		
whole, per 450 g (1 lb)	8 minutes Stand 5 minutes. For detailed technique, see joint on bone for roasting	Wash and drain chicken. Ensure that no giblets are left inside. Stand chicken in shallow dish. Brush with baste. Cover with film and slit twice. After standing time, remove film. Lift chicken out of dish, retaining hot juices for gravy, soup, etc., though it is advisable to skim off fat before use. If preferred, cook in roasting bag. **Note:** For larger birds, start breast-side down then turn over half way through cooking.
Chicken Portions		
225 g (8 oz)	4 minutes Stand 5 minutes	Wash and dry chicken. Stand on plate, cover with film and slit twice.
350 g (12 oz)	6 minutes Stand 5 minutes	Wash and dry chicken. Stand on plate. If several portions, place thin parts towards centre of plate. Cover with film and slit twice.
Duck		
whole, per 450 g (1 lb)	8 minutes Stand 5 minutes. For detailed technique, see joint on bone for roasting.	Wash and drain duck. Stand on rack in shallow dish, breast side down. Cover with film and slit twice. Half way through cooking, remove film and carefully turn duck over. Re-cover with film and slit twice. After cooking remove film. Lift duck out of dish and wrap in foil for duration of standing time. Do not use roasting bag or duck will be greasy. Crisp skin by placing bird under a hot grill for a few minutes if liked.
Duck Portions	As for chicken portions.	As for chicken portions. Drain after standing.

	COOK/HEAT FULL POWER	COMMENTS
Goose (about 4.5kg/10lb max.) per 450g (1lb)	7 minutes Stand 5 minutes. For detailed technique, see joints on bone for roasting.	Wash and drain goose. Ensure that no giblets are left inside. Put into large roasting bag. Close up end with elastic band or non-metallic tie-twist. Stand bag on large plate, shallow dish or directly on turntable. Turn over once during cooking, taking care that no juices run out of bag. Carefully lift goose out of microwave (still on its plate, dish or turntable) and stand on draining board. Open up bag and allow juices to trickle out into a bowl placed in the sink. Transfer goose to carving board and wrap with foil. Leave to stand for however many minutes are left at the end. Do not use roasting bag or goose will be greasy. Crisp skin as for duck if liked.
Turkey	See full instructions on page 170.	

Chilli Pork Chops

A simple imitation of Tex-Mex cooking with meaty pork chops submerged beneath tomatoes and red kidney beans. Serve it, piping hot and steaming, with jacket potatoes and sprouts – it will do wonders to enliven the spirits on a blustery winter day.

Preparation time: about 30 minutes

Serves 4 (F)

4 spare rib pork chops, each 225g (8oz) and fat trimmed
10ml (2tsp) chilli seasoning
5ml (1tsp) salt
1 can 400g (14oz) red kidney beans, drained
1 can 400g (14oz) tomatoes

1   Arrange chops in a square, 20cm (8inch) glass or pottery dish. Sprinkle with chilli seasoning.

2   Cover with cling film, then puncture twice with the tip of a knife. Alternatively, cover with matching lid.

3   Cook for 8 minutes at full power.

4   Uncover. Sprinkle with salt then top with beans and contents of can of tomatoes. Re-cover as before.

5   Cook 15 minutes at full power. Stand 5 minutes then serve as suggested above.

Pork 'n' Pineapple

Always popular and very much a restaurant favourite, the dish can be microwaved to perfection in 20 minutes. I serve it with Mild Curry Rice (page 211) and a salad based on watercress, crisp lettuce and diced dessert apples, all tossed in a sharpish dressing. It contrasts beautifully with the rich flavour of the pork and the sweetness of the pineapple.

Preparation time: about 28 minutes

Serves 4 (F)

4 spare rib pork chops, each 225 g (8 oz) and fat trimmed
1 can (439 g/15½ oz) pineapple rings in syrup
5 ml (1 tsp) paprika
20 ml (4 tsp) Soy sauce
2.5 ml (½ tsp) garlic granules

1 Wash and dry chops then arrange in a fairly shallow, 25 cm (10 inch) round glass or pottery dish.

2 Drain pineapple. Reserve 10 ml (2 tbsp) of the syrup for the baste and keep remainder for drinks or sauces.

3 Arrange pineapple rings over chops. Beat reserved pineapple syrup with all remaining ingredients. Spoon over chops.

4 Cover with cling film, then puncture twice with the tip of a knife. Alternatively, cover with a matching lid.

5 Cook 20 minutes at full power. Leave to stand 5 minutes before serving.

'Barbecued' Ribs

A real saving in time and kitchen smells when rib bones are cooked in the microwave, and the results are first rate. Serve them with noodles (prepared ahead of time in the microwave and kept warm) and a fresh salad made from bean sprouts and thinly sliced raw mushrooms tossed in French dressing.

Preparation time: about 25 minutes

Serves 4

BASTE
50g (2oz/¼ cup) butter or margarine, at room temperature
15ml (1tbsp) tomato ketchup (catsup)
10ml (2tbsp) Soy sauce
5ml (1tsp) paprika
1.25ml (¼tsp) garlic granules
2.5ml (½tsp) chilli sauce (hot)
RIBS
1kg (2lb) fleshy pork rib bones
which are also called sheet ribs or spare rib bones

1   To make baste, melt butter or margarine, uncovered, for about 1½ to 2 minutes at defrost setting. Stir in all remaining ingredients. Leave on one side temporarily.

2   Divide pork bones into single ribs then wash well and dry with kitchen paper. Arrange in a large dish with narrow part of bones pointing inwards.

3   Cover with cling film, then puncture twice with the tip of a knife.

4   Cook for 10 minutes at full power. Remove cling film, pour off fat then brush bones with baste, using about half the quantity.

5   Leave uncovered and cook 3 minutes at full power. Turn ribs over and brush with remaining baste. Cook, uncovered, a further 2 minutes. Arrange on 4 hot plates and serve coated with juices from dish.

Aubergine Moussaka

One of the top Greek favourites. Moussaka takes very well to being given the microwave treatment and is both moist and flavoursome. For quickness, boil aubergines in plenty of water with lemon juice added for about 5 minutes until tender, then drain.

Preparation time: about 50 minutes

Serves 8 (F)
AUBERGINES (EGGPLANTS)
675g (1½lb) aubergines (eggplants)
75ml (5tbsp) boiling water
10ml (2tsp) lemon juice

FILLING
50g (2oz/¼cup) butter or margarine
225g (8oz/2cups) onions, peeled and grated
350g (12oz/1½cups) cold cooked lamb or beef, minced (ground)
100g (4oz/2cups) fresh white breadcrumbs
450g (1lb/2⅔cups) blanched tomatoes, skinned and chopped
5-7.5ml (1-1½tsp) salt

SAUCE
40g (1½oz/6tbsp) plain (all-purpose) flour
450ml (¾pt/2cups) milk
40g (1½oz/3tbsp) butter or margarine
75g (3oz/¾cup) Cheddar cheese, grated
salt and pepper to taste

1 Cut stems off aubergines and discard. Slice fairly thinly and put into a large dish. Add water mixed with lemon juice.

2 Cover with cling film, then puncture twice with the tip of a knife. Cook 12 minutes at full power then leave to stand outside the oven for 15 minutes.

3 Prepare filling. Put butter or margarine into a dish and melt about 1¾ minutes at defrost setting. Mix in onions and cover with a plate. Cook 2 minutes at full power. Mix in rest of ingredients.

4   Drain aubergines thoroughly. Fill a 2.25 litre (4 pt/10 cup) greased dish with alternate layers of aubergine slices and meat mixture.

5   For sauce, whisk flour and milk together in a fairly large bowl until smooth. Add butter or margarine.

6   Cook at full power for 6-6½ minutes or until boiling, whisking gently at the end of every minute. Stir in cheese, season to taste and pour over Moussaka.

7   Cover with cling film, slit twice and reheat at full power for 12 to 14 minutes. Stand 8 minutes before serving.

NOTE: *The meat mixture prepared as above, topped with mashed potato and browned under a hot grill makes a splendid cottage pie.*

Beef and Mushroom Kebabs

Superior in all respects, these choice Kebabs are not for everyday eating but for the small intimate dinner party.

Preparation time: about 25 minutes

Serves 4

24 dried bay leaves
90 ml (6 tbsp) water
675 g (1½ lb) rump steak, trimmed of fat
175 g (6 oz) button mushrooms, trimmed
½ green (bell) pepper, de-seeded
½ red (bell) pepper, de-seeded
50 g (2 oz/¼ cup) butter or margarine, at room temperature
5 ml (1 tsp) paprika

1   Put bay leaves into a small bowl, add water and cover with a saucer. Heat for 2 minutes at full power to soften, otherwise the leaves will break. Alternatively use fresh bay leaves.

2   Cut meat into 2 cm (¾ inch) cubes.

3   Cut both peppers into smallish squares, put into a dish and only just cover with water. Top with an inverted plate and heat for 1 minute to soften.

4   Drain bay leaves and peppers. Thread steak, mushrooms, pepper squares and bay leaves on to 12 wooden skewers.

5   Arrange, like spokes of a wheel, in a 25 cm (10 inch) round and shallow glass or pottery dish.

6   Put butter or margarine into a cup, cover with a saucer and melt for 1½ to 2 minutes at defrost setting. Stir in paprika. Brush over kebabs. Cook, uncovered, for 8 minutes at full power.

7   Turn kebabs over and brush undersides with rest of butter mixture. Cook a further 4 minutes at full power.

8   Arrange on a bed of freshly cooked rice (brown is first choice) and coat with juices from dish.

Tomato Beef 'Cake'

Useful for a 'Mum and Toddlers' lunch, this meat loaf takes minutes to prepare and cook. It teams happily with creamy mashed potatoes and green vegetables.

Preparation time: about 15 minutes

Serves 2-3 (F)

*275 g (10 oz/1¼ cups) raw minced (ground) beef,
as lean as possible
25 g (1 oz/¼ cup) plain (all-purpose) flour
1 (size 3) egg
5 ml (1 tsp) onion salt
150 ml (¼ pt/⅔ cup) tomato juice
5 ml (1 tsp) Soy sauce
5 ml (1 tsp) dried mixed herbs*

1   Well grease a 1 litre (1¾ pt/4¼ cup) oval pie dish.

2   Mix beef with all remaining ingredients and spread smoothly into dish.

3   Cover with cling film, then puncture twice with knife tip.

4   Cook for 7 minutes at full power. Leave to stand 5 minutes.

5   Uncover. Lift out on to a warm plate with 2 spatulas, leaving behind surplus fat in dish which may have seeped out during cooking. Cut 'cake' into 2 or 3 portions and serve.

Buffet Meat Slice

Based on a continental idea, this Meat Slice can be served hot or cold and makes an excellent addition to any informal buffet or supper party.

Preparation time: about 28 minutes

Serves 8 to 10 (F)

900 g (2 lb/4 cups) raw minced (ground) beef, as lean as possible
2 (size 2) eggs, beaten
1 brown gravy cube
10 ml (2 tsp) onion salt
60 ml (4 tbsp) plain (all-purpose) flour
30 ml (2 tbsp) tomato ketchup (catsup)
10 ml (2 tsp) dried mixed herbs
10 ml (2 tsp) Soy sauce
glacé cherries, black olives and mint leaves to garnish

1   Tip meat into a mixing bowl and work in beaten eggs, crumbled gravy cube, onion salt, flour, ketchup and herbs.

2   Spread into a 1.2 litre (2 pt/5 cup) oblong greased dish, similar to a loaf tin.

3   Brush top gently with Soy sauce. Cover with cling film, then puncture twice with the tip of a knife.

4   Cook 5 minutes at full power. Leave to stand in the oven for 5 minutes. Continue to cook a further 10 minutes at defrost setting.

5   Stand 5 minutes. Uncover. Carefully drain off surplus fat from container then gently lift the Meat Slice on to a dish.

6   Garnish with pieces of glacé cherries, black olives and a few mint leaves and serve hot or cold.

Fast Beef Loaf

Full of flavour and unusually enriched with mayonnaise, this is a speedy dish to put together and can become quite habit-forming. Serve with microwaved jacket potatoes and tomato halves.

Preparation time: about 17 minutes

Serves 6 (F)

675 g (1½ lb/3 cups) raw minced (ground) beef, as lean as possible
15 ml (1 tbsp) red and green (bell) pepper flakes
20 ml (4 tsp) dried parsley
7.5 ml (1½ tsp) onion salt
30 ml (2 tbsp) plain (all-purpose) flour
50 g (2 oz/4 tbsp) thick mayonnaise
7.5 ml (1½ tsp) mustard powder
5 ml (1 tsp) gravy browning

1   Well-grease a round dish measuring 20 cm (8 inches) in diameter by 2.5 cm (1 inch) in depth.

2   Mix beef thoroughly with all remaining ingredients. Spread smoothly into dish.

3   Cover with cling film, then puncture twice with the tip of a knife. Alternatively, cover with matching lid.

4   Cook 10 minutes at full power. Leave to stand 5 minutes.

5   Uncover. Lift loaf out on to a warm plate with 2 spatulas, leaving behind surplus fat in dish which may have seeped out during cooking. Cut loaf into 6 portions and serve.

Butter Bean and Beef Stew with Tomatoes

Practical and economical, this is a good family dish and can be put together in next to no time. It is based on convenience foods and fresh meat – often an ideal combination.

Preparation time: about 33 minutes

Serves 6 (F)

1 can (425 g/15 oz) butter beans, drained
1 can (300 g/10 oz) cream of tomato soup
15 ml (1 tbsp) dried chopped onions
6 slices of feather steak (about 550 g/1¼ lb)
salt and pepper to taste

1 Combine butter beans, soup and onions together in a 20 × 5 cm (8 × 2 inch) round glass or pottery dish.

2 Cover with a plate. Cook 6 minutes at full power.

3 Uncover and stir. Arrange steak in a border round the edge. Cover with cling film, then puncture twice with the tip of a knife. Alternatively, cover with matching lid.

4 Cook 15 minutes at full power.

5 Leave to stand 10 minutes. Season to taste. Serve with creamed potatoes, brussels sprouts and microwaved carrots tossed in butter and seasoned lightly with nutmeg.

Beef in Wine

For sheer luxury, accompany the beef with Potatoes Savoyard (page 263) and cauliflower, coated with speedy Hollandaise sauce (page 76); two more treasures quickly cooked in the microwave oven.

Preparation time: about 25 minutes

Serves 6 (F)

225 g (8 oz) onions, peeled
1 garlic clove, peeled (optional)
100 g (4 oz) cup mushrooms, trimmed and outsides peeled
25 g (1 oz/2 tbsp) butter or margarine, at room temperature
450 g (1 lb) rump steak, cut into 1 cm (½ inch) cubes
15 ml (1 tbsp) tomato purée (paste)
15 ml (1 tbsp) parsley, chopped
15 ml (1 tbsp) cornflour (cornstarch)
5 ml (1 tsp) made English or French mustard
300 ml (½ pt/1¼ cups) dry red wine
5 ml (1 tsp) salt

1 Finely chop onions and garlic. Thinly slice mushrooms. Put butter or margarine in a round glass or pottery dish measuring about 20 × 5 cm (8 × 2 inches). Heat, covered, for 1 minute at full power.

2 Stir in prepared vegetables, leave uncovered and cook 5 minutes at full power. Stir in steak then move mixture to edges of dish to form a ring with a hollow in the centre.

3 Cover with a plate and cook 5 minutes at full power. Meanwhile mix together purée, parsley, cornflour and mustard. Blend in the wine. Pour gently into dish over steak and vegetables.

4 Cover with cling film, then puncture twice with the tip of a knife. Alternatively, cover with matching lid.

5 Cook beef 5 minutes at full power, stirring once. Leave to stand 5 minutes. Season with salt. Serve hot with suggested accompaniments.

'Braised' Beef

As with the Beef in Wine, I have used rump steak in this 'braise' for a finely-flavoured and rich brown beef dish which serves 6 people adequately. The meat stays tender, there is minimal waste and this top quality cut makes for succulence and speedy cooking. Accompany with microwaved boiled potatoes and broccoli coated with cheese or Hollandaise sauce (page 76).

Preparation time: about 20 minutes

Serves 6 (F)

100g (4oz) onions, peeled
150g (5oz) carrots, peeled
75g (3oz) mushrooms and stalks, trimmed
25g (1oz/2tbsp) butter or margarine, at room temperature
450g (1lb/2cups) rump steak, cut into 1cm (½inch) cubes
1 brown gravy cube
15ml (1tbsp) plain (all-purpose) flour
300ml (½pt/1¼cups) hot water
5ml (1tsp) salt
pepper to taste

1   Finely chop onions, carrots and mushrooms, either by hand with a sharp knife or in a food processor. A blender may also be used.

2   Put butter or margarine into a 20×5cm (8×2inch) round glass or pottery dish. Heat, covered, 1 minute at full power.

3   Add vegetables and steak. Mix round then cook, uncovered, for 3 minutes at full power.

4   Remove from oven. Crumble in gravy cube then stir in flour and hot water. Move mixture to edges of dish to form a hollow in the centre. Cover with cling film, puncturing twice with the tip of a knife. Alternatively, cover with matching lid.

5   Cook 8 minutes at full power, stirring once. Leave to stand 5 minutes, uncover, then add seasoning. Stir round and serve.

Curried Mince

Curry, traditionally cooked long and lovingly, responds so well to being microwaved that this anglicised Curried Mince is all yours in 20 minutes, excluding preparation time. It is fairly mild and therefore popular with children. It goes best with rice and curried lentils (Dhal, page 93).

Preparation time: about 28 minutes

Serves 4 (F)
225 g (8 oz/2 cups) onions, peeled and chopped
450 g (1 lb/2 cups) lean minced (ground) beef
15 ml (1 tbsp) plain (all-purpose) flour
15 ml (1 tbsp) mild curry powder
30 ml (2 tbsp) chutney
(I used mango but use any other to suit)
15 ml (1 tbsp) tomato purée (paste)
300 ml (½ pt/1¼ cups) boiling water
1 brown gravy cube
salt and pepper to taste

1 Put onions and meat into a 20 × 5 cm (8 × 2 inch) round glass or pottery dish and mash well together.

2 Form into a ring round edge of dish. Cover with a plate and cook 5 minutes at full power.

3 Remove from oven and mix in flour, curry powder, chutney, tomato purée and boiling water. Crumble in gravy cube. Season.

4 Cover with cling film, then puncture twice with the tip of a knife. Alternatively, cover with matching lid.

5 Cook 15 minutes at full power. Leave to stand 5 minutes, stir round and serve.

Stuffed Artichokes

Distinctly French, stuffed artichokes equate to the best in country cooking and make a highly innovative main course with new potatoes and mange-tout (snow peas).

Preparation time: about 1 hour 10 minutes

Serves 4 (F)

4 large globe artichokes
450g (1lb/2 cups) raw minced (ground) beef, as lean as possible
175g (6oz/1½ cups) onions, peeled and finely chopped
1 (size 2) egg, beaten
5ml (1tsp) mixed dried herbs
7.5ml (1½ tsp) salt
5ml (1tsp) Worcestershire sauce
30ml (2tbsp) water
150ml (¼pt/⅔ cup) tomato or mixed vegetable juice

1   Prepare and cook artichokes as given in recipe for Artichokes in Red Wine with Gribiche Dressing (page 48). Leave upside down in a colander to drain thoroughly.

2   When completely cold, turn right way up. Open out leaves and gently remove central cones. The bristly cores underneath are the 'chokes' and should be plucked out, bit by bit, with fingers. Left behind will be the much prized hearts surrounded by layers of leaves.

3   For stuffing, mix meat with onions, egg, herbs, salt, Worcestershire sauce and water. Spoon into artichoke cavities. Tie round with string. Stand, upright, in a deep glass or pottery dish.

4   Cover with cling film, then puncture twice with the tip of a knife. Alternatively, cover with matching lid.

5   Cook for 8 minutes at full power. Uncover and add juice.

6   Re-cover as before. Cook a further 8 minutes at full power. Serve hot as suggested above or, if preferred, leave until cold then chill in the refrigerator and serve with salad – blissful on a balmy summer day.

Beef in Stroganov Mood

What can I say about this creamy beef concoction, other than to re-affirm its splendour? There are many variations on a traditional Stroganov, but this one was passed on to me by Finnish friends from the east of the country, an area much influenced by the courtly cuisine of old Russia.

Preparation time: about 10 minutes

Serves 6

25 g (1 oz/2 tbsp) butter
75 g (3 oz/¾ cup) onions, peeled and grated
450 g (1 lb) rump steak
100 g (4 oz/1 cup) button mushrooms, thinly sliced
25 g (1 oz) chopped gherkins (sweet dill pickles)
1 carton (150 ml/5 fl oz/⅔ cup) soured (dairy sour) cream,
at room temperature
salt and pepper to taste

1　Put butter into a 20 × 5 cm (8 × 2 inch) round dish. Cover and heat for 1 minute at full power.

2　Cut steak into narrow strips against the grain.

3　Add onions and steak to butter. Cover with a plate. Cook 4 minutes at full power.

4　Stir in mushrooms and re-cover with the plate. Cook a further 2 minutes, turning once. Mix in gherkins, cream and seasoning to taste. Cook, uncovered, for 1 more minute at full power. Serve with rice.

Lamb Splits

A bit Balkanesque, this is one of my favourite ways of preparing neck of lamb fillet, memorable with spiced aubergine purée and microwaved Pitta or sesame bread to mop up the juices.

Preparation time: about 25 minutes

Serves 4 (F)

4 pieces of neck of lamb fillets, each 12.5-15 cm (5-6 inches) in length with total weight of 675 g (1½ lb)
75 g (3 oz/1½ cups) fresh white bread, cubed with crusts left on
75 g (3 oz) onions, peeled and cut into biggish pieces
25 g (1 oz/¼ cup) pine nuts (kernels),
toasted under grill or in microwave (see page 303)
25 g (1 oz/1½ tbsp) currants
2.5 ml (½ tsp) salt
15 ml (2 tbsp) thick Greek yoghurt
cinnamon
40 g (1½ oz) button mushrooms, trimmed
15 g (½ oz/1 tbsp) butter or margarine,
melted ¾ minute at defrost setting

1   Trim fat off lamb fillets, then make a lengthwise slit in each, taking care not to cut right through or filling will fall out.

2   Turn bread into crumbs and very finely grate onions. If you have a food processor or blender, this will save effort.

3   Mix crumbs and onions with nuts, currants and salt. Spoon equal amounts into lamb fillets.

4   Place round the edges of a 25 cm (10 inch), fairly shallow round dish to form a square. Smear tops of each with yoghurt then sprinkle with a trace of cinnamon. Stud with mushrooms and coat with melted butter or margarine.

5   Cover with cling film, then puncture twice with the tip of a knife. Alternatively, cover with matching lid.

6   Cook 14 minutes at full power. Leave to stand 5 minutes before serving.

Eastern Mint Kebabs

When there is a high proportion of meat to metal and provided the metal has no direct contact with the sides of the cooker, metal skewers may be used for the Kebabs without upsetting the action of the microwave. But if you are at all concerned, use wooden ones. Therefore tackle these Kebabs with confidence and serve them on Saffron Rice (page 207) and a Greek-style salad of mixed vegetables topped with pieces of Feta cheese, tiny black olives and a drizzle of olive oil.

Preparation time: about 25 minutes

Serves 6

900 g (2 lb) neck of lamb fillet
12 large fresh mint leaves (or used dried bay leaves,
first microwaved in a little water for 2 minutes at full power)
60 ml (4 tbsp) thick yoghurt
30 ml (2 tbsp) tomato ketchup (catsup)
1 garlic clove, peeled and crushed
5 ml (1 tsp) Worcestershire sauce

1   Trim fat off lamb then cut meat into 2.5 cm (1 inch) slices. Thread on to 6 skewers, each 10 cm (4 inches) long, alternately with mint or softened bay leaves.

2   Arrange, like spokes of a wheel, in a 25 cm (10 inch) round shallow dish. For baste, beat yoghurt with rest of ingredients. Brush about half over kebabs.

3   Cook, uncovered, for 7 minutes at full power.

4   Remove from oven and turn Kebabs over. Brush with rest of baste. Cook a further 7 minutes at full power. Leave to stand 5 minutes then serve as suggested.

Lamb and Vegetable 'Hot Pot'

If you like a conglomeration of vegetables amid the meat, this will become a favourite in no time. if you cannot abide parsnips, substitute carrots. My pet greenery with this one is deep-toned cabbage, but sprouts serve the same purpose if preferred.

Preparation time: about 45 minutes

Serves 4 to 5 (F)

550g (1¼ lb) lamb fillet
450g (1lb/4cups) potatoes, peeled and grated
225g (8oz/2cups) onions, peeled and grated
225g (8oz/2cups) parsnips, peeled and grated
30ml (2tbsp) plain (all-purpose) flour
45ml (3tbsp) cold water
300ml (½pt/1¼cups) boiling water
1 brown gravy cube
5ml (1tsp) salt
chopped parsley

1 Trim fat off lamb then cut meat into 1cm (½inch) thick pieces.

2 Put potatoes, onions and parsnips into a 20 × 5 cm (10 × 2 inch) round glass or pottery dish. Mix in meat and push towards edge of dish to form a ring.

3 Cover with a plate and cook for 7 minutes at full power.

4 Meanwhile, blend flour gradually to a smooth paste with cold water. Stir into meat mixture then add boiling water. Crumble in gravy cube and mix in thoroughly.

5 Cover dish with cling film, then puncture twice with the tip of a knife. Alternatively, cover with matching lid.

6 Cook 10 minutes at full power. Stand 5 minutes then cook a further 10 minutes at full power.

7 Stand a further 5 minutes, stir round, season with salt and serve garnished with parsley.

Luxury Lamb 'Hot Pot'

An extravagant but well worthwhile lamb casserole, full of flavour and ready in 40 minutes. No additional vegetables are necessary unless you fancy something green to offer contrast of colour and texture.

Preparation time: about 45 minutes

Serves 4 (F)

675 g (1½ lb) potatoes, peeled
225 g (8 oz) onions, peeled
100 g (4 oz) carrots, peeled
100 g (4 oz) celery, well-scrubbed
8 best end neck of lamb chops (about 1 kg/2-2¼ lb),
trimmed of fat
1 brown gravy cube
300 ml (½ pt/1¼ cups) boiling water
5 ml (1 tsp) salt
15 g (½ oz/1 tbsp) butter or margarine, melted

1 Very thinly slice potatoes, onions and carrots by hand or in a food processor. Thinly slice celery.

2 Arrange half the prepared vegetables, in layers, in a 2.25 litre (4 pt/10 cup) lightly greased casserole (Dutch oven). Top with chops. Add remaining vegetables, again in layers, ending with potatoes.

3 Cover with cling film, then puncture twice with the tip of a knife. Alternatively, cover with matching lid. Cook 15 minutes at full power.

4 Remove from oven and uncover. Crumble gravy cube into water then add salt. Pour gently down side of casserole. Drizzle butter or margarine over the top then cover as before.

5 Cook another 15 minutes at full power. Leave to stand 10 minutes. Spoon out of dish and serve.

Veal Loaf

Cut the loaf into wedges while still hot and you have a delicious main course with gravy and vegetables. Left to get cold, you can slice the loaf and serve it either as a pâté for starters or use it in sandwiches.

Preparation time: about 10 minutes

Serves 4 as a main course, 6 as a starter (F)

450g (1 lb/2 cups) raw veal, finely minced (ground)
1 garlic clove, peeled and crushed
25g (1 oz/¼ cup) plain (all-purpose) flour
2 (size 2) eggs, beaten
2.5ml (½ tsp) salt
2.5ml (½ tsp) dried thyme
5ml (1 tsp) Worcestershire sauce
grated nutmeg

1 Well-grease an oblong dish measuring 12.5 × 17.5 × 5 cm (5 × 7 × 2 inches) in depth.

2 Mix veal thoroughly with all remaining ingredients, except nutmeg, then spread into prepared dish.

3 Cover with cling film, then puncture twice with the tip of a knife. Alternatively, cover with matching lid.

4 Cook 8 minutes at full power. Remove from oven and take off cling film. Sprinkle Loaf with nutmeg and serve as suggested above.

Instant Meatball Goulash

I call this 'instant' because the dish combines fresh with convenience products and can be ready and waiting in under half an hour, depending on how quickly you move. Serve with rice or pasta and some microwaved mushrooms.

Preparation time: about 28 minutes

Serves 4 to 6 (F)

450 g (1 lb/2 cups) raw veal or turkey finely minced (ground)
50 g (2 oz/1 cup) fresh white breadcrumbs
2.5 ml (½ tsp) onion or garlic salt
1 (size 2) egg, beaten
300 ml (½ pt/1¼ cups) boiling water
1 can condensed cream of tomato soup
30 ml (2 tbsp) dried and chopped red and green
(bell) pepper flakes
10 ml (2 tsp) paprika
salt and pepper to taste
1 carton 150 ml (5 fl oz/⅔ cup) soured (dairy sour) cream

1 Mix together meat, crumbs, onion or garlic salt and egg. Shape into 12 balls and arrange round the edge of a 20 × 5 cm (8 × 2 inch) round glass or pottery dish.

2 Whisk water into soup then stir in pepper flakes and paprika. Spoon all the mixture over the meatballs.

3 Cover with cling film, then puncture twice with the tip of a knife. Alternatively, cover with matching lid.

4 Cook 15 minutes at full power.

5 Leave to stand 5 minutes then uncover and baste meatballs with tomato mixture. Adjust seasoning to taste and stir in soured cream. Reheat, uncovered, for 1½ minutes at full power.

Buffet Meatball Curry

Serves 8 (F)

Make exactly as *Instant Meatball Goulash* on previous page, subsituting minced (ground) beef for veal and using 675 g (1½ lb). Shape into 16 balls and arrange round edge of a 25 × 5 cm (10 × 2 inch) round glass or pottery dish. For sauce, smoothly mix 1 can condensed cream of tomato soup with 450 g (1 lb) peeled and chopped tomatoes, 10 ml (2 tsp) Soy sauce, 15 ml (1 tbsp) mild curry powder (or more to taste), 15 ml (1 tbsp) tomato purée (paste), 1 crumbled brown gravy cube and 60 ml (3 tbsp) mango chutney. Pour into dish over meatballs. Cover as directed above and cook 18 minutes at full power. Continue as previous recipe but, after basting meatballs with sauce, do *not* mix in soured cream. Serve with rice and salad, and extra chutney if liked.

Boiled Chicken

Often useful for making other dishes such as chicken in sauce for vol-au-vents or a quick curry, boiling a bird in the microwave is totally unproblematic and gives you moist and tender meat plus enough liquid to use for the basis of soup (chicken noodle for instance) or an appropriate sauce. If the bird is served as boiled chicken, use the vegetables as accompaniments. Otherwise serve cold with salad.

Preparation time: about 45 minutes

Serves 6 to 8

1 oven ready (broiler) chicken of about 1.5 kg (3 lb)
100 g (4 oz/1 cup) baby carrots, scraped or thawed if frozen
225 g (8 oz) onions, peeled and each cut into quarters
900 ml (1½ pt/3¾ cups) boiling water
2 small bay leaves
1 bouquet garni bag
5 ml (1 tsp) salt

1   Put rinsed bird into a 2.25 litre (4 pt/10 cup) deep glass or pottery dish.

2   Surround with vegetables then add water, bay leaves, bouquet garni bag and salt.

3   Cover with cling film, then puncture twice with the tip of a knife. Cook 30 minutes at full power.

4   Stand 10 minutes. Lift chicken out of liquid and serve hot, cold or in a made-up dish.

5   Strain liquid and reheat for 3 minutes at full power if being served straight away as soup. Otherwise leave until cold, skim off fat and use as required.

Creamy Peppered Chicken

An elegant way of preparing chicken or turkey breast fillet. It should appeal to sophisticated palates, is ideal for a dinner party and teams happily with a green salad and microwaved rice, first forked with butter and about 75 ml (5 tbsp) chopped parsley to turn it a pretty green.

Preparation time: about 25 minutes

Serves 6

25 g (1 oz/2 tbsp) butter or margarine, at room temperature
150 g (5 oz/1¼ cups) onions, peeled and finely chopped
450 g (1 lb) chicken breast fillet (or use turkey if preferred), washed and dried
15 ml (1 tbsp) cornflour (cornstarch)
30 ml (2 tbsp) water
15 ml (1 tbsp) tomato purée (paste)
20 ml (4 tsp) green peppercorns, available in cans or glass jars from speciality food shops
1 carton 150 ml (5 fl oz/⅔ cup) soured (dairy sour) cream
5 ml (1 tsp) salt

1   Put butter or margarine into a 20 × 5 cm (8 × 2 inch) round glass or pottery dish. Melt, uncovered, 1 to 1½ minutes at defrost setting.

2   Stir in onions. Cook, uncovered at full power, for 2 minutes. Leave to stand while preparing chicken. Cut, across the grain, into 2.5 cm (1 inch) wide strips.

3   Mix well with onions and butter. Cover with a plate or matching lid. Cook 6 minutes at full power.

4   Meanwhile, mix cornflour smoothly with water then add purée, green peppercorns, soured cream and salt.

5   Stir into chicken and onions then move mixture to edges of dish to form a hollow in the centre.

6   Cover with cling film, then puncture twice with the tip of a knife. Alternatively, cover with matching lid. Cook 8 minutes at full power. Leave to stand 5 minutes. Stir before serving.

Chicken and Vegetable Paprika Cream

A taste of Hungary here in the use of paprika and soured cream with chicken and vegetables. It provides a quietly subtle main course, delicately pink and perfect with small pastini – small bows or shells or even short cut macaroni.

Preparation time: about 18 minutes

Serves 4 (F)

25 g (1 oz/2 tbsp) butter or margarine, at room temperature
225 g (8 oz/2 cups) onions, peeled and chopped
1 small green (bell) pepper, de-seeded and chopped
1 small red (bell) pepper, de-seeded and chopped
175 g (6 oz/1½ cups) courgettes (zucchini), very thinly sliced
350 g (12 oz/2½ cups) chicken breast fillet, diced
15 ml (1 tbsp) paprika
45 ml (3 tbsp) tomato purée (paste)
1 carton 150 ml (5 fl oz/⅔ cup) soured (dairy sour) cream
5 ml (1 tsp) salt

1 Put butter or margarine in a 20 × 5 cm (8 × 2 inch) round dish and melt, uncovered, 1 to 1½ minutes at defrost setting.

2 Stir in onions, leave uncovered and cook 3 minutes at full power.

3 Mix in peppers, courgettes, chicken breast, paprika and tomato purée. Cover with cling film, then puncture twice with the tip of a knife. Alternatively, cover with a matching lid.

4 Cook 5 minutes at full power. Uncover. Mix in soured cream and salt thoroughly. Re-cover.

5 Cook a further 8 minutes at full power. Again stir round, adjust seasoning to taste and serve straight away with pasta. A lettuce salad, tossed in a mild French dressing, makes a worthy accompaniment.

Peanut Chicken

With shades of the Orient, I seem to have found a way of enlivening chicken joints. The mild, spicy topping is very easy to prepare and the dish goes well with those Chinese-style noodles available from most supermarkets. By way of an accompaniment, why not microwaved Chinese leaves?

Preparation time: about 24 minutes

Serves 4 (F)

900g (2lb) chicken joints
100g (4oz/½ cup) smooth peanut butter
2.5ml (½tsp) ground ginger
2.5ml (½ tsp) onion salt
7.5ml (1½tsp) Madras curry powder
Chinese barbecue sauce (Hoi Sin)

1 Arrange joints, in a single layer, around the edge of a 25cm (10inch) round dish which is fairly shallow.

2 Put peanut butter into a small dish. Leave uncovered and heat 1 minute at defrost setting.

3 Stir in ginger, onion salt and curry powder. Spread over joints.

4 Top each with a little barbecue sauce (Hoi Sin). Cover with cling film, then puncture twice with the tip of a knife.

5 Cook 16 minutes at full power. Stand 5 minutes before serving.

Normandy Apple Chicken

Stylishly-flavoured and in the traditions of French family cooking, this chicken dish is different from the usual run, slightly rustic, perfect with boiled potatoes tossed in butter and a green salad.

Preparation time: about 43 minutes

Serves 4 (F)

50g (2oz/¼ cup) butter or margarine, at room temperature
900g (2lb) chicken joints, thawed completely if frozen
175g (6oz/1½ cups) onions, peeled and chopped
225g (8oz/2 cups) cooking (tart) apples, peeled and finely chopped (cores removed)
1 garlic clove, peeled and chopped (optional)
30ml (2 tbsp) plain (all-purpose) flour
300ml (½ pt/1¼ cups) medium cider
2 brown gravy cubes
5ml (1 tsp) dried thyme
salt and pepper to taste
15ml (1 tbsp) chopped parsley

1   Put butter or margarine into a 25 × 5 cm (10 × 2 inch) glass or pottery dish. Leave uncovered and melt 1½ to 2 minutes at defrost setting.

2   Add chicken joints and toss round in the butter or margarine. Cover with cling film then puncture twice with the tip of a knife. Alternatively, cover with a matching lid.

3   Cook 15 minutes at full power.

4   Uncover then sprinkle onions, apples and garlic (if used) over chicken. Mix flour smoothly with some of the measured cider. Add remainder.

5   Crumble in the 2 gravy cubes then add thyme. Spoon liquid into dish over chicken and vegetables, etc. Cover as above. Cook 15 minutes at full power. Leave to stand 10 minutes.

6   Uncover and gently stir round. Adjust seasoning to taste and sprinkle with parsley.

Chestnut Chicken

A beauty, this one, with a classic flavour. It is most acceptable with brown rice and cooked peas, mixed together while hot with butter or margarine and a tablespoon of fresh coriander (cilantro), finely chopped.

Preparation time: about 23 minutes

Serves 4 generously (F)

50 g (2 oz/¼ cup) butter or margarine
225 g (8 oz/2 cups) onions, peeled and finely chopped or grated
1 can 430 g (15 oz) sweetened chestnut purée (paste)
2.5 ml (½ tsp) salt
4 chicken breasts, about 450 g (1 lb), washed and dried
225 g (8 oz/1½ cups) blanched tomatoes, skinned and sliced
30 ml (2 tbsp) chopped parsley

1   Put butter or margarine into a 25 cm (10 inch) round, shallow dish. Melt, uncovered, for 1½ to 2 minutes at defrost setting.

2   Mix in onions and cook, also uncovered, for 4 minutes at full power. Stir in chestnut purée then season with salt.

3   Flatten into an even layer and arrange chicken breasts on top round edge of dish. Top with tomato slices and sprinkle with parsley.

4   Cover with cling film, then puncture twice with the tip of a knife. Alternatively, cover with a matching lid.

5   Cook 10 minutes at full power.

6   Leave to stand 5 minutes. Spoon out on to 4 warm plates to serve.

Chicken with Chinese Gold Sauce

Gently sweet-sour and delicately spiced, this Chinese-style chicken speciality goes best with saffron or plain rice, cooked bean sprouts and Chinese leaves.

Preparation time: about 30 minutes plus marinating

Serves 4 (F)

900 g (2 lb) chicken joints, washed and dried
then dusted with plain (all-purpose) flour
50 g (2 oz/½ cup) onion, peeled and grated
2 garlic cloves, peeled and crushed
30 ml (2 tbsp) Soy sauce
30 ml (2 tbsp) medium sherry
30 ml (2 tbsp) sunflower oil
60 ml (4 tbsp) lemon juice
30 ml (2 tbsp) soft light brown (coffee) sugar
30 ml (2 tbsp) melted apricot jam without any
large pieces of fruit
5 ml (1 tsp) ground coriander (cilantro)
3 drops Tabasco

1   Arrange chicken joints in a fairly shallow 25 cm (10 inch) round glass or pottery dish with skin sides facing. Slash through flesh in several places with a sharp knife.

2   Beat rest of ingredients well together and pour over chicken. Cover loosely and leave to stand at room temperature for 2 hours (1½ hours in the height of summer), turning chicken joints over 3 times.

3   Finally turn the chicken joints so that skin sides are up. Cover dish with cling film, then puncture twice with the tip of a knife.

4   Cook 22 minutes at full power. Stand 5 minutes. Serve coated with pan juices, and the accompaniments suggested above.

Chicken from the Forest

A warm-hearted way of serving chicken drumsticks and a feast of a family dinner with freshly microwaved noodles or rice and vegetables.

Preparation time: about 40 minutes

Serves 4 (F)

30 ml (2 tbsp) sunflower oil or melted butter or margarine
175 g (6 oz/9 slices) streaky bacon, chopped
100 g (4 oz/1 cup) onions, peeled and chopped
1.2 kg (2½ lb) chicken drumsticks, skinned
100 g (4 oz/1 cup) button mushrooms, sliced
275 g (10 oz) jar or can tomato sauce for spaghetti
15 ml (1 tbsp) malt vinegar
15 ml (1 tbsp) lemon juice
30 ml (2 tbsp) soft light brown (coffee) sugar
5 ml (1 tsp) Continental mustard
30 ml (2 tbsp) Worcestershire sauce
chopped parsley for garnishing

1   Pour oil or fat into an oblong glass dish measuring about 35 × 23 cm (14 × 9 inches). Heat 1 minute at full power, leaving uncovered.

2   Add bacon and onions. Stir well to mix. Cook, uncovered, for 5 minutes at full power.

3   Add drumsticks, turning over in the bacon and onion mixture to coat. Arrange with the thickest parts towards edge of dish.

4   Sprinkle with mushrooms. Beat tomato sauce with vinegar, lemon juice, sugar, mustard and Worcestershire sauce. Spoon over chicken.

5   Cover with cling film, then puncture twice with the tip of a knife. Cook 15 minutes at full power. Uncover, turn drumsticks over and re-cover with film. Puncture.

6   Continue to cook for a further 15 minutes at full power. Remove from oven, leave to stand 5 minutes, uncover and sprinkle with parsley.

Pineapple Chicken Loaf

A fantasy of a loaf, with the subtle tang of pineapple and an elusive sweet-sour taste that makes it seem almost Chinese in character. Serve it cold, cut into slices, and accompany with salad vegetables.

Preparation time: about 35 minutes plus cooling time

Serves 8 (F)

450g (1lb/4cups) cold cooked chicken, finely minced (ground)
75g (3oz/¾cup) onions, peeled and finely minced
1 can crushed pineapple in syrup about 450g (1lb) in size
with a drained weight of between 225-250g (8-9oz)
2 packets (26.5g/1oz) bread sauce mix
2.5g (½tsp) salt
2 (size 3) eggs, beaten
25g (1oz/¼cup) flaked and toasted almonds (page 303)

1   Line a 900ml (1½pt/3¾cup) oblong, glass pie dish smoothly with cling film.

2   Put chicken and onions into a bowl. Fork in pineapple with its syrup, bread sauce mix, salt and eggs. Mix thoroughly.

3   Spread smoothly into prepared dish. Sprinkle with flaked almonds.

4   Leave uncovered and cook 30 minutes at defrost setting.

5   Remove from oven. Lift out of dish when lukewarm and stand on a wire cooling rack. Peel away cling film when loaf is completely cold.

Spanish Chicken

Here is a chicken dish that is vividly-coloured and tantalisingly-flavoured – a delightful weekender for a family group or small dinner party. Add 100 g (4 oz/²⁄₃ cup) peeled prawns (shrimp) after cooking for a quick paella.

Preparation time: about 45 minutes

Serves 4 generously (F)

25 g (1 oz/2 tbsp) butter or margarine
100 g (4 oz/6 slices) streaky bacon, chopped
1 garlic clove, peeled and crushed
225 g (8 oz/2 cups) onions, peeled and very finely chopped
1 can 185 g (6½ oz) red pimientos, drained and fairly finely chopped
1 can 400 g (14 oz) tomatoes
225 g (8 oz/1 cup) easy-cook, long-grain rice
5 ml (1 tsp) paprika
15 ml (1 tbsp) turmeric
175 g (6 oz/1½ cups) frozen peas
900 g (2 lb) chicken joints, thawed if frozen
Soy sauce
1 quartered fresh tomato for garnishing

1   Put butter or margarine into a fairly shallow 25 cm (10 inch) round glass or pottery dish and melt 1 to 1½ minutes at defrost setting. Leave uncovered.

2   Stir in bacon, garlic and onions. Cover with a plate and cook for 5 minutes at full power.

3   Stir in pimientos, canned tomatoes (taking care not to break them up too much), rice, paprika, turmeric and peas.

4   Stand chicken joints on top then brush lightly with Soy sauce.

5   Cover dish with cling film, then puncture twice with the tip of a knife. Alternatively, cover with matching lid. Cook 35 minutes at full power.

6   Remove from oven, uncover and serve.

Roast Turkey

When dealing with such a large bird, correct defrosting times are necessary for success.

Allow 350g (12 oz) raw weight per person

- Keep the size of turkey to be defrosted and microwaved around 4.5 kg (10 lb). It can be accomodated comfortably in most ovens (except small ones).

- Remove metal ties but keep bird in its original wrapper.

- Put into microwave, set control to defrost and leave the turkey to thaw partially for 45 minutes.

- Take out of oven, remove giblet bag if it is loose enough, then leave turkey to continue thawing overnight in the kitchen. On this basis, it makes sense to carry out the 45 minute defrost the evening before the turkey is to be cooked.

- Remove giblet bag if this has not already been done, then make sure *inside* of turkey is totally free of ice crystals. If not, leave in a sink of cold water until bird has completely and thoroughly thawed. Rinse inside and out with fresh water, dry with kitchen paper.

Alternative Method of Defrosting

1 Microwave bird for 45 minutes at defrost setting. Leave to stand 45 minutes. Check to see if giblet bag has loosened and can be removed. If not leave bag where it is. Turn bird over.

2 Microwave bird for 30 minutes at defrost setting. Leave to stand 30 minutes and check giblet bag. Remove if possible. Turn turkey over.

3 Repeat No. 2 above, removing giblet bag if it has not already been taken out.

4 Check for ice crystals and if any are still in body cavity, leave bird in a sink of cold water up to 1 hour or until completely and thoroughly defrosted.

To Cook Turkey

1 Cover wing tips and ends of legs with foil to prevent overcooking.

2 Stand turkey, breast side down, in a dish large enough to hold the bird comfortably, even if body domes up above the rim.

3 Cover with cling film, then puncture 4 times with the tip of a knife.

4 Cook at full power, allowing 8 minutes per 450 g (1 lb) for half the cooking time.

5 Remove from oven and carefully turn over so that breast of turkey is now uppermost. Brush thickly with baste (page 75), choosing a fat-based one if bird is plain, or a non-fat one if bird is self-basting* and impreganted with fat or oil. This browns the skin and makes turkey look as though it had been roasted conventionally.

6 Re-cover as before, finish cooking at full power. Transfer to carving dish.

7 Cover with foil. Leave to stand 15 minutes. Carve. Serve with gravy (page 79) made from pan juices and microwaved vegetables with trimmings to taste. Alternatively, cook turkey in a giant roasting bag, secured with an elastic band at the top. Basting will be unnecessary.

*It is not essential to brush the self-basting turkey with extra baste.

Whole Turkey Breast on the Bone

(Bought ready-prepared)

Defrost if frozen then remove wrapping. Put on to a plate, skin side uppermost. Brush with baste, cover as 'roast' turkey and cook at full power, allowing 8 minutes per 450 g (1 lb). Standing time should be about 7 minutes.

Boned Turkey Roast with Stuffing

(Bought ready-prepared)

A 'roast' of this nature, which is fairly dense, should be thoroughly defrosted and then cooked at full power for 15 minutes per 450 g (1 lb) with a 10 minute rest period in the middle and at the end. It should be unwrapped, put on to a dish and covered as roast turkey. The stringy casing should be removed before slicing. If the slices look slightly undercooked, they can be put on to individual plates, covered as for 'roast' turkey with film or with an inverted plate, and cooked at full power for about 1 to 1½ minutes extra. When choosing a joint of this kind, ensure that the weight does not exceed 1 kg (2 lb).

NOTE: *If turkey or joint has been taken straight from refrigerator, allow 1 minute extra cooking time per 450 g (1 lb).*

Mild Family Curry

For all those times when you wonder how to perk up the remains of a large family turkey or chicken, here is a recipe to set the taste buds tingling. If a hotter curry is preferred, add cayenne pepper to taste, allowing from a good pinch to a level teaspoon – or use a few drops of Tabasco.

Preparation time: about 18 minutes

Serves 4 (F)

25 g (1 oz/2 tbsp) butter or margarine, at room temperature
150 g (5 oz/1¼ cups) onions, peeled and very thinly sliced
1 garlic clove, peeled and crushed
25 g (1 oz/1½ tbsp) raisins
25 g (1 oz/¼ cup) desiccated (shredded) coconut
25 g (1 oz/¼ cup) plain (all-purpose) flour
20 ml (4 tsp) Madras curry powder
300 ml (½ pt/1¼ cups) boiling water
30 ml (2 tbsp) milk
2.5 ml (½ tsp) salt
15 ml (1 tbsp) lemon juice
350 g (12 oz/2¼ cups) cooked turkey or chicken, diced

1   Put butter or margarine into a 20 × 5 cm (8 × 2 inch) round dish. Melt, uncovered, for about 1 to 1½ minutes at defrost setting.

2   Stir in onions, garlic, raisins and coconut. Leave uncovered and cook 2 minutes at full power.

3   Mix in flour, curry powder, water, milk, salt, lemon juice and turkey. Cover with cling film then puncture twice with the tip of a knife. Alternatively, cover with a matching lid.

4   Cook 6 minutes at full power. Leave to stand 5 minutes.

5   Uncover, stir round, transfer to a warm dish and serve with freshly cooked rice, mango chutney and a salad of sliced onions, separated into rings, with thinly sliced red or green (bell) pepper. If liked, also serve a dish of plain yoghurt sprinkled with chopped preserved ginger.

Sweet-Sour Duckling

A remarkabley easy way of giving a microwaved duck a warm, golden glow and chinese flavour. It goes well with freshly cooked noodles tossed with peas and strips of omelet. Another appetising accompaniment – bean sprouts microwaved as described on page 187.

Preparation time: about 52 minutes

Serves 4

1 × 2 kg (4½ lb) duckling, thawed and weighed after giblets have been removed
40 ml (2 slightly rounded tbsp) mango chutney

1   Keep giblets from duckling and use for conventionally-cooked soup such as vegetable broth or Minestrone.

2   Wash bird inside and out under cold, running water. Dry with kitchen paper.

3   Place a plastic rack or 2 inverted saucers into an oblong dish measuring about 30 × 19 cm (12 × 7½ inches). Stand duck on top, breast side down.

4   Cover with cling film, then puncture twice with the tip of a knife.

5   Cook 20 minutes at full power.

6   Uncover. Turn duckling over carefully, using 2 wooden spoons, so that breast side is now uppermost.

7   Spread thickly with the chutney then re-cover with cling film as before. Cook a further 20 minutes.

8   Leave to stand 10 minutes. Cut into 4 portions with poultry shears and serve.

TIP: *Keep duck juices in the refrigerator overnight. Next day, remove fat and discard, then use remaining semi-jellied stock for soups, stews or sauces.*

Turkey Flan

This is an appetising flan and especially useful at Christmas or Easter when there is leftover turkey. Serve with salad or cauliflower cheese.

Preparation time: about 25 minutes

Serves 6 to 8

Base
shortcrust pastry (basic pie crust) made with
175g (6oz/1½ cups) plain (all-purpose) flour,
75g (3oz/⅓ cup) fat etc.

Filling
350g (12oz/2¼ cups) cold cooked turkey,
cut into large cubes or strips
100g (4oz) onion, peeled and cut into eighths
2 (size 3) eggs, beaten
75ml (5 tbsp) cold milk
5ml (1 tsp) salt
white pepper to taste

Garnish
sliced onion, separated into rings
chopped parsley

1   Roll out pastry on floured surface and use to line a greased round 18 cm (7 in) flan dish.

2   Prick well all over, especially where base of pastry meets sides. Bake, uncovered, for 6 minutes at full power. Gently press down any bulges with hand protected by oven glove.

3   For filling, finely mince turkey and onion. Transfer to mixing bowl then add eggs, milk, salt and pepper. Mix thoroughly and spread smoothly into pastry case.

4   Cook, uncovered, 7½ to 8 minutes at full power (or until filling is firm and set).

5   Leave to stand 5 minutes. Garnish with a border of onion rings then sprinkle with parsley. Serve hot or cold.

French Country Liver

An absolute winner for those who enjoy offal, and liver in particular. Rice, buttered carrots and Casseroled Leeks (see Vegetable Section) are admirable accompaniments.

Preparation time: about 18 minutes

Serves 4 to 6 (F)

25 g (1 oz/2 tbsp) butter or margarine
175 g (6 oz/1½ cups) onions, peeled and finely chopped or grated
450 g (1 lb) lambs' liver, cut into strips measuring 10 × 2.5 cm (4 × 1 inch)
20 ml (4 tsp) plain (all-purpose) flour
300 ml (½ pt/1¼ cups) dry red wine
15 ml (1 tbsp) dark brown sugar
1 brown gravy cube, crumbled
15 ml (1 tbsp) parsley
seasoning to taste

1 Put butter or margarine into a 25 cm (10 inch) fairly shallow round dish and melt 1 to 1½ minutes at defrost setting. Leave uncovered.

2 Stir in onions and liver. Cover with a plate and cook 5 minutes at full power.

3 Mix in all remaining ingredients except seasoning. Cover with a plate as before and cook 6 minutes at full power, stirring mixture twice.

4 Leave to stand 3 minutes then uncover, stir round and season to taste. Serve as suggested above.

Liver and Bacon

A special attraction main course made from those tubs of frozen chicken livers now readily available from supermarket chains. Diced pork or lamb liver may be used instead, soaked first for 1 hour in milk to eliminate bitterness.

Preparation time: about 30 minutes

Serves 6 (F)

175 g (6 oz/1½ cups) onions, peeled and sliced
225 g (8 oz/12 slices) streaky bacon, derinded and chopped
450 g (1 lb/2 cups) chicken livers (2 tubs), de-frosted if frozen
then rinsed and well-drained
45 ml (3 tbsp) cornflour (cornstarch)
60 ml (4 tbsp) cold water
150 ml (¼ pt/⅔ cup) boiling water
Salt and pepper to taste

1   Put onions and chopped bacon into a 1.75 litre (3 pt/7½ cup) glass or pottery dish. Leave uncovered and cook 7 minutes at full power, stirring 3 times.

2   Mix in livers, each of which should first be punctured with the tip of knife to prevent popping. Cover with a plate and cook 8 minutes at full power, stirring 2 or 3 times. Leave to stand in oven for 5 minutes.

3   Mix cornflour smoothly with cold water. Add boiling water then add to livers. Stir thoroughly.

4   Cover with a plate and cook 6 minutes at full power.

5   Stir round, season to taste with salt and pepper then serve with creamed potatoes or freshly cooked rice and a selection of vegetables to taste.

VEGETABLES

If you refer to the charts, you will see how easy it is to cook a wide selection of both fresh and frozen vegetables in the microwave without loss of colour, flavour and texture. And because the amount of cooking water is, in most instances, minimal, valuable nutrients are retained instead of being drained away at the end.

Imagination as far as flavourings and additions are concerned has been left to you but cooked vegetables can be served with sauces chosen from the Sauce Section on page 67, tossed or coated with melted butter or margarine, flavoured and garnished with a shower of chopped parsley or chives (or other fresh herbs or spices to taste), and even sprinkled with chopped nuts or grated lemon rind. Always season vegetables **after** cooking as salt tends to toughen them.

For simplicity when cooking smallish packs of frozen vegetables, leave in their original bags. Puncture each bag 2 or 3 times with the tip of a knife and stand in a dish. Cook for the length of time given in the charts, or on the bag itself, then drain and serve as previously suggested. If cooking a block of frozen vegetables, open out and put into a dish with the ice side facing. Cook as directed.

A short selection of vegetable dishes follows, ranging from Gratin Dauphinoise and Danish-Style Red Cabbage to a Spiced Aubergine Purée and Ratatouille. Even creamed potatoes, with their hundred and one uses, have been included.

Frozen Vegetables (to cook from frozen)

	COOK/HEAT FULL POWER	COMMENTS
Asparagus Spears		
225g (8oz)	6 minutes	Put into an oblong dish. Add 15ml (1tbsp) boiling water. Cover with plate or lid. Half way through cooking, separate spears and arrange in the dish with the thick ends pointing outwards. Season. Remove from dish with a fish slice to prevent spears breaking.
450g (1lb)	10 minutes	As above, adding 45ml (3tbsp) boiling water.
Beans, Broad (Lima)		
225g (8oz)	5 minutes	Put into bowl or dish. Add 15ml (1tbsp) boiling water. Cover with plate or lid. Stir half way through cooking. Season. Drain before serving.
450g (1lb)	9 minutes	As above, adding 45ml (3tbsp) boiling water.
Beans, Green, cut or whole		
225g (8oz)	6 minutes	Put into bowl or dish. Add 15ml (1tbsp) boiling water. Cover with plate or lid. Stir half way through cooking. Season. Drain before serving.
450g (1lb)	10 minutes	As above, adding 45ml (3tbsp) boiling water.
Beans, Green, sliced		
225g (8oz)	5 minutes	Put into bowl or dish. Add 15ml (1tbsp) boiling water. Cover with plate or lid. Stir half way through cooking. Season. Drain before serving.
450g (1lb)	9 minutes	As above, adding 45ml (3tbsp) boiling water.
Broccoli Spears		
400g (14oz) pack	8 minutes	Put into oblong dish. Add 30ml (2tbsp) boiling water. Cover with plate or lid. Separate half way through cooking. Season. Drain before serving.
2 × 400g (14oz) packs	14 minutes	As above, adding 60ml (4tbsp) boiling water.
Brussels Sprouts		
225g (8oz)	5 minutes	Put into bowl or dish. Add 15ml (1tbsp) boiling water. Cover with plate or lid. Stir half way through cooking. Season. Drain before serving.
450g (1lb)	9 minutes	As above, adding 45ml (3tbsp) boiling water.

	COOK/HEAT FULL POWER	COMMENTS
Carrots, baby		
225g (8oz)	8 minutes	Put into a bowl or dish. Add 15ml (1tbsp) boiling water. Cover with plate or lid. Stir half way through cooking. Season. Drain before serving.
450g (1lb)	15 minutes	As above, adding 45ml (3tbsp) boiling water.
Carrots, sliced		
225g (8oz)	5 minutes	Put into a bowl or dish. Add 15ml (1tbsp) boiling water. Cover with plate or lid. Stir half way through cooking. Season. Drain before serving.
450g (1lb)	9 minutes	As above, adding 45ml (3tbsp) boiling water.
Cauliflower Florets		
225g (8oz)	6 minutes	Put into a bowl or dish. Add 15ml (1tbsp) boiling water. Cover with plate or lid. Stir half way through cooking. Season. Drain before serving.
450g (1lb)	10 minutes	As above, adding 45ml (3tbsp) boiling water.
Corn-on-the-Cob		
1 head	6 minutes	Put on to plate. Cover with kitchen paper. Turn over twice during cooking.
2 heads	8 to 9 minutes	As above, turn over 3 times during cooking.
Courgettes (Zucchini), sliced		
225g (8oz)	5 minutes	Put into bowl or dish. Add 15ml (1tbsp) boiling water. Cover with plate or lid. Stir half way through cooking. Season. Drain before serving.
450g (1lb)	9 minutes	As above, adding 45ml (3tbsp) boiling water.
Macedoine		
225g (8oz)	5 minutes	Put into bowl or dish. Add 15ml (1tbsp) boiling water. Cover with plate or lid. Stir half way through cooking. Season. Drain before serving or using in Russian salad, etc.
450g (1lb)	9 minutes	As above, adding 45ml (3tbsp) boiling water.
Mange Tout (Snow Peas)		
225g (8oz)	5 minutes	Put into bowl or dish. Add 15ml (1tbsp) boiling water. Cover with lid or plate. Stir half way through cooking. Season. Drain before serving.
450g (1lb)	9 minutes	As above, adding 45ml (3tbsp) boiling water.

	COOK/HEAT FULL POWER	COMMENTS
Mexican Mix		
225g (8oz)	5 minutes	Put into bowl or dish. Add 15ml (1tbsp) boiling water. Cover with lid or plate. Stir half way through cooking. Season. Drain before serving.
450g (1lb)	9 minutes	As above, adding 45ml (3tbsp) boiling water.
Mixed Vegetables, Farmhouse Style		
225g (8oz)	5 minutes	Put into bowl or dish. Add 15ml (1tbsp) boiling water. Cover with lid or plate. Stir half way through cooking. Season. Drain before serving.
450g (1lb)	9 minutes	As above, adding 45ml (3tbsp) boiling water.
Onions, sliced		
225g (8oz)	3 to 4 minutes	Put into bowl or dish. Add no liquid. Cover with plate or lid. Stir half way through cooking. Drain before serving.
Peas, garden		
225g (8oz)	5 minutes	Put into bowl or dish. Add 15ml (1tbsp) boiling water. Cover with pate or lid. Stir half way through cooking. Season. Drain before serving.
450g (1lb)	9 minutes	As above, adding 45ml (3tbsp) boiling water.
Peppers (Bell), mixed, sliced		
225g (8oz)	2 to 3 minutes	Put into bowl or dish. Add 15g (½oz/1tbsp) butter or margarine but no liquid. Cover with plate or lid. Stir half way through cooking. Season. Do not drain.
Spinach, chopped		
225g (8oz)	5 minutes	Put into bowl or dish. Add 15ml (1tbsp) boiling water. Cover with plate or lid. Stir half way through cooking. Season. Drain very thoroughly before serving.
450g (1lb)	9 minutes	As above, adding 45ml (3tbsp) boiling water.
Sweetcorn		
225g (8oz)	5 minutes	Put into bowl or dish. Add 30 ml (2 tbsp) boiling water. Stir half way through cooking. Season. Drain well before serving.
450g (1lb)	9 minutes	As above, adding 45ml (3tbsp) boiling water.

Tips on Cooking Fresh Vegetables

Microwaved vegetables should be cooked either in a mixing bowl or, for convenience, a dish suitable for serving. The bowl or dish should be covered with cling film and slit twice. Alternatively, a matching lid or plate may be used for covering if stirring or rearranging is required during cooking.

Weights given are for vegetables *before* trimming, peeling, etc. It is advisable to leave firm vegetables to stand for 2 to 3 minutes after cooking but soft vegetables, such as sliced cabbage, tomato halves or mushrooms, may be served straight away. Always season after cooking (before standing) to avoid toughening.

Some vegetables actually take longer in the microwave than on the hob, but you will avoid a steamy kitchen and save on washing up.

BLANCHING IN THE MICROWAVE PRIOR TO FREEZING VEGETABLES

When carrying out this operation, allow 150 ml (¼ pint/⅔ cup) water to every 450 g (1 lb) prepared vegetables. Put both together into a dish, cover with film as directed above and allow *only half* the amount of cooking time given in the charts. Afterwards drain vegetables and rinse under cold, running water. Pack as directed in your own freezer instruction book or manual.

Cooking Fresh Vegetables

	COOK/HEAT FULL POWER	COMMENTS
Artichokes, Globe		
4	25 to 35 minutes, depending on size	Cut off stems and tips of leaves. Soak in cold water for 1 hour with leaves pointing downwards. Drain. Stand upright in a large glass or pottery dish, add 2.5 cm (1 inch) boiling water. Cover with cling film and slit twice. Drain before serving.
Artichokes, Jerusalem		
450 g (1 lb)	12 to 14 minutes	Peel artichokes and wash. Put into dish or bowl with 15 ml (1 tbsp) lemon juice and 90 ml (6 tbsp) boiling water. Cover with cling film and slit twice. Season. Drain before serving.
Asparagus		
medium to thin spears 225 g (8 oz)	10 minutes	Wash. leave whole and put into dish. Add 30 ml (2 tbsp) water. Cover with film and slit twice. Season. Drain before serving.
thick spears 225 g (8 oz)	12 minutes	As above.

TIP: *Cut a thin sliver off the root end of each asparagus spear before washing and cooking. If spears are thick, scrape downwards from tips to remove a thin layer from outside of each.*

	COOK/HEAT FULL POWER	COMMENTS
Aubergines (Eggplants)		
450 g (1 lb)	6 minutes	Cut tops (stem ends) off unpeeled aubergines and slice. Put into dish or bowl with 60 ml (4 tbsp) water and 10 ml (2 tsp) lemon juice. Cover with plate or matching lid. Stir half way through cooking. Season. Drain before serving.
Beans, broad (Lima), French or runner		
450 g (1 lb)	8 to 10 minutes	Prepare according to type of bean. Put into shallow dish with 30 ml (2 tbsp) water (60 ml/4 tbsp for broad beans). Cover with plate or matching lid. Stir half way through cooking. Season. Drain before serving.
Broccoli Spears		
3 to 4	11 minutes	Wash and shake dry. Split the spears lengthwise if thick. Put in shallow dish with 60 ml (4 tbsp) water. Cover with cling film and slit twice. Season. Drain before serving.

	COOK/HEAT FULL POWER	COMMENTS
Brussels Sprouts		
225g (8oz)	10 minutes	Wash sprouts and remove outer leaves if bruised. Make a cross cut in stem end of each. Put into shallow dish with 30ml (2tbsp) water. Cover with plate or matching lid. Stir half way through cooking. Season. Drain before serving.
Cabbage		
450g (1lb)	10 minutes	Remove any outer leaves that may be damaged or bruised. Wash cabbage and shred. Put into dish or bowl with 30ml (2tbsp) water. Cover with plate or matching lid. Stir half way through cooking. Season. Drain before serving.
Carrots, new		
225g (8oz)	12 to 14 minutes	Scrape carrots and leave whole. Put into shallow dish with 60ml (4tbsp) boiling water. Cover with cling film and slit twice. Season. Drain before serving.
Carrots, old		
225g (8oz)	8½ to 10 minutes	Peel and slice carrots. Put into shallow dish with 60ml (4tbsp) boiling water. Cover with plate or matching lid. Stir half way through cooking. Season. Drain before serving.
Cauliflower		
675g (1½lb)	10 to 12 minutes	Wash cauliflower and cut head into small florets. Put into dish or bowl with 60ml (4tbsp) water. Cover with plate or matching lid. Stir half way through cooking. Season. Drain before serving.
Celery		
350g (12oz)	10 minutes	Wash and scrub celery then slice. Put into shallow dish with 30ml (2tbsp) water. Cover with cling film and slit twice. Season. Drain before serving.
Chicory (Belgian Endive)		
225g (8oz)	8 minutes	Remove a cone-shaped bitter core from the base of each head of chicory. Wash heads gently, removing any damaged outer leaves. Put into dish with 15ml (1tbsp) lemon juice and 45ml (3tbsp) water. Cover with cling film and slit twice. Season. Drain.
Corn-on-the-Cob		
1 medium	2 minutes	Cook in own husk and silk for maximum flavour and moisture. Otherwise wrap each in cling film, slitting in 2 or 3 places. Stand 5 minutes. Unwrap, serve.
2 medium	4 to 5 minutes	
3 medium	6 to 7 minutes	
4 medium	8 to 10 minutes	

	COOK/HEAT FULL POWER	COMMENTS
Courgettes (Zucchini)		
450 g (1 lb)	7 to 8 minutes	Top and tail courgettes. Wash. Slice unpeeled and put into shallow dish. Add *no* water. Cover with plate or matching lid. Stir half way through cooking. Season before serving if liked.
Cucumber		
225 g (8 oz)	4 minutes	Peel cucumber and cut into dice. Put into shallow dish with 15 ml (1 tbsp) water. Cover with plate or matching lid. Stir half way through cooking. Season. Drain before serving.
Leeks		
450 g (1 lb)	10 minutes	Slit leeks and wash thoroughly. Trim and slice. Put into dish or bowl with 30 ml (2 tbsp) water. Cover with plate or matching lid. Stir half way through cooking. Season lightly. Drain thoroughly before serving.
Marrow (Squash)		
450 g (1 lb)	8 to 9 minutes	Peel. Slice into rings and remove centre 'cores' of seeds and fibres. Cut each empty ring into small cubes. Put into shallow dish. Add *no* water. Cover with plate or matching lid. Stir half way through cooking. Season. If necessary, drain before serving.
Mushrooms		
225 g (8 oz)	6 minutes	Wash mushrooms. Peel if necessary. Put into shallow dish with 15 ml (1 tbsp) water. Cover with plate or matching lid. Stir half way thorugh cooking. Season. Drain before serving. If preferred, omit water and cook in 15 ml (1 tbsp) melted butter or margarine. Do *not* drain after cooking but serve with juices.
Okra (Ladies' fingers)		
450 g (1 lb)	7 to 8 minutes	Top and tail washed okra. Put into shallow dish with 30 ml (2 tbsp) melted butter or margarine. Cover with plate or matching lid. Stir gently half way through cooking. Do *not* drain before serving.

	COOK/HEAT FULL POWER	COMMENTS
Onions 450g (1lb)	8 to 10 minutes	Peel onions and halve or quarter if large. Put into a dish or bowl. Add 30ml (2tbsp) water and a knob of butter or margarine. Cover with cling film and slit twice. Season. Drain if necessary before serving.
Parsnips 450g (1lb)	8 to 10 minutes	Peel and dice parsnips. Put into a shallow dish with 45ml (3tbsp) water. Cover with plate or matching lid. Stir half way through cooking. Season. Drain before serving.
Peas 450g (1lb)	9 minutes	Shell peas. Put into shallow dish with 30 ml (2 tbsp) water. Add a pinch of sugar and a sprig of mint if liked. Cover with plate or matching lid. Stir half way through cooking. Season. Drain before serving.
Potatoes, new small, in their skins 450g (1lb)	11 minutes	Wash and scrub potatoes well. Put into shallow dish with 30ml (2tbsp) water and a sprig of mint if liked. Cover with plate or matching lid. Stir half way through cooking. Season. Drain before serving.
Potatoes, old, in their jackets 1 medium potato 100g (4oz)	5 to 6 minutes Stand 5 minutes wrapped in foil or tea towel	Wash and dry potatoes thoroughly. Slit or prick skins in several places. Stand on plate or kitchen paper. Cover with more kitchen paper. Turn over twice or three times during cooking. When cooking more than one potato, leave 2.5cm (1inch) space between each. Arrange 3 potatoes in triangle; 4 in square; 5 to 8 round edge of plate or paper.
2 medium potatoes	6½ to 8 minutes Stand 5 minutes as above	
3 medium potatoes	9 to 11 minutes Stand 5 minutes as above	**Note:** Cooking times can vary enormously, depending on variety. These are the *minimum* you can expect. After cooking, potatoes should feel soft when gently squeezed.
4 medium potatoes	12 to 14 minutes Stand 5 minutes as above	For 5-8 potatoes, increase cooking times accordingly (approx. 3 minutes for each extra potato).

	COOK/HEAT FULL POWER	COMMENTS
Spinach 450g (1lb)	7 to 8 minutes	Wash very thoroughly to remove grit. Tear leaves into small pieces. Put into dish but *do not* add water. Cover with plate or matching lid. Stir half way through cooking. Season. Drain if necessary.
Spring Greens 450g (1lb)	7 to 9 minutes	Tear leaves off stalks, wash and shake dry. Shred coarsely and put into shallow dish. Cover with plate or matching lid. Stir half way through cooking. Season. Drain before serving.
Swedes (Rutabaga) 450g (1lb)	10 minutes	Peel swedes and dice. Put into shallow dish with 60ml (4tbsp) water. Cover with plate or matching lid. Stir half way through cooking. Season. Drain before serving.
Sweet (Bell) Peppers 450g (1lb)	8 minutes	Halve peppers and remove cores and seeds. Slice or chop. Put into bowl with 30ml (2tbsp) water. Cover with cling film and slit twice. Season. Drain before serving.
Tomatoes 450g (1lb)	6 to 7 minutes	Wash tomatoes and halve. Put into shallow dish, cut sides facing. Add *no* water. Cover with cling film and slit twice. If liked, brush cut sides with melted butter or margarine and sprinkle with sugar. Season before serving.
Turnips 450g (1lb)	10 to 12 minutes	Peel turnips and dice. Put into shallow dish with 60ml (4tbsp) water. Cover with plate or matching lid. Stir half way through cooking. Season. Drain before serving.

Spiced Aubergine (Eggplant) Purée

An unusual accompaniment which is a simple variation of the dip given on page 52.

Preparation time: about 15 minutes

Serves 4

Cook aubergines as directed. Drain and work to a purée with the lemon juice. Scrape into a dish and add 15 g (½oz/1 tbsp) melted butter or margarine, 15 ml (1 tbsp) finely chopped fresh coriander (cilantro), 2.5-5 ml (½-1 tsp) salt, good pinch of mixed spice and 1.25 ml (¼ tsp) paprika. Put into a dish, cover with a plate and reheat 2½ to 3 minutes at full power. Stand 1 or 2 minutes before eating.

TIP: *The purée may be made ahead of time and left, covered, in the refrigerator befor using. Either bring to room temperature before mixing with rest of the ingredients, or allow an extra ½ to 1 minute cooking time. Use olive oil instead of butter or margarine if liked.*

Bean Sprouts in Chinese-Style Sauce

Well worth a try as an accompaniment to omelets or Chinese dishes. The sprouts are also appetising with plain cooked chicken.

Preparation time: about 6 minutes

Serves 4

450g (1lb/4cups) fresh bean sprouts
10ml (2tsp) Soy sauce
5ml (1tsp) Worcestershire sauce
5ml (1tsp) onion salt

1   Toss all ingredients well together in a bowl. Transfer to a 20cm (8inch) round glass or pottery dish that is fairly deep.

2   Cover with cling film, then puncture twice with the tip of a knife.

3   Cook 5 minutes at full power. Uncover, stir round and serve.

Orange Beets

Hot beetroots in orange juice may sound unusual, but they make a lively accompaniment to pork, ham, duck and goose; certainly worth trying in the winter as a change from the more predictable and run-of-the-mill sprouts, cabbage and cauliflower.

Preparation time: about 9 minutes

Serves 4 to 6

450 g (1 lb/2⅔ cups) cooked beetroots (beets), peeled and sliced
75 ml (5 tbsp) pure orange juice
15 ml (1 tbsp) malt vinegar
2.5 ml (½ tsp) salt
1 garlic clove, peeled and crushed

1 Put beetroot slices into a fairly shallow, 18 cm (7 inch) round glass or pottery dish.

2 Beat together rest of the ingredients. Pour over beetroot. Cover with cling film, then puncture twice with the tip of a knife.

3 Cook 6 minutes at full power. Stand one minute then serve hot.

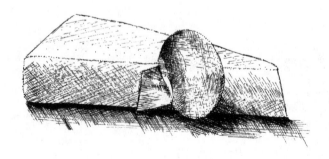

Danish-Style Red Cabbage

I've said Danish, but cooked red cabbage is eaten throughout Scandinavia and Northern Europe. It is a winter speciality, a treat with pork or goose or even sausages, and bliss to cook in the microwave where it remains slightly crisp and bright-coloured.

Preparation time: about 45 minutes

Serves 6 to 8 (F)

900 g (2 lb) red cabbage
450 ml (¾ pt/2 cups) boiling water
7.5 ml (1½ tsp) salt
225 g (8 oz/2 cups) onions, peeled and finely chopped
225 g (8 oz/2 cups) peeled cooking (tart) apples, cored and chopped
30 ml (2 tbsp) soft light brown (coffee) sugar
1.25 ml (¼ tsp) caraway seeds
30 ml (2 tbsp) cornflour (cornstarch)
45 ml (3 tbsp) malt vinegar
15 ml (1 tbsp) cold water

1   Wash cabbage, taking off any outer damaged and/or bruised leaves. Cut cabbage into pieces, minus stalks, and shred as finely as possible.

2   Put into a 2.25 litre (4 pt/10 cup) glass or pottery dish with 300 ml (½ pt/1¼ cups) boiling water and 5 ml (1 tsp) salt. Mix well. Cover with a plate and cook 10 minutes at full power.

3   Stir round then add rest of water, salt, onions, apples, sugar and caraway seeds. Mix thoroughly. Cover with cling film then puncture twice with the tip of a knife.

4   Cook 20 minutes at full power, stirring twice. Remove from oven. Blend cornflour smoothly with vinegar and cold water.

5   Add to cabbage and stir well to mix. Leave uncovered and cook 10 minutes at full power. Stir 4 times during cooking. Remove from oven. Serve, or if possible cover, leave until cold, then refrigerate overnight. This helps to mature the flavour. Reheat, covered, 5 to 6 minutes before serving.

Sour Cabbage

I first found this tucked away in the depths of Norway's countryside, served with a hearty cafeteria meal of sausages and mash. It takes a while to cook conventionally – about 1½ to 2 hours – but the microwave does a magnificent job in about half that time at defrost setting. Like the red cabbage from Denmark, this one is also best cooked one day for the next and is not unlike mild sauerkraut. You will find the cabbage takes on a creamy gold colour and stays very slightly crisp.

Preparation time: about 50 minutes plus cooling and reheating

Serves 8 to 10 (F)

900 g (2 lb) white cabbage
90 ml (6 tbsp) water
60 ml (4 tbsp) malt vinegar
20 ml (4 tsp) granulated sugar
10 ml (2 tsp) caraway seeds
7.5 ml (1½ tsp) salt

1   Wash cabbage, taking off any outer damaged and/or bruised leaves. Cut cabbage into pieces, minus stalk, and shred as finely as possible.

2   Put into a 2.25 litre (4 pt/10 cup) dish with all remaining ingredients. Stir well to mix. Cover with cling film, then puncture twice with the tip of a knife.

3   Cook 45 minutes at defrost setting, stirring twice. Cool and leave out at room temperature overnight.

4   Before serving, reheat individual portions on side plates, covering with kitchen paper and allowing about 1 minute each at full power.

Scalloped Celeriac

Easier and quicker to cope with in the microwave than when cooked conventionally, this large, swede-shaped vegetable tasting of celery makes an exciting accompaniment to meat, poultry, egg and fish dishes and is worth a try in the winter months when it is most readily available.

Preparation time: about 30 minutes

Serves 6

900g (2lb) celeriac
300ml (½pt/1¼cups) hot water
15ml (1tbsp) lemon juice
10ml (2tsp) salt
50g (2oz/3slices) lean bacon, chopped and
microwaved for 1½ minutes at full power
300ml (½pt/1¼cups) single (light) cream
25g (1oz/½cup) potato crisps (chips), crushed

1   Peel celeriac thickly, wash well and cut each head into eighths. Put in a 2.25 litre (4 pt/10 cup) dish with hot water, lemon juice and half the salt.

2   Cover with cling film then puncture twice with the tip of a knife. Cook 20 minutes at full power.

3   Drain then cut celeriac into cubes. Return to dish in which it was cooked. Gently mix in rest of salt, bacon and cream.

4   Sprinkle with potato crisps and cook, uncovered, 4 minutes at full power. Stand for 2 minutes then serve.

Buttered Lime Carrots

An all-occasion carrot dish, unusually brightened with lime cordial. Try it with veal, turkey, game dishes or offal.

Preparation time: about 25 minutes

Serves 4 to 6 (F)

50g (2oz/¼ cup) butter or margarine
450g (1lb/4cups) carrots, peeled and grated
100g (4oz/1cup) onions, peeled and grated
15ml (1tbsp) lime cordial
5ml (1tsp) salt

1   Put butter or margarine into a 20cm (8inch) round glass or pottery dish. Melt for 1½ to 2 minutes at defrost setting. Leave uncovered.

2   Stir in carrots, onions, lime cordial and salt. Mix well and cover with cling film. Puncture twice with the tip of a knife.

3   Cook 15 minutes at full power, stirring once. Leave to stand 2 or 3 minutes before serving.

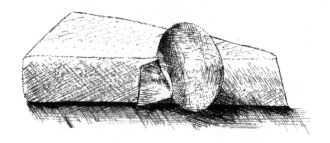

Buttered Cucumber

Cooked cucumber, with its delicate crunch and pale green colour, is a tantalising and unusual accompaniment for fish and chicken. A dinner party winner.

Preparation time: about 10 minutes

Serves 4

**1 medium cucumber (about 450 g/1 lb), peeled
25 g (1 oz/2 tbsp) butter or margarine, at room temperature
5 ml (1 tsp) salt
15 ml (1 tbsp) finely chopped parsley or dill**

1 Very thinly slice cucumber and wring dry in a tea towel.

2 Put butter into a fairly shallow glass or pottery dish measuring about 20 × 20 cm (8 × 8 inches). Or use any other shaped dish of about 1.2 litre (2 pt/5 cup) capacity. Melt, uncovered, for 1 to 1½ minutes at defrost setting.

3 Stir in cucumber and salt. Cover with an inverted plate, matching lid or cling film. If using cling film, puncture twice with tip of a knife.

4 Cook 6 minutes at full power. Uncover and stir in herbs. Serve straight away.

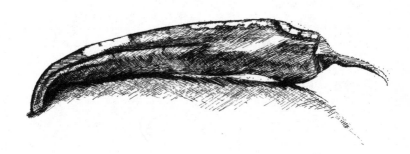

Cauliflower Camelia

Imagine a superior version of cauliflower cheese, the head of this flowery vegetable nestling under a coating of a fine, full-flavoured sauce laced with soured (dairy sour) cream. Serve it as a vegetable with beef, lamb, chicken, turkey, gammon or microwaved fish.

Preparation time: about 16 minutes

Serves 4

675 g (1½ lb) head of cauliflower, weighed after leaves and most of the woody centre stalk have been cut off
60 ml (4 tbsp) hot water
1 carton 150 ml (5 fl oz/⅔ cup) soured (dairy sour) cream
(or use Crème Frâiche)
1 (size 2) egg
7.5 ml (1½ tsp) cornflour (cornstarch)
10 ml (2 tsp) cold water
150 g (5 oz/1¼ cups) Cheshire cheese, grated
salt and pepper to taste
paprika

1   Stand cauliflower upright in deepish glass or pottery dish. Add hot water and cover with cling film. Puncture twice with the tip of a knife. Alternatively, cover with matching lid.

2   Cook for 10 minutes at full power.

3   Uncover and drain off water. Beat soured cream and egg well together. Blend cornflour with cold water an stir in.

4   Mix in cheese then season to taste with salt and pepper. Spoon over cauliflower and sprinkle with paprika. Cover as before.

5   Cook a further 3 minutes at full power. stand 2 minutes. Brown under a hot grill if liked. Serve as suggested.

Chicory (Belgian Endive) Braise

Chicory (Belgian endive) has a distinctive taste with a very slight bitterness which people either love or hate. It goes well with egg and poultry dishes.

Preparation time: about 14 minutes

Serves 4

4 heads of chicory (Belgian endive), about 675 g (1½ lb)
25 g (1 oz/2 tbsp) butter or margarine
1 chicken stock cube
15 ml (1 tbsp) boiling water
2.5 ml (½ tsp) onion salt
10 ml (2 tbsp) lemon juice

1 Trim chicory, removing any outside leaves which are bruised or damaged. Remove a cone-shaped core from base of each, as this helps to eliminate bitterness.

2 Coarsely chop chicory and put into a 1.2 litre (2 pt/5 cup) dish. Melt butter or margarine for 1 to 1½ minutes at defrost setting. Keep covered. Pour over chicory.

3 Crumble chicken stock cube into the water and stir until smooth. Blend in onion salt and lemon juice.

4 Mix well, pour into dish then cover with cling film. Puncture twice with the tip of a knife. Alternatively, cover with matching lid.

5 Cook 9 minutes at full power. Stand 1 minute then serve coated with juices from dish.

Juniper Courgettes (Zucchini)

The inclusion of juniper berries adds a gin-like and unexpected note of subtlety to the courgettes, a most pleasing accompaniment to poultry and fish dishes.

Preparation time: about 16 minutes

Serves 4 to 5

25 g (1 oz/2 tbsp) butter or margarine
450 g (1 lb) topped and tailed courgettes (zucchini),
thinly sliced
6 juniper berries, lightly crushed with the back of a spoon
2.5 ml (½ tsp) salt
30 ml (1 tbsp) finely chopped parsley

1 Put butter or margarine in a 20 cm (8 inch) round glass or pottery dish and melt, uncovered, 1 to 1½ minutes at defrost setting.

2 Stir in courgettes, juniper berries and salt and spread evenly into a layer that covers base of dish.

3 Cover with cling film then puncture twice with the tip of a knife. Cook 10 minutes at full power. Stir once.

4 Stand 2 minutes before uncovering and sprinkling with parsley.

Buttered Chinese Leaves with Pernod

A cross in texture and flavour between white cabbage and firm lettuce, Chinese leaves make a very presentable cooked vegetable and are greatly enhanced by the addition of Pernod which adds a delicate and subtle flavour of aniseed.

Preparation time: about 20 minutes

Serves 4

675g (1½ lb/6 cups) Chinese leaves, shredded
50g (2 oz/¼ cup) butter or margarine,
melted in microwave for 1½ to 2 minutes
15 ml (1 tbsp) Pernod
2.5 ml (½ tsp) salt

1 Mix all ingredients well together in a 1.75 litre (3 pt/7½ cup) glass or pottery dish.

2 Cover with cling film, then puncture twice with the tip of a knife. Alternatively, cover with matching lid.

3 Cook 12 minutes at full power, stirring twice. Leave to stand 5 minutes then serve.

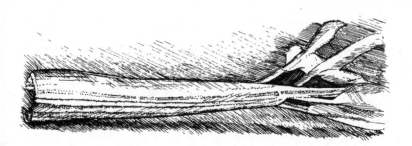

Wine-Braised Leeks with Ham

An interesting accompaniment to poultry and lamb; a perfect winter vegetable dish when made with slim and elegant leeks.

Preparation time: about 20 minutes

Serves 4

4 to 5 narrow leeks, 450g (1lb)
25g (1oz/2tbsp) butter or margarine, at room temperature
225g (8oz/1cup) mild and lean ham, fairly finely chopped
60ml (4tbsp) red wine
black pepper to taste

1   Trim roots from leeks then cut off all but 10cm (4inches) of green 'skirt' from each. Slit leeks carefully in half lengthwise, almost to top.

2   Wash gently under cold, running water, making sure earth and grit have been thoroughly removed.

3   Melt butter or margarine, uncovered, in an oblong dish measuring 25×20cm (10×8inches). Allow about 1 to 1½ minutes at defrost setting, then rotate dish until base is completely covered with fat.

4   Add leeks, arranging them in a single layer. Sprinkle with ham and wine. Season to taste with freshly ground black pepper.

5   Cover with cling film, then puncture twice with the tip of a knife. Alternatively, cover with matching lid.

6   Cook leeks 15 minutes at full power, turning dish twice. Uncover and serve straight away.

Casseroled Leeks

Serves 4

Chop slit leeks and put into a 1.75litre (3pt/7½cup) dish. Add 25g (1oz) melted butter or margarine mixed with 60ml (4tbsp) chicken stock and salt and pepper to taste. Cover as directed above. Cook 10 minutes at full power.

Fennel with Tarragon

A sophisticated vegetable with a mild aniseed flavour, fennel is companionable with fish or chicken and is an elegant dish cooked as suggested below.

Preparation time: about 33 minutes

Serves 4

900 g (2 lb) fennel
50 g (2 oz/¼ cup) butter or margarine
2.5 ml (½ tsp) salt
7.5 ml (1½ tsp) Bordeaux mustard
30 ml (2 tbsp) medium sherry
2.5 ml (½ tsp) dried tarragon

1 Wash and dry fennel. Cut off any bruised or damaged pieces but leave on 'fingers' and 'fronds'.

2 Melt butter or margarine, uncovered in cup, for 1½ to 2 minutes at defrost setting. Gently beat in salt, mustard, sherry and tarragon.

3 Cut each head of fennel into quarters, working from top to bottom and retaining 'fingers' and 'fronds'.

4 Arrange in a 25 cm (10 inch) round and fairly shallow glass or pottery dish. Coat with the butter or margarine mixture.

5 Cover with cling film, then puncture twice with the tip of a knife.

6 Cook for 20 minutes at full power. Leave to stand 7 minutes. Serve as suggested.

Creamed Mushrooms

The last time I ate anything like these luxurious creamed mushrooms was in Poland where the people pride themselves not only on the quality of their fungi, but also the way they are cooked.

Preparation time: about 15 minutes

Serves 6 to 8

25 g (1 oz/2 tbsp) butter or margarine
450 g (1 lb) button mushrooms
30 ml (2 tbsp) cornflour (cornstarch)
30 ml (2 tbsp) cold water
1 large carton, 300 ml (10 fl oz/1¼ cups) soured (dairy sour) cream
10 ml (2 tsp) salt

1   Put butter or margarine into a 2.25 litre (4 pt/10 cup) dish and melt 1 to 1½ minutes at defrost setting. Leave uncovered.

2   Mix in mushrooms, cover with a plate and cook 5 minutes at full power, stirring twice.

3   Remove from oven and uncover. Blend cornflour smoothly with water then beat into soured cream. Add to mushrooms then combine thoroughly with a wooden spoon.

4   Cover as above and cook 7 minutes at full power, stirring 3 or 4 times. Season with salt. Serve straight away.

Creamed Potatoes

Potatoes boiled in the microwave never fall to pieces, retain their flavour and colour, and have an excellent texture. Nutrients are conserved because the amount of water used for boiling is minimal, fuel is saved and there is no pan to wash – you can cook the potatoes in the serving dish.

Preparation time: about 18 minutes

Serves 2 to 3

450g (1lb) old potatoes (4 medium or 2 large)
60ml (4tbsp) boiling water
15g (½oz/1tbsp) butter or margarine
60-75ml (4-5tbsp) milk
salt and pepper
15ml (1tbsp) chopped parsley (optional)

1   Wash potatoes then peel thinly. Cut each medium potato into 8 chunks; large ones into 16.

2   Put into 1.2litre (2pt/5cup) glass or pottery dish with the water. Cover with cling film, then puncture twice with the tip of a knife. Alternatively, cover with matching lid.

3   Cook 10 minutes at full power. Stir twice. Leave to stand 3 minutes, uncover and pour off any leftover water.

4   Add butter or margarine and mash well.

5   Beat in milk. Season to taste. When potatoes are light and creamy, 'rough up' with fork then reheat, uncovered, 1 to 1½ minutes at full power. Sprinkle with parsley before serving.

NOTE: *For 3 to 5 people, use 900g (2lb) potatoes and 90ml (6tbsp) boiling water. Allow 15 to 16 minutes at full power. Add 25g (1oz/ 2tbsp) butter or margarine and 90ml (6tbsp) milk.*

Stuffed Jacket Potatoes

Allow 2 halves per person (F)

First cook as many jacket potatoes as are required for stuffing, following instructions given in the chart on page 181.

Cheese Potatoes

Allow 2 halves per person

Cut each potato in half horizontally and scoop insides into a bowl. Mash finely then beat until light with butter or margarine, cold milk and seasoning to taste. Mix in 25 g (1 oz/¼ cup) grated Cheddar cheese and 2.5 ml (½ tsp) mustard to every potato. Return mixture to potato shells, put on a plate, cover with kitchen paper and reheat as follows:

2 halves, 1½ to 1¾ minutes
4 halves, 2¾ to 3¼ minutes

Bacon and Cheese Potatoes

Allow 2 halves per person (F)

Make as Cheese Potatoes, but allow 50 g (2 oz/3 slices) chopped and microwaved cooked bacon to every 2 potatoes in addition to the cheese.

Blue Cheese Potatoes

Allow 2 halves per person (F)

Make as Cheese Potatoes, but substitute mashed or crumbled blue cheese for Cheddar.

Topping

If desired, sprinkle potatoes with chopped parsley, chives or paprika before reheating.

Savoyard Potatoes

Memorably appetising as a meal on its own with pickles or salad, or as an accompaniment to any number of meat and poultry dishes. For 'Château potatoes', use cider insted of stock or wine.

Preparation time: about 30 minutes

Serves 6 (F)

900 g (2 lb) potatoes, peeled and cut into wafer thin slices
1 garlic clove, peeled and crushed, mixed with
75 g (3 oz/⅓ cup) butter or margarine, melted
175 g (6 oz/1½ cups) grated cheese – Gruyère or Emmental
are ideal but for greater economy, use Cheddar or Edam
5 ml (1 tsp) salt
pepper to taste
300 ml (½ pt/1¼ cups) chicken stock,
made with cube and water or white wine
paprika

1   Grease a 25 cm (10 inch) round glass or pottery dish, of about 5 cm (2 inches) in depth, with butter or margarine.

2   Fill with alternate layers of potatoes, two-thirds of the garlic and butter or margarine mixture, and the same amount of cheese. Begin and end with potatoes and season between layers.

3   Gently pour stock or wine down side of the dish. Trickle rest of butter over and sprinkle with remaining cheese. Add a dusting of paprika. Cover with a lid or cling film, then puncture twice.

4   Cook for 20 minutes at full power. Leave to stand 5 minutes in the oven, uncover and serve.

Dauphinoise Potatoes

Serves 6 (F)

Make as the Savoyard Potatoes, substituting long life milk for the stock or wine. Garlic may be omitted and the top sprinkled with a little nutmeg either with, or instead of, paprika.

Ratatouille

Temperamentally Mediterranean, Ratatouille is a warmly-flavoured pot-pourri of semi-exotic vegetables, melded together by gentle cooking. Again very much at home in the microwave, serve Ratatouille with meat, egg and poultry dishes or, for vegetarian tastes, spoon over rice, pasta or bulgar. The flavour is improved if Ratatouille is cooked one day for the next and reheated, covered, for about 7 minutes at full power.

Preparation time: about 45 minutes

Serves 6 to 8 (F)

60 ml (4 tbsp) sunflower oil
175 g (6 oz/1½ cups) onions, peeled and chopped
1 garlic clove, peeled and crushed
225 g (8 oz/2 cups) courgettes (zucchini), thinly sliced
350 g (12 oz/3 cups) aubergines (eggplants), cubed
100 g (4 oz/1 cup) red or green (bell) pepper, deseeded and chopped
1 can 200 g (7 oz) tomatoes
20 ml (4 tsp) tomato purée (paste)
20 ml (4 tsp) soft light brown (coffee) sugar
10 ml (2 tsp) salt
45 ml (3 tbsp) chopped parsley

1 Pour oil into a 2.25 litre (4 pt/10 cup) glass or pottery dish. Heat 1 minute at full power. Leave uncovered.

2 Add onions and garlic. Mix in well then cook, uncovered, for 4 minutes at full power.

3 Stir in courgettes, aubergines, red or green pepper, tomatoes, purée, sugar, half the salt and half the parsley. Cover with cling film, then puncture twice with the tip of a knife.

4 Cook for 20 minutes at full power. Uncover and stir. Add rest of salt and parsley. Leave uncovered and continue to cook 8 to 10 minutes at full power or until most of the liquid has evaporated. Stir at least 4 times. Cool and cover.

Boiled Sweet Potatoes

Becomingly increasingly more available in the UK via supermarket chains and some greengrocers, these yellowy-fleshed vegetables are packed with Vitamin A. Their own natural sweetness enables them to be used as an ingredient in sweet dishes and surprisingly they also make a subtle accompaniment to poultry, ham and game. In North America, sweet potatoes are cubed then fried with sugar and fat to give them a candied appearance. They are then eaten with the Thanksgiving Day roast turkey. Yams are another 'breed' of sweet potato but are moister, deeper-toned and with a higher sugar content.

Preparation time: about 15 minutes

Serves 4 (F)

450 g (1 lb) sweet potatoes or yams
60 ml (4 tbsp) boiling water

1   Peel and dice potatoes and put into a 1 litre (1¾ pt/4¼ cup) dish. Add water. Cover with cling film, then puncture twice with the tip of a knife. Alternatively, cover with matching lid.

2   Cook 10 minutes at full power, stirring once. Leave to stand 2 or 3 minutes, drain and serve.

Mâitre D'Hotel Sweet Potatoes

Serves 4

After draining potatoes, toss with butter and sprinkle liberally with chopped parsley.

Creamed Sweet Potatoes

Serves 4

Boil sweet potatoes as directed above. Drain and mash finely. Beat with 15-25 g (½-1 oz/1-2 tbsp) butter or margarine and 45-60 ml (3-4 tbsp) warm milk. Season to taste and put into serving dish. Reheat, uncovered, for 1 to 1½ minutes at full power.

RICE AND PASTA

Cooking rice and pasta in a microwave is not necessarily speedier in time, but fuel costs are reduced by at least half, minimal involvement is required of the cook, there are no sticky saucepans to clean up afterwards and the kitchen stays steam-free and fresh – important considerations, particularly in summer when one tries to keep the room cool and comfortable, and in winter when getting rid of steam and condensation often involves a blast of cold air from an open window or back door.

There are other advantages to be gained as well. Rice grains retain their shape and do not disintegrate into a mush, they absorb all or most of the liquid as good rice should and are independent of each other, remaining dry, firm, separate and, once forked through, light and fluffy into the bargain. And this applies equally to the most popular types: American long grain, easy-cook, Italian short grain, slender Indian Basmati and round grain pudding rice.

Pasta reacts as favourably as rice and whether it be broken spaghetti or any of the small varities such as macaroni or shells, it rarely overcooks and, almost without exception, stays firmly 'al dente' in texture, true to Italian tradition.

One tip worth remembering. Rice should be covered while cooking, pasta on its own uncovered unless the recipe states otherwise.

Easy-Cook, Long Grain or Basmati Rice

(F)

Put 225 g (8 oz/1 cup) rice into a fairly large glass or pottery dish. Add 600 ml (1 pt/2½ cups) boiling water and 5 ml (1 tsp) of salt. Stir round. Cover with cling film, then puncture twice with the tip of a knife. Cook 16 minutes at full power. Leave to stand 8 minutes so that rice grains absorb all the liquid. Remove film, fluff up with a fork, adding 15-25 g (½-1 oz/1-2 tbsp) butter or margarine if desired.

Saffron Rice

(F)

Microwave as above, adding 6 or 8 saffron strands at the same time as the salt. Alternatively, add 2.5 ml (½ tsp) turmeric and half the quantity of costly saffron.

Chicken or Beef Rice

(F)

Microwave as above, adding boiling chicken or beef stock instead of water. Reduce salt to 2.5 ml (½ tsp).

Tomato Rice

(F)

Microwave as above, adding half boiling water and half boiling tomato juice or dissolve 15-30 ml (1–2 tbsp) tomato purée (paste) in the 600 ml (1 pt/2½ cups) water.

Herb Rice

(F)

Microwave as above, adding 5 ml (1 tsp) dried mixed herbs with the salt.

Parsley Rice

(F)

Microwave as above, adding 45 ml (3 tbsp) of parsley at the very end when forking through.

Pineapple Rice

(F)

Microwave as above, then fork in 175 g (6 oz/1½ cups) cut up fresh pineapple at the end. Arrange on plates and garnish with rolls of ham.

Sweetcorn and Chicken Rice

(F)

Microwave as above, adding 100 g (4 oz/¾ cup) frozen sweetcorn, 50 g (2 oz/½ cup) chopped red (bell) pepper and 175 g (6 oz/1¼ cups) cut-up cooked chicken with the water and salt. Allow 18 minutes cooking time then stand 8 or 9 minutes. Sprinkle with paprika before serving.

Brown Rice

Nutty-flavoured and nutritious, brown rice makes a pleasant change from white, although it needs a longish time in the microwave to tenderise. The advantage over conventional cooking is a saving of about 15 minutes, no attention and a kitchen that remains completely cool and fresh. Brown rice is delicious with almost everything, but is especially appetising with poultry, veal, lamb, offal and scrambled eggs or omelets.

Preparation time: about 45 minutes

Serves 3 to 4 (F)

5 ml (1 tsp) salt
100 g (4 oz/½ cup) brown rice
300 ml (½ pt/1¼ cups) boiling water

1   Put all ingredients into a 2 litre (3½ pt/8½ cup) glass or pottery dish and stand on a plate in case water boils over.

2   Stir round to mix. Cover with cling film, then puncture twice with the tip of a knife. Alternatively, cover with matching lid.

3   Cook 35 minutes at full power. Leave to stand 10 minutes.

4   Uncover and fluff up by stirring with a fork.

Pilau Rice

Middle Eastern in origin, Pilau Rice (also called Pilav, Pilaf or Pilaff) has many facets, but this version is one of the simplest and enhanced with raisins and toasted pine nuts. Partner it with roast lamb or chicken joints though vegetarians may well settle for omelets.

Preparation time: about 30 minutes

Serves 4 (F)

30 ml (2 tbsp) sunflower oil
175 g (6 oz/1½ cups) onions, peeled and grated
225 g (8 oz/1 cup) easy-cook, long grain rice
600 ml (1 pt/2½ cups) boiling chicken or vegetable stock
50 g (2 oz/⅓ cup) seedless raisins
25 g (1 oz/¼ cup) toasted pine nuts (page 303)
2.5 ml (½ tsp) salt

1 Pour oil into a 20 cm (8 inch) fairly deep and round glass or pottery dish and heat 1 minute at full power. Leave uncovered.

2 Stir in onions and rice. Leave uncovered and cook 4 minutes at full power.

3 Mix in remaining ingredients. Cover with cling film then puncture twice with the tip of a knife.

4 Cook 17 minutes at full power.

5 Leave to stand 8 minutes, so that rice grains absorb all the liquid.

6 Uncover, fluff up with a fork and serve.

Mild Curry Rice

Attractively flavoured and coloured, this Mild Curry Rice makes an amiable accompaniment to fish, egg and poultry dishes and should please all those who enjoy oriental food.

Preparation time: about 32 minutes

Serves 6 to 8 (F)

25 g (1 oz/2 tbsp) butter or margarine
275 g (10 oz/2½ cups) onion, peeled and grated
225 g (8 oz/1 cup) basmati rice
1 large bay leaf
2 cloves
seeds from 4 opened-out cardamom pods
45 ml (3 tbsp) mild curry powder
5 ml (1 tsp) salt
600 ml (1 pt/2½ cups) boiling chicken or vegetable stock
45 ml (3 tbsp) mango chutney

1   Melt butter or margarine in a 2.25 litre (4 pt/10 cup) glass or pottery dish for 1 to 1½ minutes at defrost setting. Leave uncovered. Add onion. Cook, uncovered, for 5 minutes at full power.

2   Stir in all remaining ingredients. Cover dish with cling film, then puncture twice with the tip of a knife.

3   Cook 18 minutes at full power.

4   Leave to stand 8 minutes, so that rice grains absorb all the liquid. Uncover.

5   Fluff up with a fork and serve.

Peanut Rice

An attractive accompaniment – serve it with poultry or fish, even hardboiled (hardcooked) eggs for a vegetarian-style main course.

Preparation time: about 30 minutes

Serves 6 to 8 (F)

225 g (8 oz/1 cup) easy-cook, long grain rice
50 g (2 oz/½ cup) toasted peanuts (page 304), skins rubbed off
then nuts coarsely chopped
600 ml (1 pt/2½ cups) meat or vegetable stock
5 ml (1 tsp) dried dill weed
2.5-5 ml (½-1 tsp) salt
15 g (½ oz/1 tbsp) butter or margarine, at room temperature

1   Sprinkle rice into a large and fairly shallow glass or pottery dish. A comfortable size is one measuring about 25 cm (10 inches) in diameter by 5 cm (2 inches) in depth.

2   Stir in rest of ingredients. Cover with an inverted plate or cling film. If using the latter, puncture twice with the tip of a knife. Alternatively, cover with matching lid.

3   Cook 15 minutes at full power. Leave to stand 5 minutes.

4   Uncover and fluff up rice by tossing gently with a fork. Serve hot.

Brazil Nut Rice

Serves 6 to 8 (F)

If you have a food processor, thinly slice 50-75 g (2-3 oz/½-¾ cup) brazils. Toast under the grill. Add to the rice instead of peanuts.

Eastern Gold Rice

A fluff of brilliant colour and a warm flavour reminiscent of the Middle East. A lovely accompaniment to kebabs or lamb roasts.

Preparation time: about 22 minutes

Serves 6 (F)

50g (2oz/⅓cup) dried apricots
hot water
25g (1oz/¼cup) pine nuts
225g (8oz/1cup) easy-cook, long grain rice
1 chicken stock cube
600ml (1pt/2½cups) boiling water
5ml (1tsp) salt
2.5ml (½tsp) saffron strands, crushed in a pestle and mortar

1   Wash apricots thoroughly and put into a cup. Add hot water to cover. Top with a saucer. Microwave for 2 minutes at full power. Drain. Snip into small pieces with scissors.

2   Toast pine nuts under the grill until deep gold, or follow microwave directions on page 303.

Tip rice into a deep dish. Crumble over stock cube then mix in water, salt and saffron. Add prepared apricots and nuts.

4   Stir round. Cover with cling film, then puncture twice with the tip of a knife. Alternatively, cover with matching lid.

5   Cook for 15 minutes at full power.

6   Uncover then fluff up with a fork. Serve hot.

Spaghetti with Sweet-Sour Sauce

Appetising and colourful, I can see this easy-style main course becoming a firm family favourite with its oriental overtones.

Preparation time: about 30 minutes

Serves 4

225 g (8 oz/2 cups) spaghetti, snapped into thirds
900 ml (1½ pts/3¾ cups) boiling water
7.5 ml (1½ tsp) salt
10 ml (2 tbsp) sunflower oil
50 g (2 oz/¼ cup) butter or margarine
225 g (8 oz/2 cups) onion, peeled and chopped
350 g (12 oz) pork fillet, cut into thin strips
1.25 ml (¼ tsp) dried minced garlic
20 ml (4 tsp) tomato purée (paste)
15 ml (1 tbsp) cornflour (cornstarch)
1 can (350 g/12 oz) pineapple chunks
75 g (3 oz/¾ cup) red (bell) pepper, deseeded and chopped
75 g (3 oz/¾ cup) green (bell) pepper, deseeded and chopped
1.25 ml (¼ tsp) ground ginger
15 ml (1 tbsp) Soy sauce
salt and pepper to taste

1 Put spaghetti into a 2.25 litre (4 pt/10 cup) glass or pottery dish. Add boiling water, salt and oil. Cook, uncovered, for 10 minutes at full power. Stir at least 3 times. Remove from oven.

2 Cover with a plate and leave to stand while preparing sweet-sour mixture. Put butter or margarine into 1.75 litre (3 pt/7½ cup) glass or pottery dish and melt 1 to 1½ minutes at defrost setting. Add onions. Cover dish with plate and cook 2 minutes at full power.

3 Gently stir in all remaining ingredients. Cover with a plate or matching lid. Cook 15 minutes, stirring 3 times.

4 Reheat spaghetti for 2 minutes. Drain. Spoon into a serving dish and top with sweet-sour pork mixture. Serve.

Italian-Style Risotto

Classic, as only an Italian dish can be, this Risotto contains the marrow from a beef bone, its fair share of wine and one of the country's most renowned cheeses – Parmesan – sprinkled over the top.

Preparation time: about 25 minutes

Serves 4 to 6 (F)

50g (2oz/¼ cup) butter
100g (4oz/1cup) onions, peeled and chopped
25g (1oz) beef bone marrow, sliced or diced (optional)
225g (8oz/1cup) easy-cook, Italian round grain rice
450ml (¾pt/2cups) boiling chicken stock
300ml (½pt/1¼cups) dry white wine
4 saffron strands soaked in an egg cup of water
2.5ml (1tsp) salt
50g (2oz/½cup) grated Parmesan cheese

1   Put half the butter into a 1.75 litre (3pt/7½ cup) glass or pottery dish and melt for 1 to 1½ minutes at defrost setting. Leave uncovered.

2   Stir in onions and bone marrow if using. Cook, uncovered, 5 minutes at full power, stirring twice.

3   Mix in rice, boiling stock and the wine. Cover with a plate or matching lid and cook 14 minutes at defrost, stirring twice with a fork.

4   Uncover. Add rest of butter, saffron strands and liquid, salt and 25g (1oz) Parmesan cheese.

5   Cook at full power, uncovered, until rice grains have absorbed all the mixture; depending on the rice this could take from 4 to 8 minutes. Fork-stir at the end of every 2 minutes, working gently to prevent breaking up the rice.

6   Spoon out on to plates and sprinkle each portion with rest of Parmesan cheese.

Dry Pasta – to cook

Serves 4 (F)

Choose spaghetti (broken into thirds to ensure even cooking), macaroni, shells, bows, wheels or any other fancy shapes. Allow 225 g (8 oz/2 cups) for 4 people. Put into a large glass or pottery dish. Add 900 ml (1½ pt/3¾ cups) boiling water, 5 ml (1 tsp) salt and 10 ml (2 tsp) sunflower oil as it helps to prevent the pasta from sticking together. Leave uncovered. Cook 12 to 15 minutes at full power, stirring gently 4 times. Remove from oven, cover and leave to stand for another 6 to 8 minutes or until pasta swells and absorbs most of the liquid. Drain and use as required. For very small pasta (pastini) and vermicelli, cook at full power for 7–10 minutes only.

Fresh Pasta – to cook

Serves 4

Follow directions above but allow only 600 ml (1 pt/2½ cups) boiling water to 225 g (8 oz/2 cups) fresh pasta. Cook, uncovered, for half the time of dry pasta. Cover. Stand 5 minutes then drain and serve.

TIP: *All pasta is improved if, after draining, it is tossed with a little olive oil, butter or margarine for extra glisten.*

Spaghetti Bolognese

Serves 4

Cook dry or fresh pasta as above. Drain. Transfer to 4 plates. Coat with Bolognese sauce, given on page 73. Sprinkle each serving with grated Parmesan cheese.

Pasta Ham Casserole

Fast food from home makes appetising sense and this carefree casserole is both filling and nutritious, a good companion to salad or cooked vegetables such as beans, peas, sprouts or even a mixture.

Preparation time: about 25 minutes

Serves 4

225g (8oz/2 cups) pasta shells
900ml (1½ pt/3¾ cups) boiling water
7.5ml (1½ tsp) salt
10ml (2 tsp) sunflower oil
1 can condensed cream of mushroom soup
100g (4oz/1 cup) lean ham, chopped
100g (4oz/1 cup) button mushrooms, sliced
5ml (1 tsp) prepared mustard
seasoning to taste
100 g (4oz/1 cup) Cheddar cheese, finely grated

1   Put pasta shells into a large glass or pottery dish. Add boiling water, salt and oil. Cook, uncovered, for 10 minutes at full power. Stir 3 times with spoon, taking care not to break up shells.

2   Remove from oven, cover with a plate and leave to stand for 10 minutes. Drain and return to dish.

3   Stir in soup, ham, mushrooms and mustard. Season to taste with salt and pepper. Sprinkle with cheese.

4   Leave uncovered and re-heat 5 minutes at full power.

Spaghetti Carbonara

A classic from Italy, delightfully simple to make and with an element of chic. Serve it with a green salad tossed in a mild dressing and garnish with black olives, capers and rolls of anchovy fillets.

Preparation time: about 25 minutes

Serves 6

225g (8oz/2 cups) spaghetti, snapped into thirds
900ml (1½pt/3¾cups) boiling water
7.5ml (1½tsp) salt
10ml (2tbsp) sunflower oil
200g (7oz/10slices lean bacon, chopped
30ml (2tbsp) milk
2 (size 2) eggs
100g (4oz/1cup) Cheddar or Gruyère cheese, finely grated
60ml (4tbsp) double (heavy) cream
salt and pepper to taste
paprika

1 Put spaghetti into a 1.75litre (3pt/7½cup) glass or pottery dish. Add boiling water, salt and oil. Cook, uncovered, for 15 minutes at full power. Stir at least 3 times. Remove from oven.

2 Cover with a plate and leave to stand a further 5 minutes when spaghetti should be more swollen and a little bit softer. Drain and return to dish. Re-cover with a plate to keep hot.

3 Put chopped bacon into a separate small dish. Cover with a plate and cook 4 minutes at full power, stirring once.

4 Add to spaghetti. Beat milk and eggs with cheese, cream and seasoning to taste. Add to spaghetti. Toss with 2 spoons. Cover with plate again then reheat 5 minutes at full power to give egg and milk mixture a chance to scramble.

5 Uncover. Toss gently to mix and sprinkle with paprika. Serve straight away, while still very hot.

Family Pasta Pot

A useful dish if you happen to have leftover meat to use up such as boiled bacon, cooked smoked gammon, even sausages. It's an economical meal for midweek with plenty of colour and flavour. Serve it with Brussels sprouts and carrots, or braised red cabbage for novelty.

Preparation time: about 30 minutes

Serves 4 generously

25g (1oz/2tbsp) butter or margarine, at room temperature
175g (6oz/1½cups) onions, peeled and chopped
225g (8oz/2cups) pasta bows or shells (uncooked)
225g (8oz/1⅓cup) tomatoes, blanched and skinned then chopped
350g (12oz/2½ cups) boiled bacon, gammon or cold cooked sausages, cubed
750ml (1¼pt/3cups) hot stock, made with cubes and water
5ml (1tsp) salt
5ml (1tsp) dried mixed herbs
15ml (1tbsp) tomato purée (paste)

1 Put butter or margarine into a 1.75-2 litre (3-3½pt/7½-8½cup) round glass or pottery dish. Leave uncovered and melt for 1 to 1½ minutes at defrost setting. Stir in onions. Continue to cook, still uncovered, for 2 minutes at full power.

2 Mix in pasta bows or shells and tomatoes then add meat.

3 Combine stock with rest of ingredients, pour into dish of pasta and mix well. Cover with cling film, then puncture twice with the tip of a knife. Alternatively, cover with a matching lid.

4 Cook 25 minutes at full power, stirring twice.

5 Uncover. Stir round and serve with accompaniments as suggested above.

Tortellini Verdi

Compact little cases of fresh pasta, enclosing a cheese, vegetable or meat filling, are becoming increasingly available from supermarket chains and speciality food shops. Cooking them in the microwave poses no problems at all and in fact they work beautifully, retaining a pale green colour and 'al dente' or firm texture which all Italian cooks recommend. Whether green or white, toss with butter, margarine or olive oil and serve with a dusting of grated Parmesan cheese. Or add to clear soup as a starter.

Preparation time: about 15 minutes

Serves 3 to 4 as a main course; 8 as a starter in soup

225-250 g (8-9 oz/2 good cups) fresh tortellini (green or white)
600 ml (1 pt/2½ cups) boiling water
5 ml (1 tsp) salt

1 Put all ingredients into a 1.75 litre (3 pt/7½ cup) glass or pottery dish.

2 Cook, uncovered, for 10 minutes at full power. Stir 4 times.

3 Continue to cook a further 3 to 5 minutes when tortellini should be plump and almost double in size.

4 Drain and serve as suggested above.

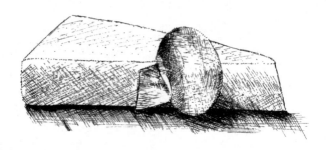

Lasagne

Serves 4 to 6 (F)

Grease a 20 cm (8 inch) square glass or pottery dish and fill with alternate layers of no-need-to-pre-cook lasagne sheets and Bolognese sauce (page 73), beginning with a thin layer of Bolognese. Cover with Cheese sauce (page 69). Sprinkle top with 25 g (1 oz/¼ cup) grated Parmesan cheese, 25 g (1 oz/2 tbsp) melted butter or margarine and paprika. Cook, uncovered, for 15 minutes at full power. Leave to stand 5 minutes then cook a further 15 minutes or until lasagne feels soft when a knife is plunged down through the centre. The time will vary depending on whether the sauces were hot, warm or cold.

TIP: *Make sure your Bolognese mixture is good and moist as the lasagne sheets need this to soften during cooking.*

Lasagne Verdi

Serves 4 to 6 (F)

Use green lasagne instead of white.

Brown Lasagne

Serves 4 to 6 (F)

Use wholewheat (brown) lasagne instead of white.

FRUIT

Fruit, like vegetables, behave extremely well in a microwave. Defrosting from frozen is quick and efficient and cooking fresh fruit couldnt be simpler. You used to have to stew fruit in quite heavy syrup to preserve its colour and texture. But in the microwave you only need to sweeten to taste as the fruit will keep its shape and colour without any difficulty whatsoever.

Defrosting Frozen Fruit

	DEFROST SETTING	COMMENTS
Apples 450g (1lb)	7 minutes Stand 8 minutes	Put into dish or bowl. Cover with plate or matching lid. Stir gently when partially thawed, bringing softer fruit from edge of dish to centre.
Blackberries 450g (1lb)	8 minutes Stand 7 minutes	As above.
Blackcurrants 450g (1lb)	5 minutes Stand 6 minutes	As above.
Cherries 450g (1lb)	4 minutes Stand 5 minutes	As above.
Gooseberries 450g (1lb)	7 to 8 minutes Stand 7 minutes	As above.
Rhubarb 450g (1lb)	8 minutes Stand 8 minutes	As above.
Strawberries 450g (1lb)	6 minutes Stand 6 minutes	As above.

Cooking Fresh Fruit

	COOK/HEAT FULL POWER	COMMENTS
Apples 450g (1lb)	7 to 8 minutes	Peel, core and slice apples. Put into dish or bowl with 30ml (2tbsp) boiling water. Sprinkle with caster (superfine) sugar to taste. Cover with plate or matching lid. Stir during cooking. For pulpy fruit allow 1 minute *less* cooking time than suggested, beat fruit to purée *then* stir in sugar to taste. Cover. Reheat 1½ minutes when sugar should have dissolved completely. Remove from oven and stir round.
Apricots 450g (1lb)	8 to 9 minutes	Halve, stone and wash apricots. Put into dish or bowl with 60ml (4tbsp) boiling water. Sprinkle with caster (superfine) sugar to taste. Cover with plate or matching lid. Stir during cooking. For pulpy fruit, see apples.
Blackberries 450g (1lb)	5 to 7 minutes	Hull the berries and wash well. Put into dish or bowl with 30ml (2tbsp) boiling water. Sprinkle with caster (superfine) sugar to taste. Cover with plate or matching lid. Stir during cooking. For pulpy fruit, see apples.
Blackcurrants 450g (1lb)	8 to 10 minutes	Remove currants from stalks and wash well. Put into dish or bowl with 60ml (4tbsp) boiling water. Sprinkle with caster (superfine) sugar to taste. Cover with plate or matching lid. Stir during cooking. If skins remain tough, cook for an extra ½ minute. For pulpy fruit, see apples then blend currant and sugar mixture to smooth purée in food processor or blender.
Damsons 450g (1lb)	8 to 10 minutes	Wash damsons and slit each with sharp knife. Put into dish or bowl with 60ml (4tbsp) boiling water. Sprinkle liberally with caster (superfine) sugar to taste. Cover with plate or matching lid. Stir during cooking. Do not pulp because of stones.

	COOK/HEAT FULL POWER	COMMENTS
Gooseberries 450g (1lb)	6 to 7 minutes	Top and tail gooseberries. Wash and put into dish or bowl with 60ml (4tbsp) boiling water. Sprinkle liberally with caster (superfine) sugar to taste. Cover with plate or matching lid. Stir during cooking. For pulpy fruit, see apples.
Peaches 450g (1lb)	5 to 7 minutes	Halve, stone and wash the peaches. Put into dish or bowl with 30ml (2tbsp) boiling water and 15ml (1tbsp) lemon juice. Sprinkle with caster (superfine) sugar to taste. Cover with plate or matching lid. Stir during cooking. For pulpy fruit, see apples.
Pears 450g (1lb)	8 to 10 minutes	Peel, halve and core the pears. Arrange in a dish or bowl. Put 45ml (3tbsp) boiling water into a jug. Partially dissolve 50g (2oz) sugar in the water and add 3 or 4 cloves. Pour over fruit and cover bowl with plate or matching lid. Stir during cooking but take care not to break up the pear halves. Do not pulp.
Plums and Greengages 450g (1lb)	5 to 7 minutes	Stone and wash the fruit. Put into dish or bowl with 60ml (4tbsp) boiling water. Sprinkle with caster (superfine) sugar to taste and the grated peel of half a lemon. Cover with plate or matching lid. Stir during cooking. For pulpy fruit, see apples.
Rhubarb 450g (1lb)	7 to 9 minutes	Trim and wash the rhubarb and cut into small pieces. Put into dish or bowl with 30ml (2tbsp) boiling water. Sprinkle liberally with caster (superfine) sugar and the grated peel of one lemon or small orange. Cover with plate or matching lid. Stir during cooking. For pulpy fruit, see apples.

PUDDINGS
AND DESSERTS

Puddings and desserts, the treat of the nation, are represented here in all their glory and if you are astonished at a baked apple taking only 5 minutes to cook in the microwave, you will be even more suprised to learn that a steamed suet pudding takes even less!

Speed, economy of fuel and almost instant success characterise this collection of old and new favourites but, for more detailed guidelines, I would ask you please to read the introduction to the cake section as part of it is applicable to this section as well.

Louisiana Spice Pie

Remarkable for its beautiful flavour and texture, an ideal dinner party show-piece. It is made with a filling of spicy sweet potatoes and is a variation of a dessert I tried out when visiting the deep south of the USA.

Preparation time: about 45 minutes

Serves 8

shortcrust pastry (basic pie crust)
made with 175 g (6 oz/1½ cup) plain (all-purpose) flour
and 75 g (3 oz/⅓ cup) fat etc
1 egg yolk, beaten

Filling
450 g (1 lb) sweet potatoes, freshly cooked
as directed on page 205
75 g (3 oz/⅓ cup) caster (superfine) sugar
7.5 ml (1½ tsp) mixed (apple pie) spice
3 (size 2) eggs
150 ml (¼ pt/⅔ cup) cold milk
25 g (1 oz/2 tbsp) melted butter

1   Roll out pastry fairly thinly and use to line a 20 cm (8 inch) glass or pottery fluted flan dish. Prick well all over, especially where sides join base.

2   Cook, uncovered, for 6 minutes at full power. If pastry has bulged in places, press down gently with oven-gloved hands.

3   Brush all over with yolk to seal up holes then cook, uncovered, 1 minute at full power. Leave to stand while making filling.

34   Drain sweet potatoes and mash finely or, for smoother texture, work to a purée in blender or food processor.

5   Tip into bowl and leave until cold. Add remaining ingredients and beat well until smoothly mixed. Spoon into pastry case.

6   Cook for 22 to 25 minutes at defrost setting, when filling should be set. Leave until just warm then cut into portions and serve topped with lightly whipped cream or vanilla ice cream.

Semolina Milk Pudding

Satiny-smooth and easily and cleanly made in the microwave, the Semolina (cream of wheat) Pudding can cook in its own serving dish.

Preparation time: about 9 minutes

Serves 4

50g (2oz/⅓cup) semolina (cream of wheat)
50g (2oz/¼cup) caster (superfine) sugar
600ml (1pt/2½cups) cold milk
15g (½oz/1tbsp) butter or margarine

1   Tip semolina into a serving dish. Mix in sugar and milk. Cook, uncovered, for 7 to 8 minutes at full power when pudding should have come to the boil and thickened.

2   Whisk hard at the end of every minute. Finally mix in the butter or margarine. Spoon into dishes and serve while hot.

Flavoured Semolina Milk Pudding

Serves 4

Flavour to taste with vanilla essence (extract) or grated lemon rind, adding it at the same time as the butter or margarine.

Blackberry and Lemon Pudding

Fragrant and slightly gooey, this is one of the best autumnal puddings I have ever made in the microwave. It's a treat with double cream or custard.

Preparation time: about 16 minutes

Serves 6

225g (8oz/2cups) blackberries, washed and drained
finely grated rind and juice of 1 medium lemon
225g (8oz/2cups) self-raising flour
100g (4oz/½cup) butter or
block margarine, at room temperature
100g (4oz/½cup) dark brown (coffee) sugar
2 (Size 3) eggs, beaten
60ml (4tbsp) cold milk

1   Well-grease a dish measuring 18cm (7inches) in diameter by 7.5cm (3inches) in depth.

2   Crush blackberries. Combine with grated lemon rind and juice. Set aside.

3   Sift flour into a bowl. Rub in butter or margarine finely. Toss in sugar.

4   Using a fork, stir to a softish consistency with the fruit mixture, eggs and milk.

5   Spread into prepared dish and cook, uncovered, for 7 to 8 minutes at full power. Pudding is ready when it rises to top of dish and just loses its shiny top.

6   Leave to stand 5 minutes. Loosen edges then turn out on to a warm dish. Note that pudding will drop slightly but this is perfectly satisfactory.

TIP: *Sometimes soft brown sugar develops lumps, so check carefully and break down any that have formed be pressing against the sides of a bowl with the back of a wooden spoon. Alternatively, rub between fingertips.*

Nectarine and Blueberry Crumble

Try this exquisite crumble with its vibrant colour, perfumed flavour and enticing crown of spicy sweetness. Cosseted in a blanket of cream, there is little to better such a stunning sweet.

Preparation time: about 15 minutes

Serves 6 (F)

450g (1lb) nectarines
225g (8oz/2 cups) blueberries
60ml (4tbsp) cold water
75g (3oz/⅓ cup) caster (superfine) sugar

TOPPING
175g (6oz/1½ cups) wholemeal (graham) flour
75g (3oz/⅓cup) butter or margarine, at room temperature
10ml (2tsp) cinnamon
75g (3oz/⅓cup) demerara (light brown) sugar

1 Puncture skin of nectarines by nicking once or twice with a knife. Put into a bowl and cover with boiling water. Leave 2 minutes. Drain, rinse with cold water then remove skins.

2 Cut each nectarine in half then twist to separate. Remove stones and cut flesh into slices. Put into a buttered glass or pottery soufflé-type dish, about 1.75 litre (3pt/7½ cups).

3 Mix in blueberries and water. Cover with a lid or cling film, then puncture twice with the tip of a knife.

4 Cook 5 minutes at full power. Add sugar and stir to melt.

5 For crumble, put flour into a bowl. Rub in butter or margarine finely. Toss in cinnamon and sugar. Sprinkle thickly over fruit mixture. Leave uncovered.

6 Cook 4 minutes at full power. Remove from oven, stand 2 minutes then spoon on to plates.

NOTE: *For a crispier topping brown briefly under a pre-heated grill before serving.*

Cherry Orchard Pudding

Cascading with cherries and sauce, flavoured with lemon and light as a feather, here is a stupendous pudding which cooks in 9 minutes.

Preparation time: about 15 minutes

Serves 6

1 can 200 g (14 oz) cherry pie filling
225 g (8 oz/2 cups) self-raising flour
100 g (4 oz/½ cup) butter or margarine, at room temperature
100 g (4 oz/½ cup) caster (superfine) sugar
finely grated rind of 1 lemon
2 (size 2) eggs
75 ml (5 tbsp) cold milk

1 Well-grease a 1.75 litre (3 pt/7½ cup) round soufflé-type glass or pottery dish. Cover base with whole can cherry pie filling.

2 Sift flour into a bowl. Rub in butter or margarine finely with fingertips. Toss in sugar and lemon peel.

3 Beat eggs and milk add to mixture and using a fork, mix to a soft consistency.

4 Spoon gently and evenly over cherries. Leave uncovered and cook 9 minutes at full power.

5 Leave to stand 3 minutes then turn out into a dish (not a plate as the cherries and liquid will flow over the sides). Spoon portions on to plates and serve either as it is, or accompany with cream, ice cream or custard.

Chocolate Mousse

The now famous Chocolate Mousse that has made such a noteworthy contribution to gracious living. It is child's play with a microwave.

Preparation time: about 5 minutes plus chilling time

Serves 4

1 bar 100g (4oz/⅔cup) plain (semi-sweet) chocolate, broken into pieces
15g (½oz/1 tbsp) butter
4 (size 3) eggs, at room temperature, separated

1 Put chocolate into a glass or pottery bowl or basin. Add butter.

2 Leave uncovered and heat for 3½ to 3¾ minutes at defrost setting or until both have melted. Stir once.

3 Beat in egg yolks. Whip egg whites to a stiff foam and fold smoothly into chocolate mixture with a large metal spoon.

4 Divide equally between 4 wine-type glasses and chill in the refrigerator until firm.

Chocolate Mocha Mousse

Serves 4

Make as Chocolate Mousse (on page 232) but beat in 10 ml/
2 teaspoons instant coffe powder with egg yolks.

Chocolate Rum, Sherry or Peppermint Mousse

Serves 4

Make as Chocolate Mousse (on page 232) but beat in 5 ml/
1 teaspoon rum, sherry or peppermint essence with the egg
yolks.

Chocolate Orange Mousse

Serves 4

Make as Chocolate Mousse (on page 232) but beat in 7.5 ml/
1½ teaspoons very finely grated orange rind with egg yolks.

Chocolate Cream Mousse

Serves 4

Make as Chocolate Mousse (on page 232). When set, decorate top
with softly whipped cream.

Bread and Butter Pudding

Very few can resist the temptation of one of Britain's best loved puddings and although the microwave version lacks the traditional golden brown and crispy top, it passes muster all the same and is much appreciated by all ages.

Preparation time: about 40 minutes

Serves 4 to 6

6 medium or 4 large slices of white bread
50g (2oz/¼ cup) butter, softened
50g (2oz/⅓ cup) currants
50g (2oz/¼ cup) caster (superfine) sugar
600ml (1pt/2½ cups) cold milk
3 (size 3) eggs
25g (1oz/2tbsp) demerara (light brown) sugar
grated nutmeg

1 Leave crusts on bread then spread slices with butter, taking it right to the edges. Cut each slice into 4 squares.

2 Well-butter a 1.75 litre (3pt/7½ cup) deepish glass or pottery dish. Arrange half the bread squares over the base, buttered sides facing.

3 Sprinkle with currants and caster sugar then top with remaining bread squares, also buttered sides facing.

4 Pour milk into a bowl, leave uncovered and warm for 3 minutes at full power. beat in eggs then pour gently over bread and butter in dish.

5 Sprinkle with the demerara sugar and nutmeg. Leave uncovered and cook 30 minutes at defrost setting. Stand for 5 minutes before serving or brown under a pre-heated grill to crisp top, if liked.

Baked Egg Custard

Well-liked by almost everyone. Egg Custard responds happily to microwave treatment and shows no signs of separating out or behaving in a temperamental fashion. If you follow the directions...

Preparation time: about 10 minutes plus setting time

Serves 3 to 4

300 ml (½ pt/1¼ cups) evaporated milk or
single (light) cream (for extra richness)
3 (size 3) eggs
1 extra (size 3) egg yolk
100 g (4 oz/½ cup) caster (superfine) sugar
5 ml (1 tsp) vanilla essence (extract)
2.5 ml (½ tsp) grated nutmeg

1   Pour milk or cream into a jug. leave uncovered and warm 1½ to 2 minutes at full power.

2   Whisk in eggs, egg yolk, sugar and vanilla essence. Strain into a 1 litre (1¾ pt/4¼ cups) buttered glass or pottery dish then stand in a second dish, capacity 2 litres (3½ pints/8½ cups).

3   Pour sufficient boiling water into the large dish until it reaches the level of custard in the smaller dish.

4   Sprinkle top of custard with nutmeg then cook for 6 to 8 minutes at full power when custard should be only just set.

5   Take smaller dish of custard out of the larger dish and wipe the sides dry. Leave to stand until centre has set. Serve warm or cold.

Jamaican Pudding

An exotic harmony of flavours characterise this very slightly stodgy pudding – the sort of thing to drool over. It is at its best with single cream or very rich chocolate ice cream.

Preparation time: about 22 minutes

Serves 6

1 can 376 g (13 oz) crushed pineapple
225 g (8 oz/2 cups) self-raising flour
100 g (4 oz/½ cup) butter or block margarine,
at room temperature
100 g (4 oz/½ cup) soft light brown (coffee) sugar
2 (size 3) eggs
45 ml (3 tbsp) cold milk
30 ml (2 tbsp) dark rum
15 ml (1 tbsp) demerara (light brown) sugar

1   Well-grease a round dish measuring 18 cm (7 inches) in diameter by 7.5 cm (3 inches) in depth.

2   Cover base of dish with half the pineapple and liquid from can. Leave remainder on one side.

3   Sift flour into bowl. Rub in fat finely then toss in sugar. If sugar seems at all lumpy, continue to rub in until mixture looks like small breadcrumbs.

4   Add eggs, milk, rum and rest of pineapple with liquid from can. Fork-stir to a soft consistency.

5   Spread over pineapple in dish. Cook, uncovered, for 9 minutes at full power.

6   Leave to stand 10 minutes. Invert carefully on to a warm plate then sprinkle with the demerara sugar. Serve while still hot.

Blackcurrant Stodge Pudding

I am including this recipe at the special request of my husband and son who regard stodgy, sticky puddings as one of life's ultimate delights. I do not subscribe to that view but as men seem to dote on schoolboy desserts, who am I to argue?

Preparation time: about 17 minutes

Serves 6

275 g (10 oz/2½ cups) self-raising flour
150 g (5 oz/⅔ cup) butter or margarine, at room temperature
100 g (4 oz/½ cup) soft light brown (coffee) sugar
2 (size 3) eggs, beaten
1 can 400 g (14 oz) blackcurrant pie filling
45 ml (3 tbsp) cold milk

1   Well-grease a 1.75 litre (3 pt/7½ cup) round soufflé-type glass or pottery dish.

2   Sift flour into a bowl. Rub in butter or margarine finely. Toss in sugar.

3   Mix to a soft consistency with eggs, pie filling and cold milk, stirring briskly with a fork.

4   Spoon into prepared dish. Leave uncovered and cook 9 minutes at full power.

5   Stand 5 minutes, turn out on to a warm dish and spoon into portions. Good with thick cream.

Steamed Suet Syrup Pudding

Unbelievably light in texture and beautifully spongy, this pudding cooks in under five minutes and looks and tastes as though it had been steamed for hours. No mean achievement!

Preparation time: about 8 minutes

Serves 4

45 ml (3 tbsp) golden (light corn) syrup
100 g (4 oz/1 cup) self-raising flour
pinch of salt
50 g (2 oz/½ cup) finely shredded (chopped) packet suet
50 g (2 oz/¼ cup) caster (superfine) sugar
1 (size 3) egg
90 ml (6 tbsp) cold milk
5 ml (1 tsp) vanilla essence (extract)

1   Well-grease a 1.2 litre (2 pt/5 cup) pudding basin. Pour syrup into base.

2   Sift flour and salt into a bowl. Toss in suet and sugar.

3   Beat egg with milk and essence. *Add all at once* to dry ingredients and stir briskly with a fork to mix.

4   Spoon into basin, cover with cling film, then puncture twice with the tip of a knife.

5   Cook 4 to 4½ minutes at full power or until mixture reaches top of basin and just meets the film.

6   Remove from oven, leave to stand 2 minutes then uncover. Turn out on to a plate and serve portions with cream, custard or one of the sweet sauces from the Sauce Section.

Alternative Flavours

Serves 4

Make as Steamed Suet Syrup Pudding, using honey, jam, marmalade or lemon curd instead of syrup.

Jam Sponge Pudding

As light as a puff of wind with a fluffy texture and high-rise finish.

Preparation time: about 15 minutes

Serves 4 to 6

45 ml (3 tbsp) red jam
175 g (6 oz/½ cup) self-raising flour
pinch of salt
75 g (3 oz/⅓ cup) butter or margarine, at room temperature
75 g (3 oz/⅓ cup) caster (superfine) sugar
2 (size 3) eggs
45 ml (3 tbsp) milk

1   Spoon jam into a 1.5 litre (2½ pt/6 cup) well-greased pudding basin.

2   Sift flour and salt into a bowl. Rub in butter or margarine finely then toss in caster sugar.

3   Beat eggs and milk together using a fork, then stir into dry ingredients to make a soft consistency. Spoon into the prepared basin and leave uncovered.

4   Cook 7 to 8 minutes. Leave to stand 3 or 4 minutes then invert on to a plate. Serve with cream or custard.

Orange Jam Sponge Pudding

Serves 4 to 6

Make as above, but add the finely grated rind of 1 medium orange with the sugar. Add about 2.5 ml (½ teaspoon) orange essence with eggs and milk.

Alternative Flavours

Serves 4 to 6

Use 5 ml (1 teaspoon) of any essence (extract) to taste, adding it with the eggs and milk. Use syrup or honey instead of the jam.

Spirited Christmas Puddings

Makes 2, each enough for 10 servings

Make up Spirited Christmas Cake mixture as directed on page 264. Divide remaining half of mixture between 2 well-greased glass or pottery pudding basins, each 900 ml (1½ pt/3¾ cups). Leave uncovered. Cook individually, allowing 5 minutes at full power, a rest period of 5 minutes then a further 2 minutes cooking at full power.

The puddings may be flamed with alcohol and eaten straight away or left until cold, wrapped in greaseproof paper, over-wrapped with foil and left to mature for several weeks. For reheating instructions, see Convenience Food Chart on page 38.

Special Plum Pudding

Fabulous. Every year requests pour in for these rich and fruity Christmas puddings which, until now, I have always steamed conventionally. But they work just as well in the microwave, take 14 to 15 minutes each to cook and no steamy kitchen. The inclusion of cherry pie filling gives them instant maturity so they can be made just before Christmas.

Preparation time: about 18 minutes

Makes 2

225 g (8 oz/4 cups) soft white breadcrumbs, freshly made
100 g (4 oz/1 cup) plain (all-purpose) flour
5 ml (1 tsp) mixed (apple pie) spice
5 ml (1 tsp) cinnamon
1.25 ml (¼ tsp) ginger
1.25 ml (¼ tsp) nutmeg
175 g (6 oz/¾ cup) soft dark brown (coffee) sugar
275 g (10 oz/2½ cup) finely shredded (chopped) suet
675 g (1½ lb/4 cups) mixed dried fruit
3 (size 3) eggs, beaten
1 can 400 g (14 oz) cherry pie filling
30 ml (2 tbsp) black treacle

1 Well-grease 2 × 900 ml (1½ pt/3¾ cups) basins.

2 Tip crumbs into a bowl. Sift in flour, spice, cinnamon, ginger and nutmeg.

3 Add sugar, suet and dried fruit then mix to a softish mixture by stirring in the eggs, cherry pie filling and black treacle.

4 When evenly combined, spread smoothly into prepared basins. Leave uncovered then cook each pudding for 6 minutes at full power.

5 Stand 5 minutes then cook a further 3 minutes, turning twice. Remove from oven and leave until lukewarm in the basins.

6 Turn out on to greaseproof paper and wrap when cold. Overwrap with foil and store in the cool until required. Reheat as directed in the chart on page 38. Decorate. Flame with alcohol.

Calypso Pudding

One of those soft and comforting puddings, always welcome in the depths of winter with an overcoat of hot custard. It cooks in around 8 minutes.

Preparation time: about 10 minutes

Serves 4 to 5

225g (8oz/2cups) self-raising flour
100g (4oz/½cup) butter or margarine (or mixture),
at room temperature
100g (4oz/½cup) caster (superfine) sugar
2 (size 2) eggs, well-beaten
75ml (5tbsp) crushed pineapple with syrup
15ml (1tbsp) liquid coffee and chicory essence (extract)

1   Well-grease a 1.75litre (3pt/7½cup) straight-sided round dish. A glass or pottery soufflé dish is ideal.

2   Sift flour into a bowl. Rub in fats finely. Toss in sugar.

3   Using a fork, stir to a soft consistency with the eggs, pineapple and coffee.

4   Spread smoothly into prepared dish. Leave uncovered and cook 6½ minutes at full power.

5   Invert on to a plate and if centre still looks sticky, return to oven and cook an extra 1 to 1¼ minutes.

6   Spoon into bowls and coat with hot custard.

Lime Floss

Not for haute cuisiners but certainly for Mum, Dad and the children who all look forward to something light and refreshing at the end of a filling meal. It's nourishing too.

Preparation time: about 5 minutes plus setting time

Serves 4 generously

1 lime flavour packet jelly
hot water
300 ml (½ pt/1¼ cups) cold Egg Custard sauce (page 81)
or the same amount of canned custard
2 (size 2) eggs, separated
2.5 ml (½ tsp) lemon juice
hundreds and thousands (sugar strands) for decoration

1   Divide jelly up into cubes and put into a measuring jug. Cover with a saucer and melt for 2 to 2½ minutes at defrost setting.

2   Make up to 300 ml (½ pt/1¼ cups) with hot water then whisk into Egg Custard sauce or canned custard. Follow by beating in yolks.

3   Cover. Leave until cold then refrigerate until just beginning to thicken and set.

4   Whisk egg whites and lemon juice to a stiff snow. Beat one-third into jelly mixture then fold in remainder.

5   Divide equally between 4 dishes and set in the refrigerator. Sprinkle with hundreds and thousands before serving.

Lemon Floss

Serves 4 generously

Just as cooling and tangy, make as above but use a lemon jelly instead of lime.

Orchard Fruit Crush

What a blissful flavour this sweet has, yet it's the easiest thing in the world to put together and, with its glowing colour, contributes admirably to autumnal mellowness. It is quite splendid with a topping of whipped cream, dusted prudently with very finely grated lemon rind and cinnamon.

Preparation time: about 4 minutes plus setting time

Serves 4

1 tangerine flavour packet jelly
hot water
225 g (8 oz/2 cups) blackberries, washed
and crushed with a fork
apple juice
75 ml (5 tbsp) whipped cream
7.5 ml (1½ tsp) grated lemon rind
2.5 ml (½ tsp) cinnamon

1 Divide jelly up into cubes and put into a measuring jug. Cover with a saucer. Melt for 2 to 2½ minutes at defrost setting.

2 Stir in hot water and blackberries then make up to 600 ml (1 pint/2½ cups) with apple juice. Leave until cold.

3 Refrigerate, covered, until just beginning to thicken and set. Spoon into 4 dishes and leave in the refrigerator until firm.

4 Top with cream then sprinkle with the lemon rind and cinnamon.

Wine-Spiced Peaches

For sophisticates, I present a heady and sweet-smelling dessert to savour with pleasure. Serve it with pieces of bought or homemade sponge cake, crisp biscuits or wedges of gingerbread.

Preparation time: about 18 minutes plus chilling time

Serves 6 to 8

8 large peaches
lemon juice
300 ml (½ pint/1¼ cups) dry red wine
175 g (6 oz/¾ cup) caster (suprfine) sugar
5 cm (2 in) piece of cinnamon stick
4 cloves
2 medium oranges, peeled and thinly sliced

1 Puncture skin of peaches by nicking once or twice with a knife. Put into a bowl and cover with boiling water, leave 2 minutes. Drain and cover with cold water. Drain again and remove skins.

2 Cut each peach in half and twist to separate. Remove stones. Brush halves all over with lemon juice.

3 Put wine, sugar, cinnamon and cloves into a 20×5cm (8×2inch) round dish. Cover with an inverted plate and heat 4 minutes at full power.

4 Stir round, add peaches (cut side down) and baste with wine mixture. Stud here and there with orange slices and cover with cling film, puncturing it twice with the tip of a knife. Alternatively, cover with a matching lid.

5 Cook 10 minutes at full power. Leave to cool then refrigerate until well-chilled before serving.

Apple Snow

This light dessert should be well-received, flavoured as it is with apple purée and the ever popular vanilla.

Preparation time: about 8 minutes plus chilling time

Serves 4

1 packet 31g (1.1oz) vanilla blancmange powder
450ml (¾pt/2cups) cold milk
45ml (3tbsp) caster (superfine) sugar
100g (4oz/1cup) apple purée (apple sauce)
2 (size 2) egg whites
2-3 drops lemon juice
a few fresh mint leaves

1 Tip blancmange powder into 1.2litre (2pt/5cups) bowl and mix smoothly with 60ml (4tbsp) of the measured milk.

2 Heat rest of milk, uncovered, for 4 minutes at full power. Blend with blancmange mixture then stir in the sugar.

3 Return to oven and cook, uncovered, at full power until mixture boils and thickens; about 2½ minutes. Beat at the end of every ½ minute to ensure smoothness.

4 Remove from oven and whisk in the apple purée. Cool to lukewarm. Whisk egg whites to a stiff snow with lemon juice. Fold into blancmange mixture gently and smoothly with a large metal spoon.

5 Spread evenly into a bowl then cover and chill several hours in the refrigerator. Before serving decorate with a few mint leaves.

Cranberry Parfait

A luscious dessert which I learned how to make in Finland from locally grown berries: smaller than the ones we normally see and with a wonderful wild and woodland taste and aroma.

Make up any of the Cranberry sauces given on page 80. Leave until completely cold. Whip 300 ml (½ pt/1¼ cups) double (heavy) cream and 30 ml (2 tbsp) milk until thick. Fold in the Cranberry sauce then divide mixture between 6 dishes. Refrigerate at least 2 hours before serving.

Compote of Arabian Nights

The subtle tones of this sweet are reminiscent of magic carpets and mosques, sand dunes and palm trees, gardens and orchards in far-off lands. It's mystical hot and even more so cold as the flavours intensify and the whole thing becomes perfumed with roses and apricots. A 7-minute wonder.

Preparation time: about 15 minutes

Serves 6

450 g (1 lb) fresh dates, at their best during the winter months
450 g (1 lb) bananas, just ripe but not bruised
juice of ½ lemon
45 ml (3 tbsp) apricot brandy
2.5 ml (½ tsp) rose flavouring essence (extract)
20 ml (4 tsp) demerara (light brown) sugar

1 Skin dates, slit each in half and remove stones. Put into a 1.75 litre (3 pt/7½ cup) serving dish.

2 Peel bananas and slice directly on top of dates. Sprinkle with lemon juice then add apricot brandy and rose essence.

3 Toss gently together and sprinkle with the sugar. Cover with cling film, then puncture twice with the tip of a knife.

4 Cook 7 minutes at full power. Serve as suggested above.

Honeyed Raspberry Marshmallow Dream

I make this in the winter with frozen raspberries and think of summer. This top drawer sweet can be put together in under 10 minutes and then served hot or cold with sponge cake and cream. It has a wonderful fragrance, is a delight to eat and eminently suitable for entertaining.

Preparation time: about 10 minutes plus optional chilling time

Serves 6

450g (1 lb/4 cups) raspberries, thawed if frozen
30 ml (2 tbsp) clear honey
1 packet 140 g (4½ oz) pink and white marshmallows

1   Put raspberries and honey into 1.75 litre (3 pt/7½ cups) dish. Cover with a plate and cook 5 minutes at full power.

2   Remove from oven and uncover. Arrange marshmallows close together on top, forming a wide border.

3   Leave uncovered and cook a further 3 minutes at full power. If serving cold, cool off in the kitchen, cover and refrigerate about 8 hours. If serving hot, spoon on plates and serve straight away.

'Mulled' Pineapple

A wonderful way with fresh, ripe pineapple. It has a unique fragrance and needs no accompaniments at all, just appreciative diners.

Preparation time: about 18 minutes plus chilling time

Serves 8 to 10

225 g (8 oz/1 cup) caster (superfine) sugar
150 ml (¼ pt/⅔ cup) cold water
1 whole pineapple
6 cloves
5 cm (2 in) piece of cinnamon stick
good pinch nutmeg
60 ml (4 tbsp) ruby port
15 ml (1 tbsp) brandy

1 Put sugar and water into a 2.25 litre (4 pt/10 cup) dish. Stir round and cover with a plate. Cook 8 minutes at full power.

2 Meanwhile, peel pineapple and cut flesh into wedges. Removal of centre core is a matter of personal choice but it is not necessary.

3 Add to dish with rest of ingredients. Stir well to mix. Cover with cling film, then puncture twice with tip of a knife.

4 Cook 10 minutes at full power.

5 Remove from microwave, leave until cold then refrigerate overnight. Before serving, bring back to room temperature and spoon into dishes.

TIP: *The pineapple may be served hot but is not as flavoursome.*

Lemon Spiced Pears

A palate tingler this one – dessert pears coated in a spicy lemon sauce.

Preparation time: about 15 minutes plus chilling time

Serves 6

75g (3oz/6tbsp) soft light brown (coffee) sugar
300ml (½pt/1¼ cups) water
60ml (4tbsp) dry white wine
5cm (2in) piece of cinnamon stick
3 cloves
6 medium-sized dessert pears (not over-soft)
packet lemon meringue pie filling mix
150ml (¼pt/⅔cup) milk, at room temperature
10ml (2tsp) finely grated lemon rind
extra shreds of lemon rind for decoration

1 Put sugar, water, wine, cinnamon stick and cloves into a 1.75 litre (3pt/7½ cup) dish. Heat 3 minutes, uncovered, at full power.

2 Remove from oven. Peel pears, leaving in stalks. Stand upright in dish. Baste with syrup mixture. Slide dish into a roasting bag and loosely seal top with a non-metal tie.

3 Cook 6 to 8 minutes at full power.

4 Remove from microwave and carefully strain syrup from pears directly into a jug. Stir in lemon filling mix. Cover with a saucer. Cook 2 minutes at full power or until mixture comes to the boil. Whisk every ½ minute.

5 Cool slightly then beat in milk and lemon rind. Refrigerate pears and lemon sauce until well-chilled. Pour some sauce over pears before serving and decorate with strips of lemon rind. Hand extras sauce separately.

Baked Apples

As though by magic these puff up like soufflés in minutes, and may be cooked individually or in a group. The flavour is very fresh and more fruity than if baked conventionally.

Wash and dry as many even-sized cooking (tart) apples as are required, up to a maximum of 4. Remove cores from stalk ends then score a line round each apple with a sharp knife, about one-third of the way down from the top. Fill with sugar and/or dried fruit, honey, jam or even lemon curd. Top each with 5 ml/ 1 teaspoon of butter or margarine.

For 1 apple: Stand on a plate and leave uncovered. Cook 3 to 4 minutes at full power.

For 2 apples: Arrange in a small dish. Cook 5 minutes.

For 3 apples: Arrange like a triangle in a dish. Cook 6 to 7 minutes.

For 4 apples: Arrange in a dish to form a square. Cook for 8 to 10 minutes.

NOTE: *Cooking time will depend on the size of apples.*

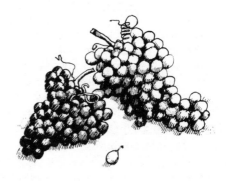

CAKES AND BISCUITS

Cakes in a microwave work like a charm and what they sometimes lack in colour, they make up for in texture and flavour. They will never give you that crusty finish associated with conventional baking but a dusting of icing or caster sugar, a topping of glacé icing, a casing of butter cream or a whoosh of whipped cream all serve to cover, camouflage if you like, the pale tops and sides of light-by-nature cakes although chocolate, spice or even coffee ones can stand on their own feet.

And the speed is incredible. A sponge in 4 minutes, a Christmas cake in 30, shortbread in 20 and cheesecake in 12. Plus, of course, a cool kitchen and no tins to clean. Cakes of all kinds can be made in glass china, pottery or firm plastic dishes. For total cleanliness and ease of removal, the dishes may be base and side lined smoothly with cling film, or greased and the bases lined with greaseproof (waxed) or non-stick parchment paper. The advantage of film is that the cakes can be lifted out of the dishes without being inverted; useful if the texture is fragile like a sponge.

One trick is essential for success. The cake mixture itself (with the exception of fatless sponges) should be made wetter than usual to prevent dryness.

When the cake is ready, based on the timings given in individual recipes, it may still look fractionally damp on top. This is quite in order. As it cools in the dish, the heat will spread from the outside through to the centre and after about 15 minutes or so standing time, the cake should be completely cooked. If not, give it an extra half to one minute, checking every 15 seconds. Even after a cake has been turned out, seemingly cooked, the base may be runny. All that is then necessary is to return the inverted cake, on its plate, to the microwave for a brief spell of cooking, again checking ever 15 seconds. The thing to avoid is overcooking, otherwise the cake will dry out and harden.

Sponge Cake

Here is the traditional fatless sponge which is a perfect specimen and takes only 4 minutes to cook.

Preparation time: about 20 minutes plus cooling time

Serves 6 (F)

75g (3oz/⅓ cup) caster (superfine) sugar
3 (size 3) eggs, at room temperature
75g (3oz/¾ cup) plain (all-purpose) flour,
sifted twice for maximum aeration

1   Line a 18cm × 10cm (7 × 4 inch) round glass dish smoothly with cling film. Make sure the dish is the same diameter top and bottom.

2   Tip sugar into a bowl and warm 2 minutes at defrost setting. Add eggs and whisk steadily until mixture is as thick as whipped cream and very pale in colour.

3   Lightly cut and fold in flour with a metal spoon, cutting side edge of spoon along base of bowl and flipping mixture over and over on itself until smoothly and evenly combined.

4   Spoon into prepared dish, leave uncovered and cook 4 minutes at full power.

5   Remove from oven and leave to stand 10 minutes before lifting out of dish (by holding edges of cling film) and transferring to a wire rack.

6   Peel film away when cake is completely cold. Afterwards dust with caster sugar,cut into wedges and eat the same day; fatless sponges go stale quickly and are best made and consumed within hours.

NOTE: *Cake will rise up to the top of the dish during the initial stages of cooking and fall to a depth of 5 to 7.5 cm (2 to 3 inches).*

Jam and Cream Sponge

Serves 6 (F)

Make Sponge Cake as directed (on page 253). When completely cold, split in half horizontally and sandwich together with jam and whipped cream. Dust with either caster (superfine) or icing (confectioners') sugar.

Chocolate Nut Gateau

Serves 8 (F)

Make Sponge Cake as directed (on page 253) then split in half horizontally when completely cold. For Chocolate Cream, melt a 100 g/4 oz bar plain chocolate as directed in the chart on page 38. Leave until cool but still liquid. Whip 300 ml (½ pint/1¼ cup) double (heavy) cream until thick. Gently whisk in melted chocolate alternately with 30 ml/2 tbsp of milk. Sandwich cake together with just under half the Chocolate Cream. Pile remainder thickly over the top then stud with hazelnuts or walnuts. Chill lightly before serving. To ring the changes, fill split cake with a little apricot jam. Spread Chocolate Cream over the top and sides then dust with a sifting of drinking chocolate powder. Decorate with nuts. Chill lightly before serving.

Genoese Cake

This is an enriched version of the Sponge Cake and much favoured by chefs. It, too, lends itself to variations and creative fantasies, but needs lightness of hand to achieve best results.

Make exactly as Sponge Cake on page 253 but increase sugar by 25 g (1 oz/2 tbsp) and eggs to 4 instead of 3. *Gently and lightly* cut and fold in 50 g (2 oz/¼ cup) melted unsalted butter alternately with 100 g (4 oz/1 cup) plain (all-purpose) flour. leave uncovered and cook 5½ to 6 minutes at full power. Stand for 7 minutes, remove from dish and cool as directed for the Sponge Cake. Dust with caster sugar before serving.

Citrus Cream Torte

Serves 8 (F)

Split Genoese Cake in half horizontally when completely cold. Sandwich together with fine shred orange marmalade. Coat top and sides with 300 ml (½ pt/1¼ cups) whipped double (heavy) cream, sweetened to taste with sifted icing (confectioners') sugar and flavoured with the finely grated rind of 1 lemon. Dust lightly with instant coffee powder. Chill briefly before serving.

Orange Cream Rum Torte

Serves 8 (F)

Make as above but flavour sweetened whipped cream with 10 ml/ 2 teaspoons finely grated orange rind and 30 ml/2 tbsp rum. Sprinkle with finely crushed chocolate flake bar. Chill briefly before serving.

Strawberry and Cream Cake

Serves 8 (F)

Make as above. Split in half horizontally and fill with 225 g (8 oz/ 2 cups) sliced strawberries mixed with 150 ml (¼ pt/⅔ cups) sweetened whipped cream. Mound top with a further 150 ml (¼ pt/⅔ cup) whipped cream and stud with berries.

Victoria Sandwich Cake

A fine-textured cake, Britain's favourite and a joy to microwave.

Preparation time: about 15 minutes plus cooling time

Serves 8 (F)

175 g (6 oz/1½ cups) self-raising flour
pinch of salt
175 g (6 oz/¾ cup) softened butter or margarine
175 g (6 oz/¾ cup) caster (superfine) sugar
3 (size 3) eggs, at room temperature
45 ml (3 tbsp) cold milk

1 Well-grease 2 × 20 cm (8 inch) round glass heat-proof dishes of about 5 cm (2 inches) in depth. Line bases with rounds of greaseproof (waxed) paper.

2 Sift flour and salt on to a plate. Put butter or margarine and sugar into a bowl and cream until very light and fluffy in consistency; also much paler than its original colour.

3 Beat in eggs, one at a time, adding 15 ml/1 tablespoon sifted flour with each.

4 Lastly fold in rest of flour alternately with milk. When evenly combined, spread smoothly into prepared dishes. Cover each with cling film, then puncture twice with tip of a knife.

5 Cook cakes individually for 4 minutes at full power.

6 Remove from oven and uncover. Leave until lukewarm then invert on to greaseproof (waxed) or parchment paper sprinkled with caster sugar. Leave until cold.

7 Sandwich together with jam or lemon curd.

NOTE: *For a quick version of above, sift flour into a bowl with 7.5 ml/ 1½ teaspoons baking powder. Add all remaining ingredients and beat well until smooth. Divide between prepared dishes and cook as above.*

Vanilla and Other Flavouring Essences

(F)

Add 5 ml/1 teaspoon vanilla or other essence (extract) to fat and sugar before creaming.

Fresh Lemon or Orange

(F)

Add 10 ml/2 teaspoons finely grated lemon or orange rind to fat and sugar before creaming.

Nut

(F)

Add 50 g (2 oz/½ cup) finely chopped walnuts to mixture after beating in eggs. Allow an extra ½ minutes cooking time.

Cup Cakes

Makes 18 (F)

Spoon cake mixture into 18 double thickness paper cake cases. Stand, 6 at a time, on turntable in a ring. Allow plenty of space between each then bake 2 to 2½ minutes or until well-risen. Remove outer cases when cold. Decorate when cold with a dusting of icing sugar or by coating tops with glacé icing, made by sifting 225 g (8 oz/1 cup) icing (confectioners') sugar into a bowl and mixing to a fairly stiff icing with fruit juice, cold coffee or alcohol. Decorate with nuts, glacé cherries, chocolate drops etc.

Fairy Cakes

Makes 18 (F)

Make as for Cup Cakes. Add 50 g (2 oz/3 tbsp) currants after beating eggs. Allow an extra ½ minute cooking time.

Seed Cakes

Makes 18 (F)

Make as for Cup Cakes. Add 10 ml/2 teaspoons caraway seeds and 5 ml/1 teaspoon vanilla essence (extract) to the creamed mixture.

Fruit and Nut Cup Cakes

Makes 18 (F)

Make as for Cup Cakes. Add 25 g (1 oz/1½ tbsp) sultanas (golden raisins) or raisins and 25 g (1 oz/¼ cup) chopped walnuts or hazelnuts after beating in the eggs.

Hasty Madeleines

Makes 18 (F)

Make Cup Cakes as directed. When just cold, spread tops of each with red jam and sprinkle with dessicated (shredded) coconut. Top each with a ½ a glacé cherry and 2 angelica leaves.

Tip for Fancy Gateau

Make up the Victoria Sandwich Cake as directed, then turn into Gateaux by following any of the ideas given in the recipes for Sponge and Genoese Cakes. Instead of cream, use Butter Cream made by creaming 175 g (6 oz/¾ cup) softened butter (unsalted for preference) with 225 g (8 oz/1 cup) sifted icing (confectioners') sugar, 15 ml/1 tablespoon milk and flavourings to taste. Colour, if liked, with a few drops of edible food colouring.

Family Fruit Cake

The sort of cut-and-come-again cake that is close to the heart of all families. It cooks in an amazing 7 minutes and keeps perfectly in an air-tight container.

Preparation time: about 28 minutes plus cooling time

Serves 8 (F)

225 g (8 oz/2 cups) self-raising flour
pinch of salt
7.5 ml (1½ tsp) mixed (apple pie) spice
100 g (4 oz/½ cup) butter or margarine, at room temperature
100 g (4 oz/½ cup) soft light brown (coffee) sugar
175 g (6 oz/1 cup) mixed dried fruit (fruit cake mix)
2 (size 3) eggs
75 ml (5 tbsp) cold milk
75 ml (5 tbsp) icing (confectioners') sugar

1 Sift flour, salt and spice into a bowl. Rub in butter or margarine finely. Toss in sugar and fruit.

2 Beat eggs and milk and add in one go, then stir to a soft consistency with a fork.

3 Spread evenly into a 20 cm (8 inch) round glass dish (deep and straight-sided), closely lined with cling film. Leave uncovered.

4 Cook for 6½ to 7 minutes at full power when cake should be well-risen and beginning to pull away from sides.

5 Remove from microwave and leave to stand 15 minutes. Lift out on to a wire cooling rack and carefully peel away film.

6 When completely cold, dust top with sifted icing sugar.

Chocolate Christmas Cake

Unusual to say the least is this deeply dark chocolate Christmas cake filled with vanilla butter cream and snow-iced in traditional style.

Preparation time: about 20 minutes plus cooling time

Serves 10

30 ml (2 tbsp) cocoa (unsweetened chocolate) powder
60 ml (4 tbsp) boiling water
175 g (6 oz/¾ cup) butter or block margarine,
at room temperature and soft
175 g (6 oz/¾ cup) soft dark brown (coffee) sugar
5 ml (1 tsp) vanilla essence (extract)
3 (size 3) eggs, at room temperature
175 g (6 oz/1½ cups) self-raising flour
15 ml (1 tbsp) black treacle

FILLING
75 g (3 oz/⅓ cup) butter, softened
175 g (6 oz/¾ cup) icing (confectioners') sugar, sifted
10 ml (2 tsp) cold milk
5 ml (1 tsp) vanilla essence (extract)

ROYAL ICING
2 (size 4) egg whites
350 g (12 oz/1½ cups) icing (confectioners') sugar, sifted
2.5 ml (½ tsp) lemon juice
2 or 3 drops glycerine (to prevent icing from hardening too much)

1 Line a 20 cm (8 inch) straight-sided, soufflé type dish with cling film, making sure it is as smooth as possible and pressed well into the edges where sides meet base.

2 Mix cocoa powder smoothly with boiling water and set aside.

3 Cream butter, sugar and essence together until light and fluffy. Beat in eggs singly, adding 15 ml/1 tablespoon of flour with each. Fold in rest of flour with black treacle.

4 When smooth and evenly combined, transfer to prepared dish. Leave uncovered and cook 6 to 6½ minutes at full power. Cake is ready when well-risen and just no longer damp-looking on top. *Do not overcook* or cake will toughen and shrink.

5 Remove from oven and leave to stand until lukewarm. Lift out of dish and place on a wire cooling rack.

6 Peel back film and leave cake until cold. Remove film altogether and cut cake into 3 layers.

7 To make butter cream filling, beat butter until light then gradually whisk in sugar. Add milk and essence, mix well. Use to sandwich cakes together.

8 For icing, whisk whites to a light foam (not stiff). Gradually beat in sugar to form soft peaks. Then mix in lemon juice and glycerine.

9 Swirl over top and sides of cake and transfer to a board. When half set, add seasonal decorations to taste. Leave 1 day before cutting.

Devil's Food Cake

American inspired, this is a dark-as-night chocolate cake with the texture of velvet and flavour of heaven. It converts easily into a party gateau, just as easily into a tea table centrepiece or, with a dusting of icing sugar, into a family-style cake which the children will adore. Best whizzed in a food processor, you can have the whole thing ready in well under 30 minutes.

Preparation time: about 20 minutes plus cooling time

Serves 8 generously (F)

100 g (4 oz) plain (semi-sweet) chocolate, at room temperature
25 g (1 oz/¼ cup) cocoa (unsweetened chocolate) powder
225 g (8 oz/2 cups) plain (all-purpose) flour
5 ml (1 tsp) bicarbonate of soda (baking soda)
150 g (5 oz/⅔ cup) butter, at room temperature
200 g (7 oz/scant cup) soft light brown (coffee) sugar
2 (size 2) eggs
2.5 ml (½ tsp) vanilla essence (extract)
150 ml (¼ pt/⅔ cup) buttermilk
45 ml (3 tbsp) cold milk

1 Line a 17 × 9 cm (7 × 3½ inch) soufflé-type dish with cling film. making sure it lies smoothly over base and sides.

2 Break up chocolate and put into a glass or pottery dish. Leave uncovered and melt 3 to 3½ minutes at defrost setting. When ready, the chocolate will remain in its original shaped pieces but should be soft when touched. Remove from microwave and scrape into food processor bowl.

3 Add all remaining ingredients and blend until smooth. Stop machine, wipe down sides of bowl with spatula and continue to run machine for a further ½ minute.

4 Transfer to prepared dish, leave uncovered and cook 8 minutes at full power.

5 Remove from oven. Cool to lukewarm in the dish (the cake drops to 6 cm (2½ inches) in depth and shrinks away from the sides) then carefully lift out on to a wire cooling rack. peel back film and leave until completely cold.

Family Devil's Food Cake

Serves 8 generously

Cover top with a lacey doyley then dredge with icing (confectioners') sugar, first tipped into a fine mesh sieve (strainer). Carefully lift off the doyley and the pattern will remain on top.

Chocolate Rum Gateau

Serves 8 to 10

Make cake as previously directed then cut in half horizontally. To make Rum Butter Cream, beat 175 g (6 oz/¾ cup) softened butter until very light in texture. Gradually beat in 350 g (12 oz/1½ cups) sifted icing (confectioners') sugar alternately with 50 g (2 oz/½ cup) melted plain chocolate and 15 ml/1 tablespoon dark rum. Set aside one quarter then use remainder to fill cake and cover top and sides. Coat sides with finely chopped walnuts or toasted almonds and transfer to a plate. Decorate top with a piping of remaining butter cream then stud with walnut or toasted almond halves and halved green glacé (candied) cherries. Chill before serving.

Moon Dust Cake

Serves 8 (F)

Make cake as previously directed and halve horizontally. Whip 150 ml (¼ pt/⅔ cup) double (heavy) cream until thick then stir in 50 g (2 oz/½ cup) grated milk chocolate, 15 ml/1 tablespoon caster (superfine) sugar and 5 ml/1 teaspoon finely grated lemon rind. Sandwich cake together with cream then swirl remainder thickly over the top. Chill in the refrigerator before serving.

Spirited Christmas Cake

A special cake laden with fruit and alcohol, this will suit any festive occasion. It is extravagant but the mixture not only makes one family-sized cake, but also 2 succulent Christmas puddings (see page 240). When cold, the cake should be wrapped in greaseproof paper, overwrapped with foil and stored in the cool until ready for coating with almond paste and, subsequently, white icing. To make the cake only, halve ingredients and use 3 (size 4) eggs.

Preparation time: about 1¼ hours plus cooling time

Serves about 15 to 16 (F)

450 ml (¾ pt/2 cups) sweet sherry
150 ml (¼ pt/⅔ cup) brandy
10 ml (2 tsp) mixed (apple pie) spice
5 ml (1 tsp) vanilla essence (extract)
20 ml (4 tsp) soft dark brown (coffee) sugar
225 g (8 oz/1½ cups) sultanas (golden raisins)
225 g (8 oz/1½ cups) seedless raisins
225 g (8 oz/1½ cups) currants
50 g (2 oz/¼ cup) chopped mixed peel
50 g (2 oz/¼ cup) glacé (candied) cherries, chopped
100 g (4 oz/¾ cup) dried apricots, snipped with scissors into small pieces
100 g (4 oz/¾ cup) cooking dates (in a block), finely chopped
finely grated rind of 1 orange
100 g (4 oz/1 cup) walnuts or toasted almonds (page 303), coarsely chopped
225 g (8 oz/1 cup) unsalted butter, melted
350 g (12 oz/1½ cups) soft dark brown (coffee) sugar
225 g (8 oz/2 cups) self-raising flour
5 (size 2) eggs, well-beaten (at room temperature)

1 Put sherry and brandy into a *large* bowl. Cover and bring to the boil, allowing 6 to 7 minutes at full power.

2 Add spice, essence, the 20 ml (4 tsp) of sugar, sultanas, raisins, currants, mixed peel, glacé cherries, apricots, dates, orange peel and nuts. Mix in very thoroughly.

3 Cover with a plate and warm through for 15 minutes at defrost setting. Stir 4 times.

4 Remove from oven and cover. Leave to stand overnight for flavours to mature. Work in melted butter, sugar, flour and the eggs.

5 Spoon half the mixture into a 20 cm (8 inch), 1.75 litre (3 pt/7½ cup) capacity soufflé or other similar glass or pottery dish, first lined completely with cling film.

6 Leave uncovered and cook for 30 minutes at defrost setting. Leave to stand inside oven for a further 10 minutes.

7 Remove from oven and cool to lukewarm. Carefully lift out of dish the the aid of the film and transfer cake to a wire cooling rack.

8 Peel away film and leave cake until completely cold before wrapping as previously directed. Allow to mature for at least 2 weeks before covering with almond paste.

Coffee Apricot Gateau

A showpiece for special occasions, this luscious gateau can be made in next to no time and is much less complicated to put together than it looks. Freeze in a rigid container with lid to prevent spoiling the coating.

Preparation time: about 30 minutes plus cooling and chilling

Serves 8 (F)

4 digestive biscuits (graham crackers), finely crushed
225 g (8 oz/1 cup) butter or block margarine, at room temperature
225 g (8 oz/1 cup) soft dark brown (coffee) sugar
4 (size 3) eggs, at room temperature
225 g (8 oz/2 cups) self-raising flour
45 ml (3 tbsp) coffee and chicory essence (extract)

FILLING AND TOPPING
1 can, 425 g (15 oz) apricot halves
300 ml (½ pt/1¼ cups) double (heavy) cream
30 ml (2 tbsp) coffee and chicory essence (extract)
75 g (3 oz/¾ cup) flaked and toasted almonds

1 Dust base and sides of 2 round glass or pottery buttered dishes, each 20-21 cm (8-8½ inches) in diameter by 2.5-3 cm (1-1½ inches) in depth with crushed biscuits.

2 Cream butter or margarine and sugar together until light and fluffy. Beat in eggs singly, adding 15 ml (1 tbsp) of flour with each. Fold in rest of flour alternately with coffee essence. Divide between the 2 dishes and level surface. Leave uncovered. Bake individually, allowing 5 minutes at full power.

3 Leave in dishes until lukewarm then carefully turn out and cool on wire rack.

4 To complete, drain apricots and coarsely chop up 2 of the halves. Whip cream until thick. Fold in coffee essence.

5 Take out a quarter of the cream and gently stir in chopped apricots. Use to sandwich cake together. Transfer to a serving plate. Spread rest of cream over top and sides then decorate top with apricots. Press almonds on sides then chill 1 hour.

Best Brownies

Moist and out-of-this-world are the only ways to describe these North American-style chocolate squares, my best yet.

Preparation time: about 15 minutes plus cooling time

Makes 12 (F)

75 g (3 oz/¾ cup) self-raising flour
25 g (1 oz/¼ cup) cocoa (unsweetened chocolate) powder
100 g (4 oz/½ cup) butter or margarine, at room temperature
225 g (8 oz/1 cup) soft dark brown (coffee) sugar
5 ml (1 tsp) vanilla essence (extract)
2 (size 3) eggs, at room temperature
45 ml (3 tbsp) milk
icing (confectioners') sugar for the top

1   Line an oblong dish, with a base measurement of 30 × 15 cm (12 × 6 inches), smoothly with cling film.

2   Sift flour and cocoa powder on to a plate. Put butter or margarine and sugar into a bowl. Add essence and beat until creamy and soft.

3   Beat in eggs individually then, with a metal spoon, stir in flour mixture alternately with milk.

4   When evenly combined, spread smoothly into the prepared dish and cover with cling film. Puncture twice with the tip of a knife.

5   Cook for 6 minutes at full power. Remove from oven and remove cling film cover. Leave Brownies in the dish until lukewarm.

6   Lift out, with cling film lining, on to a wire rack. Allow to cool completely, cut into 12 squares and turn upside down. Sprinkle thickly with sifted icing sugar before serving. Store leftovers in an airtight container.

Chocolate Crunch Cake

For the grand occasion, when entertaining special friends, here is a sumptuous chocolate cake made from melted chocolate and butter, enriched with eggs and liqueur, and patchworked with biscuits, fruits and nuts. It cooks, literally, in the refrigerator but the microwave makes fast work of melting the necessary ingredients and, where the chocolate is concerned, prevents overheating and spoilage.

Preparation time: about 13 minutes plus chilling time

Serves 12

200g (7oz/scant 2 cups) plain (semi-sweet) chocolate, at room temperature
225g (8oz/1 cup) unsalted butter (not margarine as cake may not set), at room temperature
2 (size 2) eggs
50g (2oz/½ cup) coarsley chopped nuts, either walnuts, hazels, brazils, toasted cashews or toasted almonds
75g (3oz/¾ cup) mixture of halved glacé (candied) cherries and pieces of crystallised (candied) pineapple or papaya
25-50g (1-2oz/¼-½ cup) crystallised (candied) ginger, coarsely chopped (optional)
20ml (4tsp) sifted icing (confectioners') sugar
15ml (1tbsp) fruit liqueur – apricot, cherry, banana or the melon liqueur called Midori
225g (8oz/2 cups) milk chocolate digestive biscuits (graham crackers), each broken into 8 pieces

1   Line a 20 × 5 cm (8 × 2 inch) round glass or pottery dish with cling film.

2   Break up chocolate and put into a large bowl. Leave uncovered and melt 4 to 5 minutes at defrost setting. When ready, the chocolate will remain in its original shaped pieces but should be very soft when touched. Remove from microwave.

3   Cut butter into chunks and put into a dish. Leave uncovered and melt 2 to 3½ minutes at defrost setting. Beat into the chocolate.

4 Carefully break eggs into a cup and pierce the yolk of each with the tip of a knife. Leave uncovered and warm ½ a minute at defrost setting. Beat well.

5 Stir into chocolate and butter mixture then work in nuts, glacé and crystallised fruits, ginger (if used), sugar and liqueur. Finally and gently fold in the biscuits with a large metal spoon.

6 Transfer as smoothly as possible to prepared tin or dish, cover with foil and chill overnight in the refrigerator.

7 Lift out, peel away cling film and transfer to an attractive serving plate. Cut into small wedges to serve.

TIP: *Leave cake in the refrigerator in between servings as it tends to soften at room temperature.*

Chocolate Crunch Rum Cake

Serves 12

Make as previously directed but use rum instead of fruit liqueur.

Chocolate Crunch Coffee Cake

Serves 12

Make as previously directed but use coffee liqueur instead of fruit. Alternatively, and for a cake without alcohol, dissolve 15 ml (1 tbsp) instant coffee powder in hot water and use instead of liqueur.

Golden Spice Cake

A delight for all those who prefer not to use butter – this cake is based on vegetable oil and has a remarkably light texture.

Preparation time: about 15 minutes plus cooling time

Cuts into 10 pieces

225 g (8 oz/⅔ cup) golden (light corn) syrup
150 ml (¼ pt/⅔ cup) water
75 ml (3 tbsp) sunflower or other vegetable oil
2 (size 3) eggs
45 ml (3 tbsp) apricot jam
225 g (8 oz/2 cups) self-raising flour
2.5 ml (½ tsp) bicarbonate of soda (baking soda)
5 ml (1 tsp) cinnamon
5 ml (1 tsp) ground ginger

1 Line closely with cling film an oblong glass dish measuring 30 × 19 cm (12 × 7½ inches) at the top, sloping to a base measurement of 25 × 16 cm (10 × 6½ inches).

2 Put syrup into a bowl and melt 2 minutes, uncovered, at defrost setting. Beat in water, oil, eggs and jam.

3 Sift in dry ingredients and mix briskly together until smooth. Spread smoothly into prepared dish. Cover with cling film, then puncture twice with the tip of a knife.

4 Cook 7 minutes at full power, turning once. Remove from oven and uncover. Leave until almost cold then invert on to an oblong or oval dish or plate, first dusted with icing sugar.

5 If top seems very damp and cake obviously undercooked, return to oven and continue to cook a further minute or two until just dry.

6 Leave until cold and dust top with more sifted icing sugar. Cut into 10 pieces. Store leftovers in an airtight container.

Toffee Triangles

A version of flapjack, but this time moist and succulent. Ideal for coffee mornings and informal parties.

Preparation time: about 15 minutes plus cooling time

Makes 8

100 g (4 oz/½ cup) butter
50 g (2 oz/¼ cup) golden (light corn) syrup
25 g (1 oz/1½ tbsp) black treacle
100 g (4 oz/½ cup) soft dark brown (coffee) sugar
225 g (8 oz/scant 2 cups) rolled oats

1 Well grease a 20 cm (8 inch) round glass or pottery dish of about 5 cm (2 inches) in depth.

2 Put butter, syrup, treacle and sugar into a bowl. Leave uncovered and heat for 5 minutes at defrost setting.

3 Stir in oats then spread evenly into prepared dish. Leave uncovered and cook 4 minutes at full power.

4 Stand 3 minutes then cook a further 1 minute at full power. Leave until quite cool then cut into 8 triangles with a sharp, round-ended knife.

5 Remove from dish when cold and store in an airtight container.

Muesli Toffee Triangles

Makes 8

Just as delicious but made with muesli. Follow above recipe but use *unsweetened* muesli mix instead of oats.

Gingerbread

Come Hallowe'en and who can resist the heart-warming aroma of ginger-bread wafting from the kitchen? It's a lovely winter cake and cooks in 3 to 4 minutes in the microwave. Best left a day before cutting.

Preparation time: about 20 minutes plus cooling time

Cuts into 8 large pieces (F)

175 g (6 oz/1½ cups) plain (all-purpose) flour
15 ml (1 tbsp) ground ginger
5 ml (1 tsp) mixed (apple pie) spice
2.5 ml (½ tsp) bicarbonate of soda (baking soda)
100 g (4 oz/⅓ cup) golden (light corn) syrup
25 g (1 oz/1½ tbsp) black treacle
25 g (1 oz/2 tbsp) soft dark brown (coffee) sugar
40 g (1½ oz/3 tbsp) lard or white cooking fat
1 (size 1 or 2) egg, well-beaten
60 ml (4 tbsp) cold milk

1 Have ready an oblong pie dish with rim, the inside measuring about 19×12.5×6 cm (7½×5×2¼ inches). Line base and sides smoothly with cling film. Alternatively, use a 15 cm (6 inch) glass or pottery soufflé-type dish.

2 Sift flour, ginger, spice and bicarbonate of soda into a fairly large mixing bowl.

3 Put syrup, treacle, brown sugar and lard or cooking fat into a separate bowl. Heat 2 to 3 minutes at full power or until fat has just melted. Do not cover. Remove from oven and stir well to blend. Add to dry ingredients with egg and milk.

4 Mix to a fairly soft consistency with a fork, stirring briskly without beating. Pour into dish and leave uncovered. Cook 3 to 4 minutes at full power. When ready, Gingerbread should be well-risen with a hint of a shine across the top.

5 Leave to stand 10 minutes. Lift out of dish and stand on wire rack. Peel away film from sides to allow steam to escape. Remove film from underneath when Gingerbread is cold.

Lemon Cheesecake

This creamy cheesecake is best made one day and eaten the next.

Preparation time: about 20 minutes plus cooling time

Serves 10

BASE
75g (3oz/⅓cup) butter, at room temperature
175g (6oz/1½cups) digestive biscuits (graham crackers), crushed
50g (2oz/¼cup) caster (superfine) sugar

FILLING
2 packets each 200g/7oz cream cheese or
450g/1lb medium fat curd (smooth cottage) cheese
75g (3oz/⅓cup) caster (superfine) sugar
2 (size 1 or 2) eggs, at room temperature
5ml (1tsp) vanilla essence (extract)
15ml (1tbsp) cornflour (cornstarch)
finely grated rind and juice of 1 lemon
150ml (¼pt/⅔cup) double (heavy) cream
1 carton 150ml (5floz/⅔cup) soured (dairy sour) cream

1 Melt butter, uncovered, for 2 to 2½ minutes at defrost setting. Stir in biscuit crumbs and sugar. Line a 20×5cm (8×2inch) round glass or pottery dish with cling film. Cover base and sides evenly with biscuit mixture. Leave uncovered and cook 2½ minutes at full power.

2 For filling, beat cheeses until soft and light then whisk remaining ingredients except soured cream. Pour into crumb case. Cook 10 to 12 minutes at full power. The cake is ready when there is some movement to be seen in the middle and the top rises up slightly and just begins to crack.

3 Remove from oven and spread with soured cream which will set on top as the cake evens out and cools.

TIP: *For strawberry or raspberry cheesecake, purée 100g (4oz) fruit and add instead of the lemon and vanilla.*

Shortbread

Because Shortbread should, traditionally, remain pale after cooking, a microwave oven does it full justice and the results are excellent.

Preparation time: about 24 minutes plus cooling time

Cuts into 12 wedges

butter for greasing
225g (8oz/1cup) butter, at room temperature
100g (4oz/½cup) caster (superfine) sugar
350g (12oz/3cups) plain (all-purpose) flour, sifted
extra caster (superfine) sugar

1   Grease the base and sides of a 20×5cm (8×2inch) round glass or pottery dish with butter.

2   Beat butter and sugar until light and creamy. Stir in flour and spread into prepared dish. Prick all over with a fork.

3   Leave uncovered and cook 20 minutes at defrost setting.

4   Remove from oven and sprinkle with 10-15ml (2-3tsp) extra caster sugar.

5   Cut into 12 wedges and leave in the dish until cold. Carefully lift out and store in an airtight container.

Extra Crisp Shortbread

The addition of semolina to the ingredients, and a different method of making, results in a somewhat more crisp shortbread than the one above with a slightly coarse-grained texture.

Preparation time: about 25 minutes plus cooling time

Cuts into 12 wedges

325 g (11 oz/1¾ cups) plain (all-purpose) flour
25 g (1 oz/¼ cup) semolina (cream of wheat)
225 g (8 oz/1 cup) butter, at room temperature
100 g (4 oz/½ cup) caster (superfine) sugar
extra caster (superfine) sugar

1 Sift flour into a bowl then toss in semolina. Rub in butter finely. Add sugar.

2 Knead by hand to a dough and spread over a buttered round glass or pottery dish measuring 20 × 5 cm (8 × 2 inches). Use fingers to ease dough over base of dish then spread evenly with a knife to make sure there are no thin patches.

3 Prick well over with a fork. Leave uncovered and cook 20 minutes at defrost setting.

4 Remove from oven and sprinkle with 10-15 ml (2-3 tsp) extra caster sugar.

5 Cut into 12 wedges and leave in the dish until cold. Carefully lift out and store in an airtight container.

Orange or Lemon Shortbread

Cuts into 12 wedges

If making version 1, add the finely grated rind of 1 orange or lemon whilst beating butter and sugar.

If making version 2, add the same amount of rind at the same time as the 100 g (4 oz/½ cup) caster sugar.

Dutch-Style Cinnamon Shortbread

Cuts into 12 wedges

Sift flour with 20 ml (4 tsp) cinnamon. After spreading either version of shortbread smoothly into dish, brush top with double cream instead of sprinkling with sugar. Leave it for a few minutes to sink in. Gently press 25 g (1 oz/¼ cup) flaked and toasted almonds (page 303) on to top of shortbread by way of decoration. Cook, cool and store as directed.

Cake Mixes (Sandwich varieties)

Make up as directed, whisking for *half* the time recommended to prevent over-aeration and a texture full of holes. When adding the second amount of water, *include 1 extra tablespoon.* Divide mixture between 2 × 20 cm (8 inch) round glass dishes lined with cling film. Cover with more film and puncture twice with tip of a knife. Cook individually, allowing 2½ to 3 minutes each at full power. Cool about 5 minutes then uncover. Invert on to a wire cooling rack and leave until completely cold before filling as specified on the packet. Decorate as liked.

BREADS, BUNS AND PIZZAS

Yeast mixtures take well to microwave treatment, the dough rises in about half the time and the resultant dough is well-textured, good-natured and easy to handle. It depends for its success on short bursts of microwave energy followed by periods of standing time. This technique warms the dough in a controlled way, the heat is evenly distributed while the dough is standing, and the process is clean and carefree. Because yeast is killed by excessive heat and immediately stops acting as a raising agent, times given should be closely followed; overheating is damaging.

The risen dough may subsequently be shaped as desired and baked conventionally or, in some cases, cooked in the microwave. What *is* important to remember is that once the dough is in a container, it must be allowed to rise – or prove – the second time round in a warm place *outside* the microwave oven.

Included in this section, in addition to yeasted goods, are traditional-style soda breads, some rather super bun scones (biscuits) for the tea table, and an old-fashioned fruited malt loaf.

NOTE: *For easy kneading use a food processor. But if adding fruit, knead it in by hand at the end.*

White Bread Dough

A standard dough which can be used to good advantage in the microwave for Bap loaves and rolls.

Preparation time: about 45 minutes plus baking time

Makes 1 loaf or 16 rolls

5 ml (1 tsp) caster (superfine) sugar
300 ml (½ pt/1¼ cups) water, with the chill off
10 ml (2 tsp) dried yeast
450 g (1 lb/4 cups) plain strong (bread) flour
5 ml (1 tsp) salt
25 g (1 oz/2 tbsp) butter or margarine

1   Put sugar into a large cup or jug and mix with 90 ml (6 tbsp) of water. Warm in the microwave oven for 1 minute at defrost setting, leaving uncovered. Remove from oven.

2   Stir in yeast. Stand about 10 minutes when yeast brew should foam up in the cup or jug and look like a glass of beer with a head.

3   Meanwhile, sift flour and salt into a bowl. Warm in the microwave, uncovered, for 1 minute at defrost setting.

4   Rub in butter or margarine finely then mix to a dough with yeast mixture and remaining water.

5   Knead thoroughly until no longer sticky and satiny-smooth, allowing about 10 minutes.

6   Place in a lightly greased or oiled large bowl then cover bowl, not dough itself, with a piece of greased or oiled cling film. Puncture twice with the tip of a knife.

7   Warm in the microwave for 1 minute at defrost setting. Rest 5 minutes. Repeat 3 or 4 times until dough has doubled in size. Re-knead briefly then use conventionally or in the recipes which follow.

NOTE: *For quickness use easy blend dried yeast, omit sugar and stages 1 and 2 and add it to dry ingredients before mixing in in water (stage 4).*

Brown Bread Dough

Follow recipe for White Bread Dough, substituting wholemeal (graham) flour or granary meal. Alternatively, use half wholemeal and half white.

Bap Rolls

Makes 16 (F)

Use white or brown risen dough for these and knead lightly after the first rising. Divide into 16 equal-sized pieces and shape into flattish rounds. Arrange round the edge of 2 large greased and floured dinner plates, putting 8 rounds onto each. Cover with kitchen paper and return to the microwave. Warm 1 minute at defrost setting then rest for 4 minutes. Repeat 3 or 4 times or until Baps double in size. Sprinkle with white or brown flour and leave uncovered. Cook each plate of rolls for 3 minutes at full power. Cool Baps on a wire rack.

Bap Loaf

Makes 1 (F)

Use white or brown risen dough, knead lightly after first rising then shape into a round of about 5 cm (2 inches) in height. Transfer to a greased and floured dinner plate. Cover with kitchen paper and return to microwave. Warm 1 minute at defrost setting then rest for 4 minutes. Repeat 3 or 4 times or until loaf doubles in size. Sprinkle with white or brown flour and leave uncovered. Cook 4 minutes at full power. Cool on a wire rack.

Fruit Baps

Rolls or loaf variation (F)

Make as above, tossing in 50 g (2 oz) dried fruit and 25 g (1 oz) caster (superfine) sugar after rubbing in butter and margarine. Cook rolls an extra ½ minute per plate and the whole loaf an extra ¾ minute.

Seed Bread

Makes 1 loaf (F)

Use white or brown risen dough, knead lightly after first rising then shape into a ball. Put into 375 ml (¾ pt/2 cup) straight-sided, greased round dish. Return to microwave and warm 1 minute at defrost setting then rest for 4 minutes. Repeat 2 or 3 times until dough has doubled in size. Brush with milk or beaten egg and sprinkle with poppy seeds, caraway seeds or toasted sesame seeds (page 304). Cover with kitchen paper and cook 5 minutes at full power, turning dish once unless oven has a turntable. Cook a further 2 minutes. Leave in the dish 15 minutes then carefully turn out on to a wire cooling rack.

TIP: *Do not eat breads or rolls until completely cold.*

NOTE: *For a crisper crust, put baps or loaves under a moderate grill after cooking in the microwave. Take care not to burn and turn once or twice to crisp and brown all sides.*

To freshen conventionally baked bread that seems stale

Put into a paper bag or stand between folds of a clean tea towel. Transfer to the microwave and heat at defrost setting until bread feels slightly warm on the surface. Eat straight away.

Fruited Malt Loaf

A genuine 'golden oldie' for those who love sticky fruit bread.

Preparation time: about 1 hour

Makes 2 (F)

5 ml (1 tsp) caster (superfine) sugar
150 ml (¼ pt/⅔ cup) water, with the chill off
10 ml (2 tsp) dried yeast
450 g (1 lb/4 cups) plain strong (bread) flour
2.5 ml (½ tsp) salt
75 g (3 oz/½ cup) mixture of sultanas (golden raisins) and raisins
60 ml (4 tbsp) malt extract
15 ml (1 tbsp) black treacle
25 g (1 oz/2 tbsp) butter or margarine
30-45 ml (2-3 tbsp) skimmed milk

1   Put sugar into a large cup or jug and mix with the water and dried yeast. Warm in the microwave for 1 minute at defrost setting, leaving uncovered. Remove from oven.

2   Leave to stand about 10 minutes when yeast brew should foam up in cup or jug. Or use easy-blend yeast and add to flour.

3   Meanwhile, sift flour and salt into a bowl then add fruits.

4   Put malt, treacle and butter or margarine into a small basin, leave uncovered and melt 3 minutes at defrost setting.

5   Add to flour with yeast liquid and sufficient milk to make a soft dough. Knead for 10 minutes then divide into halves.

6   Shape to fit 2 × 900 ml (1½ pt) oblong glass or pottery dishes, first well-greased. Cover dishes, not dough, with greased or oiled cling film. Puncture twice with the tip of a knife.

7   Warm in the microwave for 1 minute at defrost setting then rest 5 minutes. Repeat 3 or 4 times more or until loaves have doubled in size. Remove film.

8   Place side by side in the oven. Leave uncovered and cook 2 minutes at full power. Reverse position of dishes and cook a further 2 minutes. Repeat once. Leave to stand 10 minutes then turn loaves out on to a wire rack. Serve sliced and buttered.

Soda Bread

*I hesitate to call this Irish Soda Bread because on my visits to Ireland –
North or South – I soon discovered they use special flour to achieve a
wholesome, nutty-flavoured bread with a dense texture. Mine, I believe,
comes a close second performs well in the microwave in a matter of
minutes.*

Preparation time: about 20 minutes plus cooling time

Makes 4 small triangular loaves (F)

200 ml (7 fl oz/scant 1 cup) buttermilk
75 ml (5 tbsp) ordinary milk
350 g (12 oz/3 cups) wholemeal (graham) flour
100 g (4 oz/1 cup) plain (all-purpose) white flour
10 ml (2 tsp) bicarbonate of soda (baking soda)
5 ml (1 tsp) cream of tartar
5 ml (1 tsp) salt
50 g (2 oz/¼ cup) butter, margarine or white cooking fat,
at room temperature

1 Well grease a 25 cm (10 inch) dinner plate. Mix buttermilk and
milk well together.

2 Tip wholemeal flour into a bowl. Sift in white flour with bicarbonate of soda, cream of tartar and salt. Rub in fat finely.

3 Add liquid in one go then fork-stir to a soft dough. Gather
together with well-floured hands and stand on centre of plate.
Shape into a 18 cm (7 inch) round then make a deepish cross-cut
on top with a knife.

4 Dust lightly with white flour and leave uncovered. Cook for 7
minutes at full power. Bread will rise and spread.

5 Leave to stand 10 minutes. When lukewarm, lift on to a cooling rack with the help of a fish slice.

6 Separate into 4 sections and cool completely before cutting.
Store in a bread bin up to 2 days only as this type of bread is at its
best when eaten freshly made.

Soda Bran Bread

Makes 4 small triangular loaves (F)

For all those who find bran helpful in their diet, this loaf should be very welcome. Make exactly as for Soda Bread (page 282), adding 60 ml (4 tbsp) coarse bran before mixing in liquid.

Wholemeal Soda Bread

Makes 4 small triangular loaves (F)

Make as basic Soda Bread (page 282), but use all wholemeal (graham) flour and no white. Add an extra 10-15 ml (2-3 tsp) milk if necessary.

Granary Soda Bread

Makes 4 small triangular loaves (F)

Make as basic Soda Bread (page 282), but use all granary meal (flour) and no white. Increase milk by 15 ml (1 tbsp).

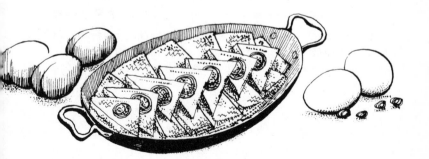

Pizzas Neapolitan

Child's play – almost – in the microwave, these are vibrant and vivacious Pizzas, reminiscent of the people of Naples and its off-shore islands.

Preparation time: about 1 hour 20 minutes

Makes 4

30 ml (2 tbsp) olive oil
100 g (4 oz/1 cup) onions, peeled and chopped
1 garlic clove, peeled and crushed
150 g (5 oz/⅔ cup) tomato purée (paste)
white or brown risen dough (page 278)
350 g (12 oz/3 cups) Mozzarella cheese, grated
50 g (2 oz/⅓ cup) anchovies in oil, drained and separated
100 g (4 oz/⅔ cup) small black olives

1 Put oil, onions and garlic into a 600 ml (1 pt/2½ cup) dish, leave uncovered and cook 5 minutes at full power.

2 Mix in tomato purée and set aside.

3 Knead dough lightly and divide into 4 equal pieces. Roll out into rounds, large enough to cover 4 greased and floured 20 cm (8 inch) dinner plates.

4 Ease dough out towards edges then warm, one plate at a time, for ½ minute at defrost setting. Rest 4 minutes. Repeat 3 or 4 times or until dough doubles in size. Leave uncovered throughout.

5 Spread each with tomato mixture then top with grated cheese. Garnish attractively with anchovies and olives then cook individually, allowing 5 minutes at full power.

Teatime Bun Scones

On a nippy winter's day, what could be more cheering than a pot of freshly brewed tea and these indulgent Bun Scones, eaten while still warm, drenched in butter and topped with summer strawberry jam or some exotic honey?

Preparation time: about 15 minutes

Makes 8 (F)

225 g (8 oz/2 cups) wholemeal (graham) flour
5 ml (1 tsp) cream of tartar
5 ml (1 tsp) bicarbonate of soda (baking soda)
1.25 ml (¼ tsp) salt
20 ml (4 tsp) caster (superfine) sugar
25 g (1 oz/2 tbsp) butter or margarine at room temperature
150 ml (¼ pt/⅔ cup) buttermilk
fresh milk or beaten egg for brushing
extra caster (superfine) sugar mixed with cinnamon
for sprinkling

1   Tip flour into a bowl then sift in cream of tartar, bicarbonate of soda and salt. Toss in sugar then rub in butter or margarine finely.

2   Using a fork, mix to a soft dough with buttermilk. Turn out on to a floured surface and knead quickly and lightly until smooth.

3   Pat or roll out to 1 cm (½ inch) in thickness then cut into 8 rounds with a 5 cm (2 inch) fluted biscuit cutter. Use re-rolled trimmings to make the required number.

4   Place round the edge of a greased 25 cm (10 inch) dinner plate. Brush with milk or beaten egg then sprinkle with sugar and cinnamon. Leave uncovered.

5   Cook for 4 minutes at full power. Leave to stand 3 or 4 minutes then transfer to a wire cooling rack. Eat while still warm as suggested above.

CONFECTIONERY

Microwave ovens weave their own special magic where sweet making is concerned and I am constantly surprised at how quick and fuss-free it is to produce the sort of confectionery one can pack up and give as gifts, offer round at home or sell at stalls gracing garden fêtes, school open days and fund-raising events for charity. A short selection follows with these major advantages:

1 They can be made in dishes instead of pans so there is less messy washing up.

2 The mixtures do not boil over.

3 The danger of burning oneself is reduced.

4 The mixtures need not be stirred all the time as when cooked conventionally – just occasionally.

Walnut Candy

A cross between toffee and fudge, this is a super confection with a lovely, old-fashioned flavour and crumbly texture.

Preparation time: about 30 minutes plus setting time

Makes 450g (1lb)

350g (12oz/1½ cups) soft light brown (coffee) sugar
150ml (¼pt/⅔cup) milk
50g (2oz/3tbsp) golden (light corn) syrup
25g (1oz/2tbsp) butter
5ml (1tsp) vanilla essence (extract)
50g (2oz/½cup) walnuts, coarsely chopped

1   Well butter a shallow dish of 1 litre (1¾ pt/4¼ cup) capacity. It makes no difference whether it is square or round.

2   Put all ingredients, except nuts, into a 1.75 litre (3pt/7½ cup) dish. Leave uncovered and cook 14 minutes at full power, stirring 4 or 5 times.

3   Remove from oven, cool 5 minutes, then stand in the sink with enough cold water to come half way up sides of dish.

4   Leave for a further 8 minutes then lift out and wipe base and sides dry.

5   Add walnuts and beat candy (hard work) for a few minutes until it starts to lighten in colour.

6   Spread into prepared dish and allow to set. Remove from dish by lifting up with a knife then break candy into pieces.

7   Store in a polythene bag or tin.

Brazil Nut Candy

Makes 450g (1lb)

Use coarsely chopped brazils instead of walnuts.

Coffee Truffles

Classy affairs, with their roots deep set in France. They are decidedly on the rich side and look elegant and presentable in sweet paper cases.

Preparation time: about 15 minutes

Makes 15

1 bar (100g/4oz) plain (semi-sweet) chocolate
50g (2oz/¼cup) butter
15ml (1 tbsp) instant coffee powder
100g (4oz/½cup) icing (confectioners') sugar, sifted
cocoa (unsweetened chocolate) powder sifted on to a piece of paper

1   Break up chocolate and put into a bowl with butter. Stir in coffee powder.

2   Leave uncovered and melt 4 minutes at defrost setting. Stir until ingredients are well mixed, making sure the coffee has dissolved.

3   Mix in icing sugar thoroughly. Leave about 5 minutes then roll into 15 balls.

4   Toss in cocoa powder and transfer to paper sweet cases. Store in the cool but not in a refrigerator as the Truffles will become too hard.

Plain Truffles

Makes 15

Make as above but omit coffee.

Vanilla, Rum or Sherry Truffles

Makes 15

Make as Coffee Truffles but omit coffee and add 5 ml (1 tsp) vanilla, rum or sherry essence (extract) instead.

Rose or Pistachio Fondants

A touch of gracious living and nostalgia with these delicately-flavoured and pastel-tinted fondants.

Preparation time: about 10 minutes plus setting time

Makes 550 g (1¼ lb)

50 g (2 oz/¼ cup) butter
30 ml (2 tbsp) milk
5 ml (1 tsp) rose or pistachio essence (extract)
450 g (1 lb/2 cups) icing (confectioners') sugar, sifted
red or green food colouring

1   Put butter, milk and essence into a 1.75 litre (3 pt/7½ cup) dish and heat 3 minutes at defrost setting.

2   Work in icing sugar then add a few drops of red or green colouring, mixing until evenly tinted.

3   Knead until smooth then roll out to 1 cm (½ inch) thickness on a surface dusted with sifted icing sugar.

4   Cut into about 30 rounds with an 2.5 cm (1 inch) fluted cutter or 70 rounds with a 1 cm (½ inch) cutter. Leave 2 or 3 hours to dry out then drop into paper sweet cases.

Dinner Party Mints

Makes about 550 g (1¼ lb)

Follow recipe for Rose or Pistachio Fondants, but use peppermint essence (extract). Tint pale green. If liked, dip one side of each in melted chocolate.

Fruit Creams

Makes about 550 g (1¼ lb)

Follow recipe above, but use orange, lemon, strawberry, raspberry or pineapple essence (extract). Tint with matching colours.

Marshmallow Raisin Fudge

Almost fool-proof, this is my favourite recipe for a speedy fudge.

Preparation time: about 7 minutes plus setting time

Makes 350g (12oz)

50g (2 oz/¼ cup) butter
50g (2 oz/¼ cup) soft light brown (coffee) sugar
30ml (2 tbsp) milk
100g (4oz) marshmallows (pink or white)
100g (4oz) icing (confectioners') sugar, sifted
50g (2oz/⅓ cup) raisins

1 Put butter into a 1.75 litre (3 pt/7½ cup) dish with sugar and milk. Heat 4 minutes at defrost setting, stirring twice.

2 Continue to cook a further 4 minutes at full power, stirring twice.

3 Mix in marshmallows. Cook ½ minute at full power. Stir and continue to cook for a further ½ minute. Mix in icing sugar.

4 Stir briskly a few times, add raisins then spread into a 1 litre (1¾ pt/4¼ cup) buttered shallow dish. Leave about 2 hours in the cool or until fudge is set.

5 Cut-up and store in an airtight tin or polythene bag.

Marshmallow Nut Fudge

Makes 350g (12oz)

Add 50g (2oz/¼ cup) chopped walnuts or toasted almonds instead of raisins.

Cherry Petit Fours

Ideal for serving with after-dinner coffee, these fanciful little mouthfuls are designed for entertaining.

Preparation time: about 5 minutes plus setting time

Makes about 12

1 bar (100g/4oz) plain (semi-sweet) chocolate
50g (2oz/¾ cup) digestive biscuits (graham crackers),
finely crushed
6 glacé (candied) cherries, halved

1   Break up chocolate, put into a bowl and melt 3 to 3½ minutes at defrost setting. Leave uncovered.

2   Stir in biscuits then transfer equal amounts to 12 paper sweet cases.

3   Top with halved cherries and leave in the cool until quite firm before serving.

PRESERVES

Making preserves in a microwave is quick, clean and safe. There are no pans of very hot jam or marmalade to contend with, no boiling over and no hassle. The technique is reliable, the preserve a bright colour and the taste is impeccable.

The same maxims apply to preserves made in the microwave as those cooked conventionally on the hob:

1 Choose sound fruit; not over-ripe.

2 Wash well.

3 Stone where possible before cooking.

4 To test for setting, use a sugar thermometer which should register 110°C (220°F). Alternatively, pour a little preserve on a cold saucer. Leave 2 minutes. If a skin forms on top which wrinkles when touched, preserve is ready. If not, cook a little longer, checking at the end of every minute.

5 Skim.

6 Spoon into clean and dry jars. Top with waxed discs. Cover and label when cold.

7 To sterilise and warm empty glass or pottery jars, pour about 45 ml (3 tbsp) water into each. Heat 1½ to 2 minutes at full power. Pour out water. Turn jars upside down to drain on a clean tea towel. If traces of water remain inside, wipe dry with kitchen paper.

8 Store preserve in a cool, dark and dry place.

Jam

Yield about 675g (1½lb)

To make jam in the microwave, keep to smallish quantities of fruit (450g/1lb). Put the fruit into a 2.25 litre (4pt/10cup) dish and cook to the pulpy stage with water, *but no sugar,* as given in the chart Cooking Fresh Fruit on page 224. Afterwards add the amount of boiling water and granulated or preserving sugar etc., given below. Stir well, return to microwave and leave uncovered. Cook 5 to 7 minutes at full power until sugar has completely dissolved, stirring twice. Continue to cook, uncovered, for 20 to 40 minutes at full power (time will depend on fruit) or until setting point is reached (see previous page). Stir frequently throughout cooking. Skim at the end. Pot, cover and label.

Apple and Blackberry

Add 15ml (1tbsp) water and 450g (1lb/2cups) sugar.

Apricot

Add 15ml (1tbsp) water, 450g (1lb/2cups) sugar and juice of ½ lemon.

Blackberry

Add 450g (1lb/2cups) sugar and 15ml (1tbsp) lemon juice but *no* additional water.

Raspberry

Cook to pulp as given in chart under Apples (page 225), allowing 4 to 6 minutes but with *no* water. Add 450g (1lb/2cups) sugar.

Strawberry

Cook to pulp as given in chart under Apples (page 225), allowing 4 to 6 minutes but with *no* water. Add 390 g (13½ oz/scant 1¾ cups) sugar and juice of half a small lemon.

Blackcurrant

Add 300 ml (½ pt/1¼ cups) water and 525 g (1 lb 3 oz/scant 2½ cups) sugar.

Gooseberry

Add 150 ml (¼ pt/⅔ cup) less 15 ml (1 tbsp) water and 450 g (1 lb/ 2 cups) sugar.

Peach

Add 45 ml (3 tbsp) water, 390 g (13½ oz/scant 1¾ cups) sugar and juice of 1 small lemon.

Plums and Greengages

Add 15 ml (1 tbsp) water and 450 g (1 lb/2 cups) sugar. Preferably remove stones before cooking.

Dried Apricot Jam

A handsomely-flavoured jam with a thousand and one uses.

Preparation time: about 50 minutes plus setting time

Makes 900 g (2 lb)

*225 g (8 oz/1⅓ cups) dried apricots, soaked overnight in 600 ml
(1 pt/2½ cups) water
900 g (2 lb/4 cups) granulated or preserving sugar
strained juice of 1 large lemon*

1 Put apricots and water into a large bowl. Cook, uncovered, for 15 to 20 minutes at full power or until fruit is soft and tender.

2 Add sugar and lemon juice. Return to microwave. Leave uncovered and cook about 5 minutes when sugar should be dissolved. Stir twice.

3 Contine to cook, uncovered, a further 20 to 25 minutes at full power or until setting point is reached. (See introduction.)

4 Leave until lukewarm then pot and cover.

TIP: *For ease of eating, snip apricots into 4 pieces before cooking.*

Mixed Fruit Marmalade

A full-flavoured marmalade which does credit to the microwave. Use plump and juicy fruits, well washed and dried before using.

Preparation time: about 2 hours 10 minutes plus setting time

Makes about 2.5-2.75 kg (5-6 lb)

2 grapefruit
2 oranges
2 lemons
900 ml (1½ pt/3¾ cups) boiling water
2 kg (4 lb/8 cups) granulated or preserving sugar

1 Peel fruit thinly and cut rind into fine, medium or thick strips, depending on personal taste.

2 Halve each piece of fruit and squeeze out the juice. Pour into a *large* bowl. Save all the pips and tie in a clean cloth with cut-up white pith. Add to bowl.

3 Add 300 ml (½ pt/1¼ cups) of the boiling water and leave to stand 1 hour. Pour in remaining water then cover bowl with cling film. Puncture twice with the tip of a knife.

4 Cook 20 to 30 minutes at full power, time depending on the thickness of the skin.

5 Uncover. Stir in sugar and return to microwave. Leave uncovered and cook about 8 minutes or until sugar dissolves, stirring 4 times.

6 Continue to cook, uncovered, for another 30 to 35 minutes or until setting point is reached. (For testing, see Jam.) Stir every 7 to 10 minutes.

7 Leave until lukewarm, remove and discarde tied-up pips and pith then transfer marmalade to clean, dry jars. Cover and label when cold.

TIP: *It is important to leave marmalade until lukewarm before potting to prevent the peel from rising up in the jars on cooling.*

Lemon Curd

Very fresh, very lemony and quite delicious! Make in small quantities and store in the refrigerator to prevent spoilage. Based on eggs and butter, the curd quickly deteriorates if left out and about.

Preparation time: about 10 minutes plus setting time

Makes about 450g (1lb)

100g (4oz/½ cup) butter
3 (size 3) eggs **plus** *1 extra yolk*
225g (8oz/1 cup) caster (superfine) sugar
finely grated rind and juice of 3 lemons

1   Put butter into a 1.2 litre (2pt/5 cup) basin and heat 4 minutes at defrost setting.

2   Add rest of ingredients, first beaten well together.

3   Leave uncovered and cook 5 minutes at full power, beating at the end of every minute with a wooden spoon.

4   When curd is thick and coats the back of a spoon in an even layer, remove from oven and spoon into 1 or 2 small clean jars or pots. Cover as for Jam (page 293).

TIP: *If curd looks a little too thin, cook for a further ½-1 minute.*

Apple Chutney

Made from garden windfalls – or even your best crop – and with the full taste of autumn behind it, chutney fares well in a microwave as you will find out when you try the recipe. A few variations follow:

Preparation time: about 50 minutes

Makes about 900 g (2 lb)

450 g (1 lb/4 cups) cooking (tart) apples, peeled and chopped
100 g (4 oz/1 cup) onions, peeled and chopped
15 ml (1 tbsp) salt
60 ml (4 tbsp) water
250 ml (12 fl oz/scant 1½ cups) malt vinegar
225 g (8 oz/1 cup) soft dark brown (coffee) sugar
1 garlic clove, peeled and crushed
100 g (4 oz/⅔ cup) chopped dates
100 g (4 oz/⅔ cup) raisins
15 ml (1 tbsp) ground ginger
5 ml (1 tsp) cinnamon
5 ml (1 tsp) mixed (apple pie) spice
1.25-2.5 ml (¼-½ tsp) cayenne pepper
1 bouquet garni bag

1 Put apples and onions into large bowl. Mix in salt and water. Cover with a plate and cook 5 minutes at full power.

2 Mix in all remaining ingredients. Leave uncovered and cook 30 to 40 minutes at full power until chutney has thickened to a jam-like consistency.

3 Stir often and cook an extra 5 to 10 minutes if necessary. Remove and discard bouquet garni bag. Leave chutney, covered with a lid, overnight for flavours to blend and mature.

4 The next day pot and cover as for Jam (page 293).

Variations

Follow basic recipe but use half apples and half pears. *Or* half apples, half topped and tailed gooseberries. *Or* half apples, half chopped green tomatoes.

DRINKS

Milk

Milk is easily heated up in the microwave and runs less risk of boiling over than if warmed conventionally in a saucepan on the hob.

To heat until hot, pour 300 ml (½ pt/1¼ cups) milk into a glass or pottery jug. Leave uncovered and heat 1½ to 2 minutes at full power.

To bring milk just up to the boil, follow directions above and heat 2½ to 3 minutes at full power.

Cocoa

1 cup

Put 15-20 ml (3-4 tsp) cocoa (unsweetened chocolate) powder into a large cup or mug (not teacup size as it is a bit too small). Mix smoothly with 15-30 ml (1-2 tbsp) cold milk. Add a further 150 ml (¼ pt/⅔ cup) cold milk and whisk gently to ensure even mixing. Leave uncovered and heat 1¾ to 2 minutes at full power or until cocoa just comes up to the boil. Add sugar to taste.

Hot Chocolate

1 cup

Make as above, using drinking chocolate powder instead of cocoa. Leave uncovered and heat 1¾ to 2 minutes or until very hot. Stir round, sweeten to taste if necessary.

Coffee with Milk

Make as cocoa, using 5-10 ml (1-2 tsp) instant coffee powder instead of cocoa.

Quick Cappucino

Fill a fairly large cup with cold, leftover strong coffee. Add 15-20 ml (3-4 tsp) low fat milk powder (milk solids) mixed smoothly with 10 ml (2 tsp) cold water. Heat about 1½ minutes at full power or until very hot and foamy. Sweeten as desired, stir round and sprinkle with drinking chocolate powder.

Reheating Leftover Coffee

Because of speed, there is no stale flavour when remains of a pot of coffee are reheated. Pour into cups and reheat, individually, for about 1 minute at full power. Add milk or cream and sugar to taste.

TIP: *A cup of tea which has gone cold can also be revitalised in this way – but don't use the stewed remains of a pot.*

Jaffa Wine Mull

Tangy, zesty and spicy – all the ingredients needed for mulled wine.

Preparation time: about 15 minutes

Serves 5 to 6

2 large grapefruit
600 ml (1 pt/2½ cups) medium dry red wine
5 cm (2 in) piece of cinnamon stick
3 cloves
100 g (4 oz/½ cup) granulated sugar
30 ml (2 tbsp) whisky or brandy

1   Halve grapefruit and squeeze out juice. Strain into a large bowl then add wine, cinnamon stick, cloves and sugar.

2   Cover with a plate and heat 6 to 8 minutes at full power, stirring twice. Remove from oven and leave to stand 5 minutes.

3   Stir round again and add whisky or brandy. Ladle into handled cups or glasses and serve.

Winter Punch

A Punch to thaw you out in a very civilised way.

Preparation time: about 14 minutes

Serves about 6

450 ml (¾ pt/2 cups) apple juice
150 ml (¼ pt/⅔ cup) ruby port
300 ml (½ pt/1¼ cups) orange juice
2.5 ml (½ tsp) cinnamon

1   Put all ingredients into a large bowl and cover with a plate.

2   Heat at full power for about 5 to 8 minutes when Punch should be hot but not boiling. Leave to stand 5 minutes. Stir.

3   Ladle into handled cups or glasses and serve.

ODDS AND ENDS

Toasting Nuts, Other Cereals and Seeds

Although microwave ovens are reputed not to brown – and for many dishes this holds perfectly true – they nevertheless have a marvellous effect on nuts, as demonstrated by the short selection of ideas below. Even if the toasting process is no swifter than it would be in a conventional oven or under the grill, the saving in fuel is appreciable, the whole operation is clean and tidy, and the browning is evenly distributed with minimal effort.

The type of dish or plate used will affect the cooking time to some extent, and nuts on a pottery plate will take marginally longer than those in a glass dish such as Pyrex.

Toasted Flaked Almonds

Spread 100 g (4 oz/1 cup) flaked almonds on to a 25 cm (10 inch) pottery plate or put into a 18 cm (7 inch) round glass dish. Leave uncovered. Toast in the microwave for 6 to 7 minutes at full power or until nuts become light golden brown. Move about with a wooden spoon or fork at the end of every minute. Remove from oven but leave on the plate or in the dish so that they go on gently cooking and crisping. When cold, store in an airtight jar or tin.

Buttered Flaked Almonds

Superb sprinkled over cooked vegetables such as cauliflower or broccoli, buttered almonds take a few minutes to prepare in the microwave and work well every time.

Put 15 g (½ oz/1 tbsp) butter into a 20 cm (8 inch) round and fairly shallow dish. Melt, uncovered, ¾ to 1 minute at full power. Add 50 g (2 oz/½ cup) flaked almonds. Cook, uncovered, for 6 minutes at full power or until golden brown. Use straight away, otherwise the butter congeals.

Toasted Whole Almonds

Make as Toasted Flaked Almonds but use 100 g (4 oz/1 cup) blanched whole almonds instead.

Toasted Cashews

Make as Toasted Flaked Almonds but use 100 g (4 oz/1 cup) cashews instead.

Toasted Hazelnuts

This technique will give you toasted nuts with skins which are easy to rub off.

Make as Toasted Flaked Almonds but use 100 g (4 oz/1 cup) hazelnuts instead. Cook for 10 minutes at full power, moving nuts with a wooden spoon or fork at the end of every 1½ minutes. Leave to cool then rub off skins with a tea-towel.

Toasted Pine Nuts

Make as Toasted Flaked Almonds but use 100 g (4 oz/1 cup) pine nuts instead.

Toasted Desiccated (Shredded) Coconut

Make as Toasted Flaked Almonds but use 100 g (4 oz/1 cup) desiccated (shredded) coconut instead and cook 5 minutes at full power.

Toasted Coconut Curls

These are curling coconut strips which look a bit like narrow noodles. To brown, make as Toasted Flaked Almonds but use 100 g (4 oz/1 cup) coconut strands (coarse shredded coconut) instead and cook 5½ to 6 minutes at full power.

Toasted Rolled Oats

Make as Toasted Flaked Almonds but use 100 g (4 oz/1 cup) rolled oats instead and cook 6½ to 7 minutes at full power.

Toasted Sesame Seeds

As these can brown suddenly and burn, a pottery plate slows down the cooking process which, in this instance, is more beneficial than glass. Make as Toasted Flaked Almonds but use 100 g (4 oz/1 cup) sesame seeds instead and cook 12 minutes at full power, moving seeds with a wooden spoon or fork at the end of every 2 minutes.

Toasted Peanuts

Spread 450 g (1 lb/4 cups) shelled peanuts over the turntable or put into a large round or square dish. Cook, uncovered, for 15 to 17 minutes at full power. Carefully turn nuts over with a spatula every 5 minutes to ensure even browning. If nuts have brown skins, rub off between palms of hands or in a clean tea-towel. Store in an airtight tin when cold. Peanuts have a natural sodium (salt) content and, when treated this way, you will find they taste as though they are very slightly salted.

Drying Herbs

If you grown your own herbs, you will know the tedium of trying to dry them successfully for winter use, especially if you are dependent on hot sun in our unpredictable climate. This is where a microwave reduces the hassle to nil and carries out the process quickly and efficiently, ensuring that your annual crop can be dealt with in minutes. Each variety of herb should be dried separately and stored in airtight jars.

Cut herbs off shrubs, remove leaves from stalks (needles in the case of rosemary) and loosely pack into a 300 ml (½ pt/1¼ cup) measuring jug, filling it almost to overflowing. Tip into a colander and rinse quickly and gently. Leave to drain then dry thoroughly between a clean, folded tea towel. Transfer to 2 sheets (one on top of the other) of kitchen paper, placed on turntable. Spread out to form an even layer. Heat for 5 to 6 minutes at full power, carefully moving herbs about on the paper 2 or 3 times. As soon as they sound like the rustle of autumnal leaves and lose their bright green colour, you can take it the herbs are dried through. If not, give them a further 1 to 1½ minutes. Remove from oven and crush by rubbing between hands. Tip into jars with airtight stoppers, label and store away from bright light.

Dried Chestnuts

Easier, I believe, to cope with than fresh ones, the microwave renders dried chestnuts cooked and usable in about 1¾ hours, without either soaking overnight or prolonged cooking.

Wash 250 g (9 oz/a good 2 cups) packet of dried chestnuts thoroughly. Put into a 1.75 litre (3 pt/7½ cup) dish and mix in 600 ml (1 pt/2½ cups) boiling water. Cover with a plate and cook 15 minutes at full power. Leave to stand 15 minutes. Cook a further 15 minutes at full power then stand for another 15 minutes. Add an extra 150 ml (¼ pt/⅔ cup) boiling water and cook a further 10 minutes at full power. Remove from oven and stir round. Cover again with a plate and leave to stand for a final 15 minutes. Stir twice every time they are cooking.

Couscous

Typically North African, Couscous is a traditional accompaniment to hearty meat stews laced with every vegetable under the hot desert sun. It can be cooked separately in the microwave and takes only a few minutes.

Preparation time: about 5 minutes

Serves 4 to 6 (F)

225 g (8 oz/2 cups) couscous
600 ml (1 pt/2½ cups) boiling water
2.5 ml (½ tsp) salt
15 g (½ oz/1 tbsp) butter, margarine or olive oil

1 Put all ingredients into a 1.75 litre (3 pt/7½ cup) glass or pottery dish.

2 Cover with a plate and cook 4 minutes at full power.

3 Uncover and fluff up with a fork. Serve very hot with stews of chicken, beef or lamb.

Crisp Breadcrumbs (Raspings)

There is no better place than a microwave oven for making fine white or brown breadcrumbs, the kind top haute cuisiners always recommend for coating foods such as turkey escalopes or fish fillets, destined to be fried conventionally in deep fat or oil. Not only is crumbing in the microwave a marvellous way of using up stale bread and end crusts of loaves, but the resultant crumbs become dry and crisp without deepening in colour to the goldfish yellow often found in packeted varieties. Once cold and popped into an airtight container, the crumbs will keep almost indefinitely in the cool.

Turn 100 g (4 oz/2 cups) stale bread (white, brown or a mixture) into crumbs, the finer the better. Tip into a 25 cm (10 inch) round dish which is not too deep – about 5 cm (2 inches) only. Cook, uncovered, at full power for 5 to 6 minutes, stirring 4 times. Remove from oven and leave until the crumbs crispen and cool, stirring occasionally. Store as recommended above.

Poppadums

If you usually grill rather than fry poppadums, you'll find microwaving them more successful – they don't brown.

Put 1 poppadum at a time on a plate or directly on the turntable. Cook at full power for 45 seconds or until starting to puff-up. Turn over and cook until puffy all over.

Cheese Fondue

The après-ski favourite of European Alpine resorts, Fondue is a hearty, sustaining meal and well-suited to blustery days and nights. It's a hospitable dish too, in that everyone circles round it and literally dips in, formality going to the winds. Fondue is quick and simple to make in the microwave. Use Cheddar and cider and omit the Kirsch if you prefer.

Preparation time: about 12 minutes

Serves 6

1 garlic clove, peeled
175 g (6 oz/1½ cups) Emmental cheese, grated
450 g (1 lb/4 cups) Gruyère cheese, grated
15 ml (1 tbsp) cornflour (cornstarch)
300 ml (½ pt/1¼ cups) dry white wine
5 ml (1 tsp) lemon juice
30 ml (2 tbsp) Kirsch
salt and pepper to taste
French bread cut into cubes for serving

1   Crush garlic into a 2.25 litre (4 pt/10 cup) glass or pottery dish. Add both cheeses, cornflour, wine and lemon juice.

2   Leave uncovered and cook until Fondue bubbles gently; about 7 to 8 minutes at full power. Stir at least 3 times.

3   Remove from oven then stir in Kirsch. Season to taste and eat by spearing a cube of bread onto a fork and swirling it round in the cheese mixture. Accompany with tots of Kirsch and hot tea.

HINTS AND TIPS

1   To have plate meals ready on tap, arrange cooked foods (such as meat and two or more vegetables) on individual dinner plates. Place the meat, poultry, bacon, sausages, hamburgers or fried fish and dense vegetables like potatoes towards the outside of the dish *without piling up*, then arrange assorted vegetables, pasta or rice in the centre. Coat with gravy or sauce. Cover with cling film. To serve, puncture film twice with the tip of a knife then reheat each plate individually from frozen. Allow 5 to 6 minutes at full power, depending on the dish. Food is ready when the base of the plate feels piping hot in the centre. Leave to stand 3 to 5 minutes before serving.

2   To soften ice cream and loosen jellies (provided they are not in metal tins or moulds), heat 45 seconds at defrost setting. Stand 2 to 3 minutes.

3   To melt golden (light corn) or other syrups and honey which have become grainy (crystallised), take metal caps off jars and warm, individually, for about 3 minutes at defrost setting, stirring once if necessary.

4   Sometimes dishes become too hot to handle as they absorb heat from the cooked food. For comfort remove from oven with gloves.

5   To soften 225 g (8 oz/1 cup) brown (coffee) sugar that has become lumpy or hard, put it into a dish with half a slice of very fresh bread. Cover and warm 1½ minutes at defrost setting. Alternatively, heat sugar with a wedge of cut fruit (pear or apple) instead of bread. Another method is to cover sugar with a piece of wet kitchen paper and use neither bread nor fruit.

Q

R

S

DEDICATION

To my brother, Dave Hampton, the Carbon Coach,
because through decades when my heart would not accept it
he knew and served the truth.

Sue Hampton interviewed by Leslie Tate, October 2020

REBELLING FOR LIFE

How has the climate crisis changed you as a person and as a writer?

It has shaken me to the core, put me on antidepressants and obsessed me. It's also reinforced the values with which I was brought up, but which I set to one side as an overworked mum and consumer. Now I feel the same love for trees that made my father weep when one of 'ours' had to be cut down, and the same connection to the natural world under threat that my busyness had blocked.

For years, as I absorbed the truth about climate, I thought that I could consider my fiction my own particular kind of activism. That was convenient, because writing is what I love and do best. It made sense because I believed in the power of fiction to effect both personal and societal change, and I haven't lost faith in that power, but scale makes a difference and eventually I recognised that without a big publisher I'm deluding myself.

In START, written before I realised just how quickly breakdown would be upon us, and what that would mean around the world, Venice goes under, and it's the alarm the West needs. It was harrowing to write, but much less harrowing than the future as science now foresees it. When I resolved to write exclusively about climate change in my novels and short stories, I had already reached a point where my self-styled *keyboard warrior* identity could no longer excuse me from physical action. My (then) publishers Magic Oxygen had already rushed out an e-book called THE BIGGEST SPLASH in which four women take direct action to new limits, shocking the few who downloaded it. After speaking at Preston New Road fracking site about the role of stories in the world, I began adapting my own experience with Extinction Rebellion 2018-19 into a novel, which I released chapter by chapter on my website, a few weeks behind real time, under the title FOR LIFE. It's now an e-book and can be downloaded for a donation to XR. It's not my story, because it's populated with fictional characters, but I've been in the same locations

7

and shared their experiences. I hoped that by giving readers on the uncommitted outskirts of rebellion an intimate insight into the movement, FOR LIFE would play a very small role in recruitment as well as fundraising. Although the backdrop for the story is largely the April Rebellion on Waterloo Bridge, I wrote postscripts in order to draw on the contexts of my arrest in Trafalgar Square that October, and my involvement in the Climate Vigil which led up to Lent this year [2020] – and, as it turned out, into lockdown.

Creating climate activists is natural for me because I know so many, and rebels bond quickly but deeply. We skip the small for the biggest issue of all and while we don't all retain the fine detail of the science – personally, emotionally, I can't – we all know the truth and we're frightened. We mourn the same loss and we live, to varying degrees, with hope as well as grief, but sometimes that's harder to believe in. When I wrote INTACT, I created a character who, like some 70%+ of the UK population, knows there is a problem and is increasingly aware of ways she could make changes in response, but as a partner and mother she's preoccupied with love on a more intimate scale. I knew I had to do for Mags what is so hard to do in person with others – to wake and shake her, and yes, to an extent break her too. I had to change that theoretical, subsidiary acceptance into the kind of fundamental, pressing and overwhelming understanding beyond knowledge that can't be unfelt or unknown. But it's a slow process, as it was for me. Because how I write is almost as important to me as what I write, I've been mindful of the danger of polemic and continued to be the kind of author who lets my characters take the lead. They have to seem almost as real to me as the crisis that is a climate and ecological emergency. So here, as in FOR LIFE, there's a strange intersection between stark, horrifying reality and imaginative belief.

The short answer to how the climate crisis has changed me as a writer is that it's preoccupied me, made me doubt the value of such indirect activism and brought me to a point where only non-violent civil disobedience is enough – and the least that I, as a privileged white woman in the UK, can do – for those suffering in the Global South, species and habitats at risk and those yet unborn.

As a person, it's made me terribly sad and utterly determined in equal measure. Having believed I don't do anger, I've found some – towards governments, corporations and much of the media. It's turned me from a vegetarian to a vegan; I haven't flown for fourteen years and won't be patronising any airline again. Bizarrely I have the confidence to address

8

a crowd, without practice or notes – even though I often choose not to speak on a Zoom when the group is small. I'm less self-conscious, though, and feel able to mix with rebels minus make-up! My relatively recent activism, involving occupations, creative protests, arrests, glue-ons and lock-ons, self-representing in court last year and now preparing for another trial, has taken me where I never expected to go: police cells, a meat wagon in handcuffs, the dock – and it was a while before I recovered from the shock. Like my character Em in THE PRISONER, I was Head Girl and top of the class. I'm shy. I stick rigidly to other rules and will take the long route round rather than tread on someone's grass. So there was a certain amount of stress and trauma to survive but I'm through it now. I've been described, after five arrests, as 'hard-core', which amuses me as a weepy Pacifist Quaker with quiet good manners. And I'm often seen as brave, which is just as ridiculous, because I'm frightened of so many things: hurting or failing others, their disapproval, saying the wrong thing or saying too little; speaking the truth with friends and family and engaging strangers at protests; dogs, rats and any animal that comes too close, especially if it's loud and jumps up; dementia and loss of love. But am I braver? It's a case of having to be, because most of all I'm afraid of doing any less than the most I personally can manage in order to bring about the change that's essential to the survival of all species including ours. Physically, I've discovered that I can endure an overnight lock-on followed by an overnight stay in a cell, in spite of health issues – which surprises me! I cared passionately about the children I taught, and being a good teacher; I cared about being the best writer I could be. But I care SO much more about this. Of course I do! When I don't respond to calls to action I feel disturbing guilt which overlays the climate grief and brings me very low.

Am I a misery? I hope that's a no, or not often anyway. In XR we recognise the importance of *regen* and for me, that means Quaker medi-tation, a walk with Leslie, time with my grandson, reading a great novel, dancing or watching a quiz show or *Strictly*, real friendship. But yes, I'm more serious than I used to be. I read climate news and reports, and download non-fiction as well as literature. So we try to celebrate the good things in our lives and the world, however small, and remember the importance of gratitude. I no longer give myself a lift with new clothes, but the fact is that my little daily gestures of dedication, to Peace, Love, Truth and Justice, bring me energising joy. And I don't care if anyone thinks I'm weird or take things too far. How far should we take protect-ing life on earth?

Another way of answering the question is to claim the certainty that the climate crisis has helped me recover my core self and the daughter my dad, a Conscientious Objector and anti-materialist, loved and inspired.

Poem written in a police cell after my arrest at Stop the Arms Fair
DSEI September 2019

No Faith in War

7 a.m.
My view is different now:
an open skyful, grubby white,
a flight path torn with roaring.
I may be lying
on the road to hell.
Top left, the concrete's dark, unyielding.
Right, leaves shift and shudder high.
Seagulls loop on the wind.
Punctuating my skyline,
magpies jut out like chimneys from a roof.
And when I close my eyes, the darkness
is a scarlet weave.
I cross my legs to still the shaking.
Constrained by pain, my body's resisting,
my hand caught tight around the lock
I hooked inside the tube
through a case that says Calvin Klein.
From the hotel, cars free to slide away
are low on my radar as cats.
Beside me leaves scud scratchy, close and wild.
Bound together in love, the three of us don't talk.
The kit keeps us apart,
held in Quaker silence,
in hope, patience, conviction,
in the PEACE stitched vivid on a cloth without an altar.

9 a.m.
My scalp and shoulders are pillowed now.
Under a banner linking legs on tarmac
and a scarf from a skip,
I'm lifted.
Around us, small but focused, a Meeting's gathered.

11

I have no needs to meet
but smiles, a little conversation,
my father's hand reaching down with the rest
to hold on.
And an end to this,
but not yet.
In Yemen roads are bloodied and skies
rain merchandise from merchandise.
We're stopping the Arms Fair.
No weapons pass.
Plush and vast, the showroom space awaits unfilled
and this road is to Emmaus.
We did it.
Grandma did it.

11 a.m.
I'm shielded under pressure.
A shower sparks firework red around my boots.
The cutters burn,
the air's industrial.
In black the team crouch, sweat and struggle,
pass surgical tools for this theatre.
It's tough, all of it,
their challenge, ours.
As an observer starts to cry,
I smile at Leslie so he knows I'm not afraid.
My fingers, trapped, arthritic, curl stiff at the core.
The drill rattles hard.
Heat circles my hand until I'm free,
escorted to the van.
My legs fold and sway
but I hear the cheers.
Handcuffed, I smile and make a peace sign
through closing doors.

About Climate Grief & Depression

When my dad was depressed we didn't use the word. I didn't even think it. He would become silent and his face would set, emptied of everything but the depression. No impish smiles, playfulness or affection. Sometimes on Sundays he would eat nothing and lie on the bed all day, face to the wall, barely moving. I'd go in, climb on the cover with him and whisper love, trying to hold his hand or stroke his head. I found it hard to bear because I adored him. He understood and supported me, the real me. When my love was not enough, it hurt. And all the time, my mum was being strong and brave, as if Daddy just wasn't well or work was difficult and everything would be fine.

I wanted to be like him, to share his passions and ideals, to write beautifully too. Now I am depressed, and I'm glad he isn't here to see it because he blamed himself for so much and was overcome by penitent guilt after those stiff, silent Sundays. He was sensitive and intense and I am drawn to that, choose it. But he was also warm, creative, clever and funny, looked like Gary Cooper and reminded me of Atticus Finch. I can't manage conflict but I recognise that anger like his, rare as it was, can be part of depression. But I'm not really comfortable with signing off, Extinction Rebellion style, with *love and rage*, even though XR is beautifully peaceful and doesn't shame, and the rage is just a burden of frustration that in spite of all we know, emissions continue to rise and the world is still, as Greta and Australia remind us, on fire.

I could call my depression climate grief and that would feel terribly true. Millions must be feeling it, some of them – cruelly – still at school. Dad felt the beginnings of it, because he could see what humans were doing to the natural world. That was why he never owned a car or took a flight. He was a Pacifist (and young Conscientious Objector) who believed in living simply in order to inflict as little damage as possible on the earth, loved trees as I have learned to do, nurtured his garden, read literature and philosophy, wrote poetry and took me to art galleries, the ballet and theatre, where we cherished what was beautiful and sad. I grew up believing they were pretty much the same thing and I don't know that I've changed my mind. Love, after all, is both, and everything. Dad's faith was individual and didn't take him to church but it was not in humanity, in spite of his reverence for imaginative and sacrificial genius. He admired Gandhi and Martin Luther King as well as Jesus, and when Mandela spoke at Southwark Cathedral he was first, he said, to applaud, but his work life as an architect exposed him to the grubbiness of greed, dishonesty and irresponsibility as well as the kind of pressure on which I don't believe many of us thrive. Dad didn't. He didn't fit the London business world any more than he'd belonged at boarding school, where he wept for home, was bullied and excelled. He despaired of human cruelty, injustice and destructiveness, of selfishness and hypocrisy, of politics and corporations. So that faith of his was itself a kind of loss and yearning, a faith in the crucified Christ rather than any resurrection. While he could put on a social show of skills, I grew to realise as a child how hard he found interaction with anyone who wasn't a soulmate. And I myself became acutely, blushingly shy – still am, in spite of public appearances of one kind or another. I suppose I've learned to appear confident, like Dad did, but I've always been full of fear and now that I'm a Quaker, my open, doubting faith accommodates uncertainty as honest and rational, marvels at mystery, calls me to activism and pretends nothing. Dad must have been almost as disappointed by my evangelical phase, when I thought all he had to do was accept Jesus as his personal Lord and he would be happily healed, as by my oh-so-normal middle-class consumption and lifestyle in my thirties and forties. Now I understand that faith is inspiration but not magic, and I'm clear that being a follower of Jesus makes more sense than ticking a doctrinal checklist of Christian beliefs. It would be wildly irrational and unfaithful to follow Jesus, or Buddha, or Mohammed, without trying to make a better world for all humans and all species. Without trying to avert climate catastrophe. It would make a mockery of love, which is the only God I am willing to obey. The Quaker phrase "attend to what love requires of you" is always with me. That's why I am a peace and climate activist. Dad would be proud if he'd lived to see me arrested and defend myself in court, but he'd be terribly sad that it's necessary. I imagine he'd feel just as I do. So I'm glad he died before it dawned on anyone that we'd finally hit a climate emergency, and before our government was peopled by callous careerists who turn their backs on refugee children and are eager to increase arms sales so Saudi Arabia can bomb school buses and hospitals, while continuing to subsidise fossil fuels here and around an endangered world.

It took me a while to recognise that I'm depressed rather than just saddened by the world. Like Dad I'm in love, in my case with a kind, funny, gifted and complex husband who stores the climate facts I struggle to retain. Unlike Dad, I have many wonderful friends. I've always been an emotional person but I've been able to switch on a smile, be the teacher, then author, *snap out of it* for social reasons. In October, I couldn't, and that scared me. I was spending more and more time disconnected from my husband and unable to call one of my closest friends. Too much silence, and not the Quaker Meeting kind, which is giving and enlightens, but the helpless, numbing, chest-tightening kind that welcomes nothing but sleep. A fear of going out and seeing someone I know and being unable to show them the Sue they expect. That heaviness I saw in Dad, immobilising and freezing. An inability to open my mouth because I just "don't know" what would help or what to do. After all, nothing the CBT therapy suggests will arrest climate breakdown. And unless I'm physically trying to do that, I feel a failure. After actions, there's a comedown. But arrests and court appearances have been harder than I anticipated and for someone who aims to please and be approved, it hurts that I'm a *criminal* now.

So I'm on antidepressants and I regret it, not because they haven't helped but because they do, so I tried to wean myself off them with a sense of shame and weakness that I know I shouldn't feel, and it's proving tough. And part of me thinks that if I was a more full-time activist I'd be and feel better. But a small part of me wishes I was in full-time functional denial instead, and not just once a day or week when I watch *Richard Osman's House of Games* or *The Greatest Dancer*. Because then happiness might be possible. It would be easy to stay afloat in the bubble of romantic commitment, regardless of the world around the two of us. I know, though, that if we're to change the future we can't delude ourselves. And in a theoretical way I know how to do that without the limiting self-absorption of depression. The secret, as always, is love. Because although anyone will understand why I linked it with sadness, the only real joy lies in loving. Love makes us vulnerable, but it's the most powerful force I know. I don't love as well as I want but I use the verb freely because that's the way I love – not just Leslie and the family closest to me but new rebel friends, old friends I haven't seen for years, Greta, Caroline Lucas, Van Gogh, Susan Fletcher's novels, the cello, Meryl Streep, Jodie Whitaker's Doctor, George Eliot, Barber's Adagio, the trilogy that began with Before Sunrise ... The snowdrops I just stood to love as they secretly stirred in the stillness; that even on a grey day, grass can blade silver; the surprise that moss can be so woolly, contoured over earth like a jumper on flesh, and a robin can pause and charm me as if I've found my way into a story that will fill me up. The way a colourless sky shines with a deeper, whiter light than anything we can create. The young kangaroo burned against the wire in a harrowing image that will always stay with me. Elephant loyalty and penguin community. The scent of hyacinths, jasmine and lily-of-the-valley. That every rainbow is exciting enough to be announced and shared from our flat. That my bare scalp feels the sun and rain more intensely now I don't hide it. The desire to express something important and wordless in dance.

With love comes gratitude and in this moment of clarity I know I have much to live for. I know I am loved. I wouldn't blame Pacific islanders and other indigenous peoples already suffering from climate change, or the people of Yemen, the Syrians of Idlib, those whose children are sick and traumatised in overcrowded refugee camps, and those enduring racist or homophobic hate fermented in countries like mine by right wing leaders, for asking what reason a privileged white woman in leafy Hertfordshire could possibly have to surrender to depression. A more pragmatic person might warn me not to ruin the rest of my life focusing on what's to come. Why not seize the day? But the truth about the climate emergency is completely overwhelming and once taken into the heart, can only direct the way we live. What I must try to hold on to is the love that makes loss real, and the hope that it will override short-termism, ambition, profit, nationalism, war ... because if protecting life on earth is not what love requires of us, I don't know what is. There's no debate, just urgency. When depression takes control of me, it means the hope is harder to hold, but nothing has really changed. My therapy beyond snowdrops is the company of rebels who share my grief, and may have treated it with Prozac too, or could. My Leslie's arms around me. Not ducking reality but finding a way through it without giving up. Now, as I write, I believe we can do it. But I accept that tomorrow I may not, that silence could isolate and disempower me as it used to steal Dad's light. That there may be more hours or days ahead when I function on auto from a hollow core. I have no solution to depression, yours or mine, but I know I must keep on loving to be lovable, to be brave, to do what must be done and know what that is. If this is familiar to you, let's join hands and rebel for life together, with love, for love's sake – but also work, day after day to build a world worth saving. To take care of those our pain can hurt, and make our own bubbles beautiful places to share in safety. To watch the snowdrops stir.

Poem written in the National Gallery café, November 2019

Without Dad

The lights didn't used to be pentagons.
Georgian perhaps, so discreet I never saw them.
You were an evacuee grown old,
steps still brisk but behind all the same,
feeling cosmopolitan with cappuccino.
Now the choices keep on coming.
I don't want to find the table
where we're sitting in your poem
because change feels raw and ruthless
and my velvet coat wore away.
As for the paintings, I can't picture them today
without your voice inside me splintering.
I carry the texture of your coat sleeve under my fingers,
more permanent than the cup that isn't china.
Am I the only one
inhabiting old spaces,
tracing what's beneath, more there than here,
and swimming years to reach us where we were
like a polar bear on a raft of ice?

Rebelling in Red

I've become a Red Rebel, and the night before our first action I was wildly excited about leading the procession into St Albans Abbey for the General Election hustings. I love dance, and more importantly I've experienced the mesmerising, slow, silent power of the Reds up close in a crowd. Watching them pass through the Love Rebellion site at the back of Downing Street in October, I felt moved and compelled as their presence calmed, stirred and hushed everything and everyone around them. And they seemed untouchable in their mysterious otherworldliness. What Reds do is theatrical and borrows from mime and the Chorus of a Greek tragedy but it feels to the observer less of a show than a strange connection, soul to soul.

When we entered the abbey we heard some people tell each other, "Extinction Rebellion," but many have never come across the Reds and I'm sure many more are unsure what it all means. I remember once hearing the phrase, *the blood of our children*, but the Reds are more goddess than ghoul. They are sad, generous and compassionate. What threatens is catastrophe but the rebels are the alarm, not the fire. Like the Furies they offer a warning, but without frightening the children. And the stillness is part of the drama. The founder, Bristol's Doug Francisco, acknowledges the potent symbolism of red, suggesting blood, flame and danger – now the death of life on earth – but also love. There are YouTube training videos showing how to simply convey that love, along with the mourning of climate grief and the powerful commitment represented by the fist lifted high while the head, lowered, prayerfully defuses aggression. No blame. The moves are simple; the key elements are the emotions vividly expressed and the desperately urgent purpose. Reds have a huddle before and after actions, and all I whispered during ours was, "With love." But we also take one another's hands, making eye contact and a deeply serious bond. We hoped for that kind of inner communication with the candidates, and with voters in the pews. But we also knew that there's a new sensitivity about hustings this year, given the toxic and divided nature of today's politics, and were prepared to be prevented.

In the taxi we talked of climate and ecological breakdown. From the moment we stepped out of the cab, we were in character. It was dark and wet as we walked from the Clock Tower to the abbey entrance, and much of the route was cobbled, sloping or uneven. We processed in line, just six of us, and eventually found ourselves, after warnings of police and security, walking in through the main entrance and beginning to walk slowly down the aisle. We were escorted by Graham, pristine in a suit and carrying white roses, and guided by local rebels. At once the stewards became jumpy but we'd agreed that we had to stay silent and dignified and glide on obliviously. Apparently Graham was told by one that we were disturbing the audience and disturbing her. Nothing has ever been more disturbing than this existential threat facing every one of us. We continued but about halfway we were stopped. I couldn't say exactly how because my head was high. We went back up a side aisle and then, in spite of repeated requests to sit down, 'performed' at the back until we had to leave to meet our cab. Some of those seated in front of us took selfies with us in the background.

Did we make an impact? Certainly, although not everyone among the thousand or so will have seen us. Did everyone know who we were and why were there? I'm sure not. I understand that sometimes the Reds are accompanied by an explainer, or leafleters, but this wasn't possible on such an occasion. Did we feel that it was worthwhile? Definitely. For a first attempt the context was challenging. Next time we may choose a high street. We have learned how to be more effective, need to use our faces more expressively, and have a plan to be escorted by a rebel carrying an Earth on fire as a back-up message. But I am completely in love with this creative, mysterious way of rebelling: a graceful, emotive and spiritual alternative to blocking roads.

We were all sadly conscious of the rebels on hunger strike outside political party headquarters and very much at risk. A few hours before our outing, more experienced Red Rebels visited them, and I can imagine the solace and strength they offered.

Poem in response to the bush fires and a searing photo of a baby kangaroo burnt against wire January 2020.

Joey

I used to
be blind inside
and hairless too.
It wasn't safe to jump,
but I learned as I grew to look out, smell grass,
taste sunlight and dust,
test the rhythm of my own lungs
at first spring.
Shy of you, for a short green while
I breathed my own air
until it caked to livid ash.
My world was boundless
till my feet stilled heavy, frayed by flame.
Do I remind you of a toy worn bare,
left behind and fit for landfill,
or a P.O.W. clinging to wire
as the shot breaks from the watchtower?

Written in the canteen at Exeter Hospital, early 2020

The food could be Styrofoam. Behind me a woman digests lies, big in bold, about a man with a good heart. And in the air, ruthlessly filtered out, is the unspoken truth we breathe. It's the truth you will deliver in court next week, the truth you voice until my body gasps, snatching at life, and I'm hyperventilating, unseen, among medics.

I walk with unreality. The pills can't screen it off and the CBT's N/A. Or fakery. Around me people function without panic attacks. As if the science is fantasy, the alarm is alarmist and the rebels are the trouble. At our table, the vocabulary is specialised: criminality, prevention of imminent harm, an existential threat, ecological emergency, the end of civilisation as we know it. And is that what this is, where we are? Above, below, across from here, the life support systems beat on. Obs are recorded. First oxygen activates tiny lungs. Somewhere in this building urgency compels action. Cardiac arrest, CPR, crash teams, high speed, high tech.

Too late.

Then you remind me of the bride smiling up, out, within. Of what we found in each other. Of love beyond ours that will be last, at the end, to die. The spirit that gives amidst the taking. How your hand feels in mine.

Where the sun rises.

21

The Trial

Marcus

Marcus Olorenshaw stood on the Central Line, pressed against his wife and pretending she was a stranger. Over breakfast she'd wanted an explanation for his grumpiness.

"You've no idea how wearisome these trials are," he'd told her, but that had been unguarded, a mistake.

"Doctor, professor or vicar? Or are you hoping for a crusty this time? A barefoot hippy for a change?"

"I don't care as long as I'm spared the speeches. They have to be told these cases are not about climate change. Or morality, either."

"Just as well I'm not recording this for Channel 4 News," she'd remarked, looking up at the kitchen clock. "Make them feel the full force of the law!"

Up closer to her than he'd been for a while, he couldn't be sure the purity of her white hair was natural. Marcus reflected that he didn't always know how to read her, and suspected the menopause. Irritation prevented him kissing her cheek when the carriage doors opened, and unless he missed it, she didn't wish him a good day. Suddenly it bothered him that he couldn't remember what bright-eyed cultural business she would be enjoying while he endured five hours of gritted teeth and fake patience. Sometimes he thought she was less than grateful for the salary he deserved – rather like these activists who failed to appreciate their freedom to set up camp on bridges and glue themselves to government buildings in a country that allowed them a platform.

So who had he got today?

Jenny

Emerging from the subway, Jenny Marsh saw from the curved and rather imposing building on the corner that they had arrived, albeit as early as Alice had warned they would. The doors were still locked. Jenny put up

22

her black umbrella and tried to share it with her daughter, who hadn't spoken for a while.

"Are you all right?" she checked, and Alice nodded.

She'd ignored Jenny's advice on dress code, although the jeans at least had two knees and her hair would look more presentable out of the rain as long as there was a brush in that old shoulder bag. Jenny looked at her phone: not one but two questions from staff who hadn't read their emails. Sighing, she replied as briefly as possible. Maybe she should have told them all why she wouldn't be in school. Tomorrow, perhaps, she could announce the verdict at morning briefing. She couldn't quite imagine the response but the younger ones might be impressed.

Now Alice was looking at her own phone. "Dad's train was delayed," she reported. "And he wants me to change my plea to guilty. But I can't."

"Well, you could ... in the sense that it's not too late."

"But I won't," said Alice, quietly. "It's important to tell the truth. Anyway, I've spent hours on my documents."

"I'm sure."

Jenny had offered to pay for a solicitor so Tony had done the same and they'd agreed to split it. But Alice was adamant that she wanted a voice, her own voice. This must mean her prep was at the expense of her coursework at the very start of her degree. Alice had been so studious before the Climate Strikes changed her. Tony had been convinced she'd fail her A Levels after the arrest in April – and she'd reminded him that a few weeks after he left them two years earlier, their daughter hadn't exactly done badly at GCSE. Alice was turning out to be less delicate than she looked, even though they were both convinced that on a vegan diet she didn't eat enough.

Jenny watched her reply to a message, probably from that housemate who'd already clocked up three arrests. Alice had said none of her uni friends could afford the train to London; Jenny hoped Tony wouldn't let her down again. She looked at her watch just as the heavy doors opened on some steps up to revolving doors and airport-style security.

"It's necessary," said Alice, and led the way.

Greg

Greg Swift was hung-over, which wasn't ideal, and spoiled the bacon sandwich he ate as he walked underground to Exit 8. For some reason no one could explain, there was only one defendant on his list. Why hadn't they batched her up like most of them? Such a waste of the court's time and money. At nineteen she was the youngest he'd had to prosecute so far, and barely looked adult in the bodycam footage, with her denim shorts and baggy Choose Love T-shirt. With luck, and no police officer required, it could all be over by lunchtime. He hadn't mentioned to Kristof what kind of case this was, not after that bedroom row about the last one with the Biology teacher, the architect, and the grandmother who used to play cello at the Royal Opera House. *"I don't know how you can live with yourself,"* Kristof had told him. *"In that case,"* Greg had said, *"I don't know how you can live with me, so feel free to fuck right off."* As if he could pick and choose, or rewrite the laws of the land. And as if Kristof did any more to save the planet than any other smartass young Londoner who shopped and partied hard and flew to European capitals for stag weekends, football or Taylor Swift.

Greg would rather spend the day with some petty criminal than a girl like Alice Marsh, but he knew the motions now. He would autopilot through them with the help of a couple of painkillers. He stepped over a surprisingly deep puddle, binned his disposable coffee cup and hurried inside.

Serena

Serena held her clipboard to her chest as she breezed in to Court Four waiting room and smelled the food. Those arrestee support people were marvellous the way they always turned up with their hummus and French bread, cookies and bananas – and filled the space with chat. The police superintendent was there again, poor chap. Hadn't he got real work to do? They exchanged friendly greetings before she checked off the defendants' names, all present. It seemed a shame that in Court Three a young girl was up on her own, with just her mother to support her, so she had a quiet word with a familiar woman wearing an Extinction Rebellion badge and sent her next-door. Serena knew by now how random the workings of the machine could be, how many embarrassing errors could turn up on the day. But it was always nice to see the climate protesters with their warm smiles and old-fashioned manners, some of them all loose with confidence and others, like the Alice girl, terribly shy. A bit traumatised already? It was a shame really but she always tried to make them feel at home, in a way.

Perhaps she'd pop back to the Alice girl and make sure she hadn't changed her mind.

Alice

Alice turned to see her father enter the courtroom and catch her eye with a look that probably meant *sorry*, although he hadn't missed much. He looked out of his depth, as if he had no idea how he came to be here, too late to see her stand and give her name, address and date of birth, to hear her asked to speak up. *Quiet*, her teachers always said, *hardworking* and *capable*. None of them ever knew who she was, so when her dad left no one knew how to help. Not that she could have told them. Now everything had changed, around and inside her, and like the criminal justice system, her parents weren't keeping up, either of them.

The judge was old, and looked as if he'd be more comfortable having drinks with the Prime Minister. He was crisp as toast, but every now and then slathered on a load of butter when he smiled. Alice didn't suppose there was anything she could say that he'd really hear, but her notes sat piled beside her aluminium water bottle. She tucked stray hair behind her ear, knowing it wouldn't stay there. She was aware of her father sitting down next to someone with a laptop who could be a law student or maybe a trainee police officer. The prosecution lawyer was delivering numbers. So many Londoners delayed and inconvenienced, so much disruption, takings lost, money spent on policing. Familiar, it still seemed strange that anyone would think it mattered, any of it, compared with climate catastrophe. But it was endless, and she had the feeling the lawyer was boring himself.

Alice told herself she must delete it all, everything but the much, much bigger facts. She must sit straight and keep her voice together, but sometimes when she read the reports, saw the melting and burning, nothing held. As if she had nowhere to stand, to exist, to count on.

She would tell both her parents afterwards, straight away, before they could forget the reasons.

Tony

Incredible, people said, about any old singer or goal, film or shoes. It was a joke, because *this* was incredible, thought Tony. This now, here: watching his girl on trial for trying to stop a madness that was even harder to believe in. Which was why he'd never really believed it, in spite of her, until he walked in to the courtroom and saw her looking so young and serious and *incredibly* brave.

She'd tried to teach him. Now he didn't need the science because she was enough. This was more than enough.

Greg

Greg had heard it all before. That Sixth IPCC report, Government adviser Sir David King, Attenborough, the John McDonnell statement that would needle Olorenshaw more than most, the claims that people were already dying that were never going to wash as imminence. The whole necessity argument was dead in the water before anyone got out of bed this morning or any other, but it didn't matter to these activists. They were all so sure they were right – even this girl who could do with a microphone, and looked like she needed a large beef burger and a mountain of fries. He didn't pay attention anymore, not to what they were saying, just to whatever detail he could find to distinguish the individual from the whole crowd. Whether this one would cry – or rather, how soon. How much Olorenshaw would put up with and how much, with well-groomed parents like hers, he'd make her pay. Last time he'd clobbered a Biology teacher he accused of rhetoric with seven hundred and seventy, which was more than Greg planned to ask from Alice Marsh, unless he decided she'd be the type to make a habit of it without a deterrent. It was all right for Kristof to be *woke* but he didn't understand. The establishment wasn't ready to allow people like her to break the law for a pat on the head; government certainly wasn't, and the Met was still reeling. The whole system was clogged up, like the traffic in London back in April when this girl was invited to leave but made four officers carry her off the bridge, arms out like a crucifix. If Kristof watched the bodycam footage the Catholic in him would see sacrifice, but that was just emotion. The law was something firmer, more rational and dependable. It was what had drawn Greg to it. That and the money. And the feeling of order, as long as there were no cock-ups.

"The science ..." she said, trying to project.

How many times! Irrelevant. A waste of breath. He could see she was a good girl but Olorenshaw wouldn't. "No reasonable people would have behaved as you did," he'd told the last guilty group. Wallop! His honour was a pompous old headmaster and Greg wouldn't want to see him lay into Alice Marsh like that, even though her intensity was no good for his headache.

Jenny

Jenny had told Alice more than once, face to face and on the phone but mostly in messaging, that she wasn't arrogant enough to dispute the scientific consensus but the methods the rebels used were never going to win hearts and minds. That frankly, the way these activists presented the problem was a bit over the top, too apocalyptic to credit, a turn-off. Alice had a way of going silent, as if she was wounded, or winded, or despairing of her mother's stupidity. But in the dock, she was as collected as a teenager could be.

"We live in a democracy with freedom of speech. Why was it necessary to break the law to make your point?"

"This is a climate emergency. The normal rules don't apply. The petitions and marches didn't change anything and we're running out of time."

"How could your actions change anything?"

"This is a climate emergency. We needed to get that message across so we had to grab the headlines, and tell people what's happening so that they demand change too. We had to wake everyone up, governments, media, industry, even the legal system."

"By sitting in a road making people late for work, for medical appointments."

"This is a climate emergency. Nothing else is really ... significant."

"Like the normal rules, apparently. Why didn't you move when Police Officer Hartley asked you?"

"This is a climate emergency."

The judge shifted in his chair but the prosecutor continued. "Why didn't you walk when you were arrested? Was it necessary to be carried by four tired and overstretched officers?"

In the video she'd looked so calm and certain. Now she looked tired and overstretched herself. The prosecution lawyer was pressing her hard and Jenny couldn't ask to see him in her office at lunchtime for a quiet word.

"This is a climate emergency."

The District Judge leaned forward a little, fingers clasped around his pen. "A court of law is not a place for mantras." The way he said the word suggested that he could think of nothing more offensive. "You can wave your banners and chant your chants at your demonstrations, not here."

Alice was silent. The prosecution lawyer hesitated.

"Have you any further questions, Mr Swift?" asked the judge, clearly hoping not.

"No, sir."

"In May Parliament agreed that this is climate emergency," said Alice.

"You may stand down, Miss Marsh."

Jenny glanced across at Tony and saw him with both thumbs up and a mouth that bit back emotion, but Alice didn't make eye contact with anyone as she crossed the courtroom. Honestly, Jenny didn't know. Had she done wonderfully, or badly? Did it make any difference anyway, when the deal was done?

Jenny had no idea how Tony did that heart thing with his fingers so quickly and effortlessly just as Alice looked in their direction, but she'd never done it in her life. He must be in practice. Alice said there was someone in his life. Of course there was ...

Tony

Tony produced a plastic bottle of water and had drunk a few sips before Alice shamed him by unsealing her reusable one. And she'd given him one just like it last Christmas too. He didn't want to fail her again. But this ... she shouldn't have to go through it. Let other activists bear the weight. He'd tried to explain that he'd lose his job in a blink if he were to do what she'd done. It was different for the young with their bright ideals, always had been.

He hoped she knew how proud he was.

Marcus

Marcus always talked about respect for these people's convictions but they thought they were above the law, and as good as said so. At least this girl didn't waste more police time questioning a busy senior officer about human rights. He was pretty sick of hearing about people's consciences, as though ordinary, law-abiding people didn't possess such a thing. "So you think the government has it all under control?" he'd been asked at breakfast, and apparently his answer that no doubt they did, and after all Britain led the way in this, had not convinced his own wife. Now that she'd forgotten her outrage at being delayed for something less than consequential in April, she was rather taken with the little Swedish zealot with plaits and an accusing frown.

He was rather relieved that his own son was too busy earning big bucks in the States to sign up to her kind of fervour. For all their eloquence and figures, most of these rebels must have mental health issues. But the father looked as starry-eyed as if she were five and just played Mary in the Nativity play. Did schools still do those, or just wiggle to Slade and Elton John?

Marcus expected Alice Marsh had a speech to deliver before he withdrew for his verdict and he wasn't going to allow more than two pages of it.

Greg

His case proved, Greg's job was done until Olorenshaw consulted him on the fine. Greg didn't normally pay attention to defendants' last-ditch attempts to cram in as much death and doom as possible. But he hadn't made up his mind about Alice Marsh, who was attractive in her own bare, otherworldly way, and obviously well outside her comfort zone – if she allowed herself one any more than a late-night kebab – but keeping her head above water, considering the melting Arctic. Not too quivery but not flat and boring either, in spite of all those reports from bodies with long names. He'd been half-expecting Olorenshaw to ban notes and would have been sorry to see the girl floundering. She wasn't, not yet, in spite of Olorenshaw's own brand of gentlemanly intimidation. This Ecocide Law stuff was quite interesting and Greg had been meaning to look it up. Now she was telling the court how she'd been inspired by that barrister Polly Higgins who'd died on Easter Sunday. Some people said Extinction Rebellion was a cult; Greg steered well clear of religion.

"Three years ago I told my parents I wouldn't go on any more family holidays that meant flying," Alice said, and added, "before they split up," so quietly that Olorenshaw asked her to repeat it. Greg remembered his own parents' divorce when he was about the same age and how long it had taken him to stop hating his mother.

"Before my parents split up."

Greg heard the pain then, the fault line that hadn't cracked open before. He would have liked to check their faces, the two of them. But Alice Marsh was back on track, except that she'd put the papers down and was winging it.

Her generation. The right to life. The right to bring a child into a world worth inheriting. It was personal now and she was exposed, real. Damaged, of course; Olorenshaw would despise her for it. Part of Greg wanted the old fart to stop her and part of him would be livid if he did.

Kristof would want to know about this but Greg really didn't want to tell him.

Jenny

Jenny embraced Alice as soon as the door closed behind the judge. "You must be exhausted. I know I am."

Alice nodded. Tony held her for a longer, firmer hug, and kissed her forehead the way he used to, a decade ago.

"Time for a coffee round the corner, do you think?"

Alice shook her head. "I don't suppose he'll take long."

Jenny didn't know what to say. Out came a teacherly, "Well done" but it was hard to feel as composed as she sounded. Because if Alice was right ... how did she sleep?

"Good luck."

It was the prosecution lawyer. Jenny smiled gratefully but Tony reacted as if an Everton fan had just sympathised over a Liverpool own goal. Clearly surprised, Alice thanked him, and for a moment she became a self-conscious schoolgirl again.

"He's young too," she told them as he returned to his laptop.

Jenny had never thought to find out how many of her students were worried about climate change. Now she would be afraid to ask.

Tony

It's so bloody unfair, Tony messaged outside the toilets. *Not the money. Criminalising people like her.* Tony hadn't actually told Jess the figure, which was a joke. The judge wanted to punish Alice – or them, her liberal, divorced parents, for failing to keep her submissive. It made him so angry. The law was so far behind reality. Like him. That was where people chose to stay, out of the loop, because the truth the scientists were offering as a warning was too hot to handle. Easier to get on with life the way people had got used to living it.

Jenny emerged from the Ladies first, her lipstick renewed, showing no trace of anything as she rummaged in her handbag rather than talk to him.

"Do you think she can stay out of trouble for nine months?" she asked him as she zipped it shut again.

"I doubt it."

"We have to persuade her. She's done enough. Why can't the adults do their bit?"

"Like us?"

He could see that made her cross. "I'm going to write to the Environment Minister. And no, I can't say who that is just now. And yes, I know it's probably a waste of time."

Alice appeared behind them.

"What's a waste of time? Was this? I hope not. I have to hope not."

Tony put his arm round her. "Come on, you need a decent lunch. I need a drink."

"I'm leaving uni. Maybe not for ever but for as long as it takes. Nobody's listening yet so the alarm's got to be louder. I need to be in London."

Tony hadn't seen it coming but now he didn't know why. He looked to Jenny. She was the one who bigged up education as the answer to everything.

"No, Alice. That's too much …" she tried.

"It may not be enough."

"Look, let's eat, all right?" he said, managing a kind of smile. "It's been tough, especially for you, and we need to regroup, stay rational. Enough drama for one day."

He knew Jenny would agree with that. Alice nodded, and pulled on a woolly hat that made her look fourteen. The court support woman with the hourglass badge came hurrying after them as they approached the revolving doors, wanting to know how Alice was and telling her how *brilliantly* she'd done. She never liked accepting praise.

"Thanks. I'm fine."

Jenny looked tense now. Tony didn't know for sure how he felt, or what he could say, over a bottle of wine, that was rational, and avoided drama.

Now the XR woman gave Alice a hug, gave her an email and headed for the Ladies.

Alice thanked her again. "See you on the streets."

Hold the Sun

I'm a trompe d'oeil,
straps slipped off behind the banner
but we're all naked,
even the old guy we're provoking,
forefinger whirling by his temple,
skin crushed by contempt.
Even the sharp suited, gelled and quiffed,
the heeled and sprayed
stepping lightly from the lair,
shades focused, hearts in hiding.
And restless Security gathered and breaking
to huddle again, bring on a sub, seek guidance from above.
Even the police liaison officer,
sweat trapped unacknowledged
inside easy-shift posture,
legs apart and smile ready.
We angle as one under a concrete sunshield.
As my scalp shines slippery
my arthritic grip locks with no key.
A captive released through glass
knows the truth we want uncovered,
seeks absolution.
SIZZLING! A SCORCHER!
A record bites the dust.
No beach, no barbecue or party
when islands drown.

Views of an Extremist Grandma

I was dismayed and quietly outraged but not entirely surprised to read that according to the police anti-terrorist group Prevent, people like me are extremists. My views themselves are seen as extreme – or were considered so, until challenged. Now the Met admits to "an error of judgement", Extinction Rebellion is no longer classified amongst extremist groups, and the requirement for schools and universities to report students who are emotional about the climate crisis, or take part in protests, has been withdrawn. But in November that directive was disseminated, and its impact is unknown. As I write, I have not seen a fulsome apology that contradicts its message, acknowledging the peacefulness at XR's core and the experience on the ground of officers who commonly describe our arrestees as *lovely*. It may be that among those citizens considered moderate by comparison with people like me, there will be a fair few who are more appalled by Prevent's judgement than by the road-blocking activities of activists. But some will agree with the original analysis, especially if they read certain newspapers, so I thought I'd spell out these contentious and apparently alarming views I hold along with my fellow-rebels.

1. I accept the scientific consensus that we are in a climate and ecological emergency, that the threat is existential and requires urgent, radical change now, not least because climate change is already killing people and animals.

2. It's my belief that love is stronger than hate or death and that there is God, or goodness, or light, in everyone.

3. I reject war and assert that only together, in peace, can we address this climate crisis.

4. I reject violence, including aggression and enmity, and the nationalism that often generates it.

5. I consider the differences between people unimportant compared

with the human needs that bind us, and the idea that one human is superior to another by virtue of race, gender, sexuality, ethnicity or religion, wealth or success, both divisive and mistaken.

6. I reject the exploitation, abuse and betrayal of animals and am committed to veganism as the most significant way, along with not flying, of reducing my carbon footprint.

7. I am convinced that only non-violent mass civil disobedience will persuade some governments, including mine, to work towards zero emissions by abandoning fossil fuels.

8. I do not consider myself a criminal because I acted peacefully out of love, in conscience, in the light of the science, as climate scientists and doctors declare necessary to prevent ecocide and the end of life on earth.

9. I consider the arms trade immoral.

10.   I believe in supporting and welcoming refugees who by definition have fled from war, oppression – or, increasingly, climate change.

These are the fundamentals that unite the vast majority of rebels, along with the hope that 1,000 humans, selected by sortition and given access to the appropriate experts, have a better chance of finding a way forward than politicians hamstrung by vested interests and tribalism. If more widely shared, these views could help us survive in a world that is more peaceful, more just and more compassionate as well as safe. Yet we are under media, government and establishment pressure to accept that all these beliefs are dangerous and that we should forget any campaigning for a better world and carry on consuming, competing, and prioritising our own personal desires, advancement and convenience. We are expected, even encouraged, to blame others for everything we lack and declare ourselves ready to fight for our country against people who are not like us, for oil, for power, for political gain. Greed is healthy for the economy, and the economy is apparently so precious that the survival of all species must be set aside in order to protect business as usual. And while in the UK and many other countries we have become used to leaders who lie and cheat for power, we are persuaded to accept the way politics is, to disconnect from it, to embrace cynicism as the adult position or to keep faith anyway that our team deserves to win regardless, because it's ours. And all of this is desirable, acceptable, and normal? None of this is extreme or dangerous???

I've met wonderful people through Extinction Rebellion, people who are genuinely trying to be good humans treading lightly on the planet, kind and courageous people willing to devote time, sacrifice earnings or degree courses, spend a great deal of money on train travel and in many cases endure arrest and criminalisation with a range of social consequences, for the least selfish of reasons. People who choose to freeze or get soaked when they could be enjoying the telly and bed, and experience the pain of antagonism or distancing when family and friends don't understand. My friend Anna Orridge called us *countercultural*, because our values are not yet mainstream, but that is changing faster than governments might wish. Of course, we are a band of individuals. Some, inside and outside Christian Climate Action, don't share my Quaker faith as a follower of Jesus; we didn't all vote for the same party although it's undoubtedly true that no rebel will vote for a Conservative manifesto that doesn't mention climate until page thirty-something. Some have professions respected by society, some live off-grid and many are creative; some look and sound conventional and others choose an alternative way to appear and use a less than standard vocabulary. Some fear it's too late and many live, as I do, with climate grief. But whatever our disagreements, mistakes and disconnections, what unites us is the biggest cause in human history, and we're not giving up.

Poem from March 2020

Climate Vigil

We sit, the three of us, under blue sky.
Mostly we're silent,
with our Earth and our symbols.
We face Parliament, a tower of scaffolding,
a gate where four police officers wait out time.
The bus ads thread by on a loop.
There's a low-slung, tin foil boast with IFLY on its number plate.
Cab drivers stare down,
accusing or weary,
before they move on.
Afternoon tea is served on the top deck
for vegan tourists
who like tablecloths
and bikers rev behind the Square,
their guttering belch grinding like gunfire.
Those who walk past glance, even read.
One smiles.
It's the children who linger, and look back.
"We should really buy that," one says,
As if the hollow globe Rachie's painting has a price.
I'm used to Quaker silence but this is busy, fuel-filled,
a point to make, a witness, a space to hold for life on earth,
a sharing and giving.
Warmed by sun, I'm drawn to blue sky,
in search of stillness, hope, God.
"Do you believe in love?" is the unspoken question
I answer with, "Yes. Absolutely."

April 2020
Solo at home, self-isolating,
I watch the candle,
its flame the only movement,
the brightest beauty.

I am the only sound,
as quietly I read the words that stir, strengthen, prick tears.
"...what love requires." "...not a notion but a way."
"All the children are our children."
"This is sacred."
I hold oh so many hands.
There's elation in belonging and serving,
in opening.
I can sing because no one hears.
I can dance with my arms.
It's love that connects in a world that may not hurry on for long,
a world that could learn from a virus
not just how to end the destruction
but to begin again,
to live.

Lockdown

Will I remember
the runners hurtling past
like bandits with weapon breath,
the measured queues in masks,
time that swelled like baking,
the skin tech couldn't touch?
Will my senses recall
the fresh taste of streets,
the unstained blue
and broadcast birds?
Will I forget
the daily final score,
graves like factory foundations,
white-cold lorries neatly tiled in wait,
end of shift faces grooved and raw
and tweets sharing loss from the void?
I want to remember the grid that grew
with quietly donated lives
honoured once weekly with saucepans and spoons.
Privilege vs exposure,
the space money makes,
the depth of the debt.
The angriest I've ever been.
What will I remember?
In separation, belonging.
In horror, courage.
In love learned,
a rainbow at the door.

A blog written in June 2020 about protesting on my high street

No Going Back

It's Sunday, so I was on my high street with a placard again, with XR friends – all of us in masks and socially distanced. When #nogoingback-sundays began we were deep in lockdown, George Floyd was still alive and there was hope that as a species and a nation we might learn from the last few months, and recognise that business as usual was already killing us before Covid-19. We're a small group of regulars and we stand in silence, appealing for climate justice and connecting with the Black Lives Matter movement. After all, like corona virus, climate change affects people of colour both disproportionately and first. If we look to the Global South, to the Pacific Islanders and indigenous peoples, we see terrible climate injustice, and those suffering have done the least to create the crisis.

For Leslie and me, this Sunday protest falls when we would otherwise be joining our fellow-Quakers for Meeting in our own homes, so we try to approach the hour meditatively or prayerfully as peaceful witness, a kind of vigil. Very few passers-by engage with us. A few hoot to show support from cars, or give us the thumbs-up – like a plaited girl of about twelve across the road, a mini-Greta – but most either ignore us or scrutinise our messaging before turning away. We've had no hostility, and it feels important as one of few actions currently available to us. But however many times I take this kind of stand, it's always a shock – that human beings are walking on past as if we and climate change don't really exist, when in fact we're acting on a scientific consensus and with love. When what's at risk and already being lost and destroyed, is everything, is LIFE ON EARTH. When the normality the government aims to revive is deadlier than the virus. When the nutters going over the top and classified last year as terrorists are actually responding rationally to the evidence as the world's experts present it. Or rather, we're under-react-ing, in our well-behaved way, because weeping and wailing would be more proportionate and trying to shut down government arguably quite reasonable since our leaders are the criminals. There's usually a point

39

when I sing internally, or remind myself to focus on the light that is both truth and love, in order to hold on to hope, because the alternative is the kind of grief that hollows out and immobilises. Then I realise that perhaps what most people are rejecting, or sidestepping, is that very grief that truth awakens and once faced can never sleep again. So I remember to understand.

Yesterday, when rebels talked to some sympathetic councillors on Zoom, everyone was very decent and polite, articulate and respectful. The meeting was seen by most as encouraging. But again there was a moment when I did weep and wail, inwardly and privately, not just with frustration at the snail's pace of change at local government level (arguably speedy relative to national government) but at reality. Underpinning our low-key conversation was impending catastrophe, with rising temperature and sea levels, extreme weather, climate refugees, and millions of deaths right now: Greta's world on fire, and at war too in more ways than one. Yet anyone overhearing without English might assume from the tone that we were debating the new colour scheme of the council chambers. We have to play this game, apparently, to avoid all the negative labels used by Cressida Dick and the Met, the *Daily Mail*, our Prime Minister and Pritti Patel. To seem mature and respectable rather than hysterical. Because right now, when people abandon democratic channels and peacefully shut down bridges, glue themselves to the Department of BSEI, sit down in airports or take down statues of men still honoured in spite of their crimes against humanity, those protesters are seen as a threat to society and decency – even though the goals of such protest are justice: climate, racial and social. The inversion is breathtaking. Yet such protesters are the modern equivalents of those radical reformers society learned in time to admire, to thank – in spite of their less than muted opposition to abhorrent norms we no longer attempt to justify. (Not even the far-right thugs do that, because they have and require no justification but ignorance and hate.)

Yes, I'm emotional, obsessed and often devastated by everything I challenge: not just climate inaction and systemic racism but the arms trade at which Britain excels along with the world's betrayal of refugees fleeing from war and oppression facilitated by the rich white nations. Isn't such emotion legitimate? I didn't expect to persuade the courts that my actions when arrested were necessary, in the attempt to prevent a greater crime, because as magistrates are advised in XR cases, they're "not about climate change or morality". The law, like governments, still sleeps, adhering to rules outdated by the present reality fronted by

40

activists but also by the United Nations and David Attenborough. As a shy person who prefers to let others do more of the talking, I sometimes conform to the low-key exterior that effectively denies that reality. I often duck the confrontation the truth would risk. But I have learned from my recent reading that racial injustice calls us to be actively anti-racist rather than just colour blind, and that only honouring the truth of lived BAME experience is enough. It's the same with climate activism. We must honour the truth of lived BAME experience of climate breakdown and of evidence uncovered over decades of scientific research, study and modelling.

Even if it makes us trouble-makers, law-breakers and extremists generally unwelcome at parties.

Another World is Possible

I chalk words on a wall.
Frail and dusty
the dream still gnaws through sun and wine
as chance decays,
alive but critical.
So hold her close,
breathe in each molecule that builds
the love of which you're made.
Then hope beyond belief
because the new beginning is a fine root through rubble,
Wind's corps de ballet white on blue,
A chain of hands across a chasm of flame,
The teeming underside,
Fear honoured wide eyed
in grief's communion
And every morning's soaring cry
undimmed, unmasked
and bravely yearning.

Short story from September 2020

The Prisoner

It had been part of the NVDA training but Em didn't really know how to *go floppy* so she just lay down on the road with her eyes on the sky. Her uni friends called her a lightweight because three drinks fuzzed everything, but in a more literal sense that worried her mother, she was an easy load. Four officers had a few metres to carry her to the van, where they carefully settled her on the step. No handcuffs. No Black Maria. Could they tell it was her first time? Worrying for Carl, who'd been stopped and searched eight times in Brixton, she hoped he was back on the grass with the banners and speakers. She was ashamed now of all the things she hadn't understood when colour blindness seemed enough and grades felt like everything.

Her ragged cardboard appeal to back the CEE Bill rested on her knees. Maybe these officers didn't know what that meant. What if any of them had read the climate science and ingested it? Could they ask to be sent elsewhere, to prevent actual crime?

"Are you OK?" asked the young woman who'd arrested her. She had painted nails that might glue on, French plaits and a small curve of studs in one ear. Em was curious. In a different world could they have been friends?

She nodded dumbly. *I was Head Girl. I think I'm in shock.* She sat up straighter and widened her eyes to find Carl filming her, his spare hand making a peace sign until he was shooed away. Just a close friend, she kept telling her parents, pretending that was cool.

Now her arresting officer wanted to know her details but wasn't she supposed to stay silent until they reached the station? Next she was ushered into one of the seats, behind a guy with a cap, a tattoo that reached out from the V-neck of his loose jumper and a grin he offered as he turned.

"Hey," he said. "All right?"

Maybe she needed a different slogan on her cardboard: *NO REGRETS BUT STILL ADJUSTING.* Or *NOT SURE WHAT TO TELL MUM AND DAD.* Of course she'd tried to explain the need for civil disobedience as opposed to emails, petitions and an allotment but they wanted someone else to save the Earth, not her.

"Have either of you been arrested before?" asked an older male officer who might not be able to catch either of them if they ran.

"Think I'll keep that to myself, mate. No offence." When the officer turned his back, he showed her five fingers spread on his shoulder and smiled. Tougher than Em's, and browner, they suggested a gardener. "But I'll tell you why we do this shit. It's scary but everyone needs to hear it."

Uniformed backs were turned but he grinned at Em as if unfazed. "Plenty of time to bend their ears if they take us to the wilds of Essex." Suddenly his face straightened and his rather bleary blue eyes looked sad, or afraid. A grey-haired woman was helped gallantly into the van even though she looked as if she walked Fells before breakfast. "Respect," he told her, and his smile was back.

One of the officers was reporting *three prisoners* and trying to find a police station with cell space. The woman who sat opposite Em adjusted her collar to reveal the white clerical kind. Her hair was cropped but thick, her jeans patched and her boots red. On her black T-shirt was the XR hourglass with a cross incorporated.

"Nice to meet you both," she said, as if she might belong to the Attenborough family. "Love and fierce love."

The gardener liked that. "Codename Seed," he said, as if that gave him pleasure.

This was how Em felt when she arrived at university: beige. Or even translucent, a shape people looked through in search of someone more interesting.

"They'll find me on the database once they've seen my bank card," said the vicar.

"What do your congregation make of this?" Seed asked cheerily.

"Ah," she said. "That's what you call a long story."

Em wasn't sure she had a story, herself, any more than a codename.

"Are you always this quiet, Emma?" asked her arresting officer, sitting down behind her. So she'd investigated her backpack already.

44

As if she was still fifteen, Em shrugged, with a tight smile, and Seed winked.

As they queued yet again, Seed told the driver he could do this in eight minutes by bike. Resisting his good humour, the officers talked mainly among themselves, ridiculing a superior they shared and comparing curries. Reverend Claire, whose mother was half-Indian and used to dance at Sadler's Wells, pointed out a care home where she'd planned to visit her father later that afternoon, and sit outside in PPE.

"You could de-arrest the vic," Seed suggested, "and drop her off while we're stuck here."

"Arrest was her choice." That was the sturdily unfit-looking older male. He sounded fractious or worn.

"It might have been God's!" Seed pointed out.

Rev Claire laughed heartily. "Indeed."

Seed said he was a pagan; Claire seemed quite happy to hear it. Apparently her father had dementia and little conversation but his eyes sometimes filled at the sight of her.

"I wish my mum was like you," Seed added, and looked out of the window at traffic that didn't move.

When they arrived at the police station they had to wait in a chill grey space that was a cross between a carport and a warehouse. A chirpy sergeant ambled out with a temperature gun and Claire said, after they'd all been declared *fit as fleas*, that thanks to the virus she'd had a *funeral-filled summer*. Em realised she couldn't in any case see her best gran for a fortnight after the Rebellion finished. Then she'd tell her all about it, and she'd be the one who was proud of her.

Even though Em still hadn't managed any words apart from *thank you*, the silence once Seed was led inside felt instantly weightier. Claire began to ask the officers questions about where they were from, and apologised for their extra-long shifts. Apparently they'd get *time and a half* and the otherwise-weary guy became animated at the prospect. Claire closed her eyes and smiled as if she'd fallen into a beautiful dream. Em wondered whether she was praying for her – asking God to make her stronger than she looked, perhaps, or to help her find her voice. *I'm in shock,* Em realised. *How weedy is that?*

"What are you studying, Emma?" asked Claire, on opening her eyes.

"History."

"The mistakes we should have learned from?"

"Mm." Suddenly Em wondered whether she'd quit. Focus on the present to secure the future.

"How will your parents react to your arrest?"

Em felt her expression of doubt morph into a grimace.

"It's hard to explain to those closest to us, isn't it?" Claire acknowledged. "But you might be surprised how much impact your action has on those who know you. I do believe public opinion is shifting. People are waking up."

Em smiled as if she believed that. Part of her did. Part of her wanted to tell Claire she was lucky to be old because her own could be the last generation in the UK to live a life unshaped and undamaged by climate chaos. Even if Carl grew to feel the same way she did, they couldn't make a family together, knowing what they knew. Could they?

She could hear another van drawing up outside. If enough people joined XR, the system couldn't handle the prisoners, the paperwork or the court appearances.

It was her turn to go inside.

There was nothing in the cell, lit by starkly unnatural light, but a long, low shelf covered with a mat and pillow of thin plastic, and a stainless steel pan without a seat or paper. Plus the kind of tiled walls public toilets boasted if they'd never been refurbed, and buttons to press to call the desk or wash her hands. Em put down the textbook she'd asked to keep with her, with no hope of processing the words or caring what they were. Carl would put the mat on the floor and meditate, possibly upside down. Presumably Claire would pray, and sing hymns, and count on God keeping her company. Em realised she had never been so alone. Picturing Carl with his eyes bright on her and his phone recording her so-called courage, she murmured, "I hope we always stay friends so don't let this faze you but it seems dishonest not to mention that I'm in love with you." Reminded of old Hugh Grant sitcoms, she shook her head. As her school-friend Janna used to say when she had a crush on her curate, *What are you like?*

Her dad said she'd changed, as if she was meant to conform like him, for money – and as if the world around her was the same as ever. But unless everything changed, there'd be no point any more.

"Carl," she whispered, "Stay safe." But no one would, unless the madness stopped.

46

Her door opened and someone different stood there in a mask.

"We need to take your fingerprints and DNA," he said flatly.

Em almost forgot her mask before following him. The room at the end of the corridor was small, and packed with what Carl would call kit. The fingerprint machine seemed erratic, refusing most images before over-ruled. The officer apologised.

"It never behaves."

But Em always had, up to now. Not a single cigarette, never mind a spliff. Now she might end up with a record. Eventually she sat for the DNA swab, and then the mugshots. Taking off her mask, she supposed that for this camera, a smile would be inappropriate, and the point was to make everyone look like a criminal.

"Thank you," she said after each process.

"We like XR," the guy said at the end. "You're all so polite."

That was a cue but she couldn't take it. As she was escorted back to the cell she glimpsed the custody desk and the back of a T-shirt she recog-nised, long black curls in a topknot, a lean neck that almost made her cry. She willed him to turn before she passed unseen. Almost too late he glanced around as he leant on the counter, and she could tell from his eyebrows that he was smiling. His peace sign became a heart space between his hands, and something in Em's chest tightened around her lungs. *"Be just as nice to him,"* she wanted to say, just as she'd almost told her parents before they met him, but they thought he was a radical influence and asked her to stay away from any Black Lives Matter march in case there was *trouble*. It made her sad that so much of her life was secret now.

Back in the cell she wondered how long she had been in custody but maybe it was best not to know. The love that mattered was the kind her old RE teacher called *agape*, the kind God would feel for humanity if God existed, which Carl thought likely – but Em was less persuaded than she'd been, on Sundays at least, before the IPCC report. There must be a word for love of Earth and everything that shared it. She realised that if she were in a wood right now she would be in no hurry to leave it. She would sit in shadow, touch the bark and name the textures, let the leaves pattern her face, breathe as if she'd just learned how, and imagine unseen lives above and below. Trees were what connected her with Carl, right at the start of that first term when they both looked up on campus at the same tracery woven by a Crimson King Maple through startling blue.

Em sat down on the cell floor and imagined it soft and warm, moist with moss. That was a challenge, given the chill hardness through her long summer skirt. Closing her eyes, she looked up and tried to feel the sun and breeze, rejoice and be glad in it. Even though Carl would do it better, with belief.

Giving up on herself, she stood and sang, quietly at first until the acoustics swelled her confidence. "People gonna rise like water, gonna turn this system round. In the words of my great-granddaughter, climate justice now."

When someone in plain clothes with a ponytail told her she was being released she realised with surprise that she had finally fallen asleep over her book, but it could have been for two hours or two minutes.

"What time is it?" she asked, feeling unsteady.

"It's four fifteen," the woman said.

Twelve hours, then, but with no interview and no solicitor. And what about Carl? At the custody desk there was a new, clean-shaven and unmasked face that reminded her of a less louche Ethan Hawke. The sergeant winced at a hyped, aggressive guy yelling and swearing behind him, and apologised for the noise.

"Sorry to keep you so long, Emma. We've been busy."

"No worries." *Well, apart from rising seas, melting permafrost, disappearing glaciers, record temperatures, floods and forest fires.* She saw her backpack sealed in large unnecessary plastic and regretted the polystyrene cups of water she couldn't resist in her cell.

"You're being released subject to further investigation. We'll contact you by post if you are going to be charged."

She nodded.

"When Extinction Rebellion began I used to tell first offenders that they'd probably hear nothing, so they might as well go away and forget all about it, but I can't promise that now."

"I can't go away and forget about anything." Em didn't know where that had come from. Had relief finally ungagged her before she could despise herself? "This is a Climate and Ecological Emergency. There's a bill we ask Parliament to pass and act on fast. We don't do this for the fun of it. I've been a bit traumatised really but that's nothing. I'm so privileged. People are dying in the Global South and the Prime Minister of the Maldives is begging for international Ecocide Law …"

Ethan was looking patient, or perhaps resigned. Perhaps it had been a long shift.

"It's ... unbelievably serious," she finished. Her voice faltered. "And we don't know what else to do to get people's attention."

"I understand," he said, and passed her some paperwork, lowering his eyes while hers filled.

Em felt a surge of desperation. When she had checked her belongings and signed off, he asked if she'd be all right to get home.

"Sure," she said, wondering what that meant to her now. She put on her denim jacket, but felt no warmer.

"Your friends are waiting outside," he told her.

"Carl ...?" Her hand mimed a topknot and curls.

"Not yet, I'm afraid. But there's quite a crowd. You lot look after each other, don't you?"

Wide-awake now, Em turned to the woman with the pony tail who began to show her out.

"Good luck," said Ethan behind her.

Through the darkness outside the glass-walled lobby she saw rebels gathered around a couple of folding chairs covered in blankets. As soon as she pressed the button to open a sliding door and stepped into a sharp morning, they began to cheer. Seed, blowing smoke from a roll-up, stamped both feet like a Flamenco dancer. Reverend Claire scuttled towards her, with her hands, clapping rapidly, held out towards her. Em felt the stretch of her smile as she pulled off her mask and smelled the coffee. There'd be vegan milk! Soon she was holding a steaming mug and answering questions as the others wanted to know whether she'd slept and whether the clatter of the half hourly check had woken her like a letterbox snapping. Whether she'd been offered the vegetable chilli or made a bad mistake with the baked beans and potato. An older couple from arrestee support wanted her details for XR records.

Claire said she was getting the night bus back to Parliament Square for the vigil and invited the others to join her.

"Sure," said a tall American blonde who might be a model. Her perfect teeth showed bright when she smiled. "All faiths and none, right?"

"I'll pass," said Seed. "I'm going to crash out on a mate's sofa. Reckon I can walk it from here." He elbowed farewells with the rest, his biggest smile for Em. Watching him walk away with a raised hand, Em pictured him at the next Rebellion, running to hug her and spin her round like a wild uncle. Unless, forgetting her completely, he walked straight on past.

"Emma, are you sure you won't come?" checked Claire.

"Thanks, but I guess my friend Carl's still in there. I'll wait for him."

The blonde knew who she meant. "Say hi from Megan. Hope they don't keep him long."

The five of them waved as they moved off, relaxed and chatting. No trace of sleep deprivation, dehydration or stress. It was shaming.

Millie, the well-wrapped woman in the opposite chair, offered her *vegan breakfast*. Choosing an apple and a date and cashew bar, Em realised she was happy to be mothered.

"First arrest, Emma?"

"Yes." She was glad of the sweetness. "But not my last." Both hands around the warm mug, she drank. "This is the best coffee ever."

She'd read that after beef and co, coffee had the biggest carbon footprint, but she'd think about that another time. Asked about her course and her parents, where she came from and how long she'd been in XR, she told a story only Carl knew. How disconnected she felt outside XR and how climate grief had sent her to the uni doctor for antidepressants she has to hide a long way under her childhood bed between terms. The words came fast and firm and every now and then her laugh surprised her.

Millie and Tom explained that they had small grandchildren they looked after twice a week and an A and E doctor for a daughter-in-law so they'd been shielding and could only support rebels this time round.

"Are you sure you want to wait for your friend?" asked Millie eventually. "We'll hang on until he gets out. It's after half-five now. The tube will be coming alive if you want to get home to bed."

Em smiled but shook her head. However long it took, she wasn't going anywhere.

Stop the Press

This protest was defined by inventiveness, humour and boisterous spirit, with solidarity and song, but it was also an expression of deep, sustained, patient and passionate commitment. Setting aside the Spooks-style excitement and tension, the purpose and its symbolism are profoundly serious.

The printing press we shut down for one night and one day represents so much that must change if we are to survive together, peacefully, as a species on this earth. Some of the papers that never reached their usual retail outlets are more toxic than others: guiltier of inciting racial hatred and hostility towards vulnerable minorities by vilifying and dehumanising refugees and Muslims. Individual newspapers are more or less divisive, manipulative and untrustworthy, but the most culpable provoke violent crime with violent rhetoric. The (70%) domination of the press by the five billionaires concerned, who abuse the power to shape discourse and public opinion with no respect for truth, is enormously dangerous and in itself a threat to democracy. Again and again, Rupert Murdoch has anointed pre-election the Prime Minister-to-be, and independent analysis of press coverage over recent years shows consistent demonisation of Jeremy Corbyn. This is a malignant oligarchy that sets the BBC News agenda and that of most other UK channels, and has, when fact-checked, been exposed repeatedly for presenting a fake but widely ingested reality. Our papers are internationally scorned.

The papers that never went to print because of our blockade celebrate British *scorchers* without reference to global heating, remain silent as the Arctic burns and the permafrost melts, and pay no attention to the overwhelming scientific consensus that without swift and radical action we face climate catastrophe here in the UK and across the world. Many climate scientists talk of a Sixth Mass Extinction event. Yet these papers' narrow jingoistic focus fails to acknowledge the suffering and fear of those in the Global South who are already experiencing destructive extreme weather of the sort we don't yet imagine here. Climate justice is racial and social justice, but the *news* they report shows little interest in such fundamental justice. It is because of the press we targeted that in spite of climate scientists, the IPCC, UN and Paris Agreement, the UK government continues to pursue the very policies that hasten climate chaos, financing fossil fuels at home and abroad, building new roads, expanding airports and bailing out airlines while claiming world leadership. It is because of their lies, vocabulary and evasions that the public doesn't vote that government out for ecocide shading into genocide. Because of their framing, those who have read the science and committed rationally and emotionally to raising the alarm are seen as the outliers, nutters, doom-mongers, extremists and even terrorists, threatening the *business as usual* from which these barons profit along with the fossil fuel industry. Business as usual will ensure the kind of horror no grandma wants her grandchild to know.

In Extinction Rebellion we speak the truth and act on it, in our lives and our activism, in the hope that civil disobedience can awaken the public taken in by the media's climate denial or vacuum. Today's blockade was an attempt to highlight the role of five billionaires in a conspiracy to lie to and mislead the British people, thus preventing the change that's so urgent and essential if we are to survive. I am a Quaker determined to do what love requires of me, and serve the truth. It is my sacred duty to rebel.

Poem from September 2020

Stop the Press

I'm straddling a tube.
Blanket-resistant, my legs
feel newborn and frosted.
On our web there's a scrum,
a mess of cross-stitch, lumpen and black,
a stranded, tentacled creature
with secret mouths
and twenty eyes.
My left hand's deep down steel,
where fingers that raced time to lock
rest stiff now in peace.
Rain, like Security, gave up,
and the dark's grown generous
as lightly it wraps us, fifty-one of us,
while we sing like Hardy villagers
at a harvest supper
of small and sentimental tragedies
scented with roses.
Empty, I savour happiness,
feel strong and sure
and numb with love.
High above from bold bamboo
the crows' nests swing,
and from the trucks the playlist jokes.

But this is serious,
is everything.
For just one day
the lies are stalled, and in their place
the truth can rise.
As fireworks splinter scarlet,
a grinding churns the air
and metal melts pungent through morning,
we lift it to the light.

Poem written for XR Grandparents and Elders' action outside
Buckingham Palace September 2020

For Nathaniel

I am here for you
because I'm Grandma
and you, firefly boy, are a spirit to power me.
But I'm here for all the grandchildren, living and unborn,
the privileged like you,
and those already dying
where we don't hear their voices
or connect with their eyes
like I meet yours.
I've learned
that we can only protect those closest to us
when we remember our love for those furthest away
We share each raging sun and rising sea and toxic breath,
all fear and hope.
With your hand in mine
I reach around the world.
Together we cry out for justice,
for life
in the name of love.

I love you

Every morning, when the door opened and the buggy bumped down the step, the child pointed at the tree.

On windy days the leaves waved wildly, and the noise was like a faraway train.

On still days, the tree sounded like a birthday party for excited butterflies. But that was only if the child listened very hard.

And whatever the weather, the tree always greeted the child.

"I love you," said the tree.

And the child loved the tree, because it was big and beautiful, strong and gentle, and so alive.

Every morning, when the door opened and the child ran out, the tree said the same thing.

"I love you."

The child's arms were too short to reach right around the trunk and hug the tree, but it was fun to try.

"Come on," said Mum. "You'll be late for school."

The child took her hand. The tree would still be there at home time.

"I love our tree," said the child, hopping.

"It's not really ours," said Mum, because the tree grew by the road, not in their garden.

That was all right because the child was getting better at sharing.

The cat next-door sometimes climbed the tree but squirrels were faster. The child liked the way they bounced along branches and gave them a quick dust with their tails. When the pine cones fell the child collected them and made them into circles and stripes and a slightly wobbly Isosceles triangle.

"I love you!" called the tree, and the child made a heart out of all ten fingers.

When birds made a nest inside the box high up on the tree trunk, the child watched through binoculars as the mother bird brought food for the babies. The child didn't like to imagine swallowing a worm, but it was thrilling to catch a glimpse of a beak opening like a capital V. The day the babies first peeked out and showed their fluffy chests was a big day too.

And then they chose a Saturday for their very first flight and the child hardly dared look in case they didn't flap their wings fast enough and dropped straight to the ground like conkers. Peeking through fingers, the child smiled and cried, "YAY!" Their wings did work out what to do, and it must be such a brave, happy feeling with the air soft around their feathers and the sun warming them at last. The world must seem amazing and they could see more of it than the child ever would, so their short lives must be exciting.

The child looked at the tree, and was sure it loved the birds too. Trees had really long lives, so long that this one might have seen people ride by in coaches pulled by horses. It might live nearly forever.

In stories old people were wise, so trees must know everything.

Soon the child was busy with homework, sports and friends, computer games and playing guitar. There wasn't as much time as there used to be for watching the tree, or listening or touching or just checking in. When the tree said, "I love you," the child didn't always hear or reply. Time moved so much faster for the child than the tree, until the child wasn't really a child any more.

"Look," said Mum, "the tree's looking tired."

"Trees don't get tired," said the child, without looking.

"I love you," said the tree, as the child slipped earbuds in.

Then a virus hit the news and worried the child's parents, and grandparents, and teachers, until the child was worried too. What about the exams? What about seeing friends? Once lockdown began there was no going out except to walk or run, and time changed. Instead of flowing on like wild-water rapids, it moved as slowly as a spill of treacle on a worktop. And it was thick with loneliness.

"Hey, old tree," said the child, stepping out in running gear.

"I love you," said the tree, as music filled the child's ears.

I used to love that tree, the child thought once it was far behind. *But I'm sure it used to be in better shape.* The child was in good shape now; reflections proved it.

More weeks went by and the child felt sad because the world was no longer the same. It felt as if roots had been dug out and left everything struggling to stand tall. The sun shone through the window, but there was nothing to smile about and it was hard to study. But that tree was still beautiful. The child remembered that humans couldn't live without trees like this one, and the world needed a lot more of them to undo the damage people had done. The child didn't want to think about that damage because it made everything hollow inside.

Looking out at the tree, the child murmured, "I love you."

How embarrassing, thought the child, glad no one could hear.

Lockdown had eased and the child's parents didn't mention the letter from the Council about the tree, because the child might be upset too. Or even try to protect it, arms round it, chained to it, when the tree surgeons came – like the people who were trying to stop trees even older than this one from being felled for a railway. They knew that made the child cross, but school had begun again and Britain was trying to get busy again, on its roads and in its shops and skies, and with its chainsaws.

Nearing home one afternoon, the child heard groans and whining. The air was full of it, and smelt of wood. Savage blades turned the last of the tree to sweet, scented dust ground out in a kind of storm. Only a bump of a stump remained, like a scar.

The child stood still and cried. What else was there to do? The wound felt fiery inside. That was where the words swelled.

I love you.

Very short story written in 2020

Edna & the Polar Bear

Edna lived mostly in an armchair that used to be as red as a tomato. Now it was brown as her tea. Edna's flat was on the top floor of a very tall old house. It was full of things that were at least as old as she was, and dustier. If she ever went out she needed a chair with wheels, but she was heavy to push and didn't like to bother people.

Sometimes Edna's words and sentences didn't really belong together but that didn't matter because she was the only one to hear them. She had neighbours below but she only saw them out of the window, setting off somewhere she didn't go, and coming back from somewhere she hadn't been. She paid someone to do her shopping and ask, "How are you doing, Edna? All right?" so she could say, "Still here, surviving. Did you get my ice cream?"

There was a cat that climbed the fire escape now and then and miaowed, so Edna let it in and called, "Coo-ee, come to Mummy!" If the cat padded over so she could stroke it, Edna purred too. But the cat didn't stay long. It had places to go and things to do.

Winters weren't as cold as they used to be and Edna missed snow like she missed deep sleep. One day when the frost was melting and branches were dripping outside her window, Edna turned to the fire escape and saw it was full to bursting with whiteness. And the whiteness was furry, with legs. It looked heavy enough to make the metal steps creak – or snap – but it made no sound.

"Oh my lollipops!" murmured Edna. "You'd better come in."

She shuffled over to turn the key. The door wasn't really wide enough for a polar bear, but like a bird through a hedge, it squeezed softly in.

"You're as lost as a sock," said Edna, back in the red armchair and trying to breathe the way the doctors liked.

Eyes like black ice met Edna's. The polar bear was more like a giant fluffy toy than a photo, and when he opened his jaws she could smell

58

vanilla. Or was it butterscotch? His teeth were as clean as his coat and he didn't scare her one bit.

"What can I do for you, sonny boy?" Edna asked.

But the polar bear said nothing. Instead he snuggled up to Edna, and leant his head on her lap. He was a mound of fur that rose and fell as his heart beat against her sore, wrinkled skin. That made Edna smile. Inside her was the stillness she used to feel when she sat on Mummy's lap for a story.

"Thank you," said Edna. "I'm glad you dropped by."

The bear rose and stretched up towards Edna's ceiling. Then he lowered himself onto all four paws, and as Edna began to feel sleepy, he drifted away like a cloud.

When Edna woke she remembered the polar bear that needed somewhere to be. She felt excited, as if Christmas was coming and she had people to share it with. For the rest of that day the sky was milky and she could see through the window that the air clung with damp fingers, but Edna had her own sunshine. It made her tap old tunes on her knees. It helped her to imagine the girl she used to be, dancing around the room to be clapped.

All the next day, Edna looked out for the polar bear. Her fingers and toes were too stiff to cross for luck but she hoped very hard, like she had when she wanted Daddy to forgive her for showing off. She talked to the bear, in case he was listening from inside her wardrobe or up on her roof. Surely he hadn't gone for ever? As the darkness wrapped the trees and the grass began to frost again, a movement caught Edna's eye.

This time the polar bear was slow and thin, and his eyes didn't shine. He looked as worn as Edna's chair.

"Oh my heart, sunny boy!" cried Edna. "Who turned off your light?"

The bear's head hung low. Stiffly Edna rose, shuffled to the freezer and opened the door on pistachio, chocolate fudge, caramel, raspberry ripple …

"You can scoff the lot," she told him. "Let's call it your birthday."

She pulled off all the lids and arranged the tubs on the table like candles on a cake. The polar bear sniffed, lifted his head and let his big red tongue dip close enough to slurp the lemon surprise. He reached his right paw across to the toffee munch and his left paw scooped the coffee crunch. Soon he wasn't very white any more, but it didn't seem right to laugh at a polar bear so far from home. Especially when he was shrinking. When he cuddled up beside her, she stroked his head and the back of his neck until he closed his eyes. His breath was as cool as snow in the air.

"Dear boy," she said. "I wish I wasn't old and useless."

Edna remembered climbing trees and waving to the things the world forgot. She remembered pretending to be a dolphin in the sea. And she remembered being a nurse, stroking the forehead of a child who didn't get better. Edna knew the polar bear didn't really need the ice cream melting in the tubs. He needed more ice than any freezer could make. What if his world wasn't cold enough to hold together and the water carried him away?

The polar bear was very still and peaceful. Every time she stroked him, there was less of him to stroke. When he shut his eyes and curled up no bigger than a cat, she lifted him onto her lap and felt the rhythm of his heart against her floppy tummy.

"I'm sorry, old boy," said Edna. "Don't go."

Still she stroked his fur until there was nothing to feel, and her eyes began to close. She felt her story drift quietly to an end.

When Edna's ice cream delivery arrived next day, she was still asleep, and her skin was cool. Her heartbeat was lost as a sock.

Edna waved goodbye to the old lady in the tea-coloured armchair. She couldn't be sure whether she was everywhere or nowhere but she wasn't shuffling any more. She wasn't stiff or sore and she wasn't alone. She could probably swim for ever, unless she stopped for a dance – or an ice cream. Wherever she was, Edna liked it better than that creaky old flat and its dusty old treasures. It was a place to belong.

Something white, sleek and strong swam through mist, paws paddling. The polar bear rippled like raspberry sauce through vanilla, and Edna swam after him, into the light.

Kit List

Thermals or sunblock,
Waterproofs perhaps.
Water always,
If only sips into emptiness.
Superglue,
D-lock or carabina.
Screwdriver, allan key,
A high-viz jacket at times.
A head for heights suspended,
An excuse for a pillow on tarmac,
A message scribed bold
On a frayed flat of card.
Yourself to share, along with the flyers.
Phone numbers stretched along skin
Between wrist and elbow,
Bust card in pocket.
A book you can count on
To stir and absorb,
Stillness through rhythm
And songs for silence.
Companionship
And all you need within.
Patience and energy,
Plans to improvise,
Readiness, careful,
And free.
A high heart
And thick skin.
Tears deep,
Facts, just enough, to retrieve and repeat.
Endless faith,
Open senses.
Yearning relentless,
Dreams beyond belief,
And safe, where it can't leave you stranded,
All the love you can find.

Short story from the collection, INSTEAD, published in 2019

The Activist

Lily considered herself an activist in her own small way, which was part-time because of the grandchildren. She'd spent a few days up at Preston New Road protesting against fracking and was almost arrested at the ExCel trying to stop the Arms Fair. It was sometimes exhilarating, because young people gave her heart when her own felt too worn to generate their energy and commitment. The spirit the campaigners shared, diverse as they were, often felt powerful in its peaceful way. There was no end to the sacrifices they were prepared to make: relationships, health, time and money. It was as if they'd rather die than facilitate killing, and that moved Lily more than she could express. But there were moments when she doubted all of it – not its rightness but its capacity to effect the changes the world needed to see. She considered herself feeble by comparison with these heroes who truck surfed or locked on, or simply sat prayerfully in the road and refused to move when she rose and sidled spinelessly to the pavement. The doubts, in herself and the possibility of a safe, peaceful world, could gather and break over everything. Except, perhaps, the time she spent with her babies.

Lily's son Jon had given her Dom and Charlie before the heart-breaking split from Amy. Lily had been determined not to lose them just because Jon only saw them at weekends, so she'd offered Amy one day's free childcare a week. Even ordinary routines took time now she was seventy-one, but every Friday she set the alarm for five-thirty and was with Dom and Charlie two hours later. Dom was approaching four and had to be taken to Nursery in the mornings. Charlie was just out of nappies at twenty months, and gathering speed on sturdy legs. Lily had vowed, privately, to do all she could to make sure they never grew into the kind of men who bullied, dominated, harassed or simply killed for control like trophy hunters, and racist thugs in or out of uniforms. They must learn right from the start to put people and peace before profit. So she had a lot to achieve on Fridays by the time Amy returned from work to find them clean in their jimjams and sometimes sleeping beautifully – as if they couldn't possibly have given Grandma Lily the run-around, made any mess, competed or cried over nothing.

With her granddaughter Min it was all very different. Min was already at school and since she lived ninety miles away, Lily's contact with her had always been limited, with a frisson. Once a month or so Min (real name Miranda) came to stay with Lily in her sixties' maisonette, bringing a spotty suitcase full of toys and books as well as clothes she'd packed herself. That could prove interesting if sleet fell and she'd overlooked the need for tights to accompany her little denim skirt embroidered with glinting golden butterflies. Min was a very independent thinker, which pleased Lily in theory more than in practice, because she disagreed with most adult ideas about what she might do, eat or wear. It seemed like a kind of reflex. So Lily had to guide her while making sure she didn't feel guided. It was a tiring kind of game, but Lily liked to think they played it together, and points she scored were shared.

Lily didn't approve of sex stereotypes – as Min's mum Jude knew well. Jude had grown into a glamour girl by sixteen, in spite of Lily's efforts to ban pink, make-up, Barbie and silly shoes until isolation meant defeat. At thirty Jude invested in false eyelashes and dyed her hair blonde, as if to poke Lily in the eye. Or, Lily supposed, to assert the independence she'd probably denied her in practice. Principles were tricky to manage. Her son-in-law Alex didn't meet Lily's criteria: he worked in advertising and didn't want to hear words like ethical, sustainable, vegan or biodegradable. She tried at times to avoid what Jude called 'the subjects' because as Jude pointed out, they knew her opinions already. After her brief exposure as a social media star – for singing and dancing along the Mall on a climate march, naming and shaming the Tories with lyrics of her own – she'd told Jude she was surprised she allowed Min into the orbit of a crazed radical, and was shown a V sign behind Min's back. Lily liked to think that when Jude finally outgrew rebelling against Mum, she'd recognise the need to resist injustice, climate chaos and war instead. But there was so little time for patience. The time to act was now.

As the Easter holidays approached, Jude and Alex wondered whether Lily would take Min for a week so they could go to the States.

"America?" echoed Lily. "By plane?"

"No, Mum, we're going to swim there."

"It's the last place on earth I'd want to patronise, even if I set aside the carbon footprint of a transatlantic flight. That warmongering madman is a threat to all things sacred ..."

"We're not going to take tea with Trump in the golden elevator!"

Lily wondered whether Jude was holding the phone at arm's length and counting, the way she used to with her own mother, but after a pause just long enough for a sigh she resumed: "Would you have Min? We don't really want to take her and you know she thinks you rock."

Lily didn't want Min taken to the homicide capital of so-called civilisation either. She said yes, having forgotten just for the moment that Dom and Charlie were coming for the second weekend of the stay.

Christmas often meant three grandchildren in one place but that wasn't Lily's, probably because Alex depended on the turkey and chipolatas Lily wouldn't serve, but partly because it would be a squeeze. Her hallway had just enough space for one person to manoeuvre past the front door, not childcare teams equipped with buggy, nappies, crib and a *Frozen* bike. Only on her seventieth birthday had she entertained all three babies at once. Min, having begun by doting on Charlie as a highly interactive kind of doll, had ended by snatching all targets from his path with grimaces and squeals.

"She's *my* grandma," she protested on a loop, claiming Lily by the lap and neck.

So Lily thought a while before ringing Jude back and explaining that it would just be "a bit too much, realistically" but was told Alex had just booked everything online. So she called Jon to see whether he could have the boys that weekend, but he would be away with his new girlfriend, one he hadn't seen fit to mention. Amy wouldn't want to miss her conference and Lily believed working mothers were entitled to careers. She would have to double her B12, get some Ginseng in, and order a few bottles of Fair Trade wine.

For five days Min was close to manageable, partly because she'd brought the tablet that was top of Lily's banned list. Guilty as Lily felt at the end of a demanding day's papier maché modelling, seed planting, cupcake baking, piano tuition and storytelling, she found herself unable to follow through the non-negotiable, even when Min sat silently transfixed on the sofa way past bedtime. She tried to restore the balance with walks in the woods for birdsong and tree identification. She even created two still, meditative minutes of what she called leaf music. But soon she was finding it hard to sleep at nights – and not just in case Min woke them both, either with a nightmare or a premature sense of morning which she sometimes signalled with bright pink lipstick (also banned).

By the time Saturday brought the boys she was ragged inside, worn away in part by unaccustomed love. It was no great surprise that the level of that love surged to a new maximum as Min allowed no space between them where Charlie or Dom could climb, and no silence for them to fill. Pinned down by kisses, Lily had to find negotiating skills she'd never needed before, maximising human resources while mindful of personal wellbeing.

"Not another dirty nappy! That's so gross!" "Why can't he eat nicely?" "Dom, just leave me alone, all right!"

"Grandma, she's mean!" "Where's Mummy?"

"Mamaaaaaaaaaaaaaaaaaaaaa!"

She tried to allocate equal rights to Grandma regardless of all other factors. Lily was reminded of nations that fought over territory, and robins too. She decided to take them all out to a zoo she didn't approve of, on the basis that they'd focus on loving the animals, but Min was the one she would have liked to strap in a buggy when she forged ahead on her own path according to her own preferences.

"Min, I only have three hands so hold on Dom's please. Or the buggy then ..." became, "Min I'm going to have to feed you to the elephants if you run off again!" but on balance she was glad Min knew enough to retort that elephants were vegetarians.

Lily could see that children today knew so much so soon, but most of it she would like to censor. She'd read about an eight-year-old in the States who was afraid her light-up shoes would get her killed if a 'shooter' came to school. An Australian gran who'd fought fracking too had told her counterparts in the UK that she'd bathed her little ones in contaminated water that burned them raw. Twitter offered images of small corpses in the Yemen. And pictures of refugee children barefoot in snow, or crouching over a fire in a camp, that made Lily ache inside whether they cried or smiled for the camera. Someone else's babies, they were victims of arms deals and war for power or oil, and she dreaded the future once climate chaos flooded cities but made wastelands where lakes and farms had been. How could any child play in the knowledge that filled her head? Some truths were too cruel to teach.

So she was shocked when Min said people killed lions for fun and asked, with tears, how they could.

"Oh, poppet, goodness knows."

"But they haven't got any, have they?"

"Any what?"

"Any goodness!"

Lily had to explain that she believed everyone could be good – was good, deep down, but made mistakes and did bad things sometimes.

"Like Dom!" cried Min.

Dom didn't seem to be listening most of the time. He was mesmerised by the lion slouching along only paces away in its enclosure. Lily was afraid that it might be suffering from mental health issues.

"Cool," Dom almost purred, and made a faint growl in his throat.

It was a good day, if a sticky one thanks to ice-cream and popcorn, and they were all asleep by seven – except Lily, who felt the loss of them already, hours before they'd be collected and her life would stretch ahead, quiet and free. There was a march against racism in London but that wasn't for another week. Lily felt the need to take action; it seemed more pressing than ever before. She was making a mixed-grain supper with tofu and salad, and imagining the scene if she'd tried to feed it to her houseguests, when the idea came to her.

Then she forgot, because there was one last failed attempt to fill Min with porridge instead of the sugary, salty cereal she had fitted into her spotty suitcase, and one last foray to the park once the boys had been collected. Lily worked hard to distract her from weepy declarations that she didn't want to leave her – not, at least, until she reclaimed Mummy with the same sort of fervour. Then, after the house fell quiet, the thought returned as more of a plan.

She could do it alone if she had to, but she'd need others to create publicity because she had a mere 8,671 followers on Twitter last time she checked, all but around 32 of them gained thanks to the Bob Marley moment captured by Al Jazeera. She'd been there as #ReggaeGran with #NoFrackingNoCrime and a rhythmic performance in baggy rainbow trousers that Jude and Jon must have found even more embarrassing from the outside. But would anyone remember? Because if they didn't, who would care?

Sometimes the fun had to stop. That would be the point, which was deeply serious.

Lily resolved that this was her time, and that she'd have to start without sharing it with anyone in case younger campaigners begged her, as a wrinkly, not to risk her health. She was scrawnier these days and she guessed she probably weighed less than usual after a week with her babies. She'd need a photo of her on the scales, preferably naked to get attention but without showing so much that she was barred by Twitter or unfollowed by thousands of disgusted scrollers who'd been put off their dinner.

The local Quakers might understand. And there was Susanna, her vigorous young dance collaborator from the march, who had organised a mass die-in with expert make-up and battle sounds, and locked on horizontally to a lorry delivering weapons to the Arms Fair. Perhaps Susanna would facilitate without fuss. Susanna wouldn't try to stop her, would she?

Because Jude would, and she'd recruit Amy and Jon.

Hey beautiful mover, replied Susanna by Messenger. *Sounds intriguing. Tell me more.*

You are serious right?

Let me digest this Lily. Are you sure you have thought this through?

What if nobody cares? Well except the full-time carers like you that is.

Yes we can meet. You are braver than I am. Say when.

You can't rush something like this.

See you soon then. Xx

Lily knew the next step had to be taken fast, before she lost the momentum that was fear and excitement and determination but bigger and tighter than all of them combined. At five-thirty the next evening she waited at Green Park for Susanna, who was working between acting jobs as a waitress in a chic burger-based café that made her sick "emotionally and physically". At first glimpse of her bounding up the steps, Lily looked down on the startling pink hair with black and white braids, the rose tattooed on her bare shoulder and the patchwork skirt billowing in the wind, and felt motherly. Perhaps daughters were always repelled by their mother's passions, but what about granddaughters? Min had suffragette spirit, like Susanna – who blew her a kiss and swayed towards her in sandals robust enough to take her up a mountain.

It was a short walk. Susanna talked about the restaurant and a waiter she'd liked until he kissed her around a corner near the bins. Lily told her about the journey and the funny things Min said on the phone. It was as if they were off for a coffee or a spot of shopping rather than to stake out an Embassy guarded by armed policemen – all of them big, British and fat. All the same, Lily thought Susanna wasn't quite at ease the way she'd seemed at the die-in she'd orchestrated, and supposed that was her fault.

As they looked across the road at the gated mansion with its minimalist garden, Susanna waved at the suited security guard behind it, dressed like a maitre d' rather than a hitman even though he might have a revolver under his jacket.

Lily asked, "You think I'm bonkers, don't you? Maybe I am."

"I think you're desperate. We all get that way if we follow what's happening."

"It's something," said Lily. "Something I can do."

"Sure. But we need to know how far we are prepared to take it …"

"People might see us on social media and join in."

"Hmm. They might."

"You don't have to join me – only film it, and work Twitter and all that."

Susanna said of course she would, as much as work hours allowed, and she'd find some students who could fill in for her. "But you dodged the question of how far you'll go. Because I'm looking at you and I wouldn't say you've got a lot of fat to lose."

"You'd be surprised."

Lily wasn't good at selfies but she knew she'd have to prove that herself. Susanna linked an arm in hers the way Jude used to do.

"I think you should set a limit. We don't have to publicise what it is, but if you want campaigning groups to get behind this they need to know. A week – five days rather than seven?"

Lily frowned. "No limit. It's not a diet."

"Lily, come on! No one wants to call the paramedics."

Lily wanted to say that people died because of arms deals, that children in Yemen died every day because of British weapons, that it wasn't about publicity but death.

"Gandhi didn't set a limit," she mumbled, immediately feeling foolish. "Not that I'm comparing … I know I'm no one. Maybe that's the point."

"OK," said Susanna, "we've seen enough. Let's grab a coffee and talk it through."

At the nearest café Lily ended up promising to listen to her body and know when to stop. Susanna called her "awesome" and "seriously crazy" and insisted that she ate some cake to store up some fuel. She shared some of the most effective campaigns she'd taken part in, or read about, and mentioned the importance of humour.

"Not a lot of that in this case," she added.

"I could tell jokes. Ladies and gentlemen, have you heard the one about the regime that bombed hospitals and weddings? And the 'civilised' – haha – country that kept on profiting from making the bombs?"

Susanna sighed. "People know. They just don't care. Or they think humans will always do that toxic shit."

Lily nodded. She could cry now. All she would prove was that however far she was prepared to go, she couldn't stop anything. But she had to try. She couldn't live with herself if she pulled back. She wouldn't be able to play like Grandma any more.

"Don't try to stop me," she said.

"All right," said Susanna, and hugged her.

Before they left the café Lily made sure there was a toilet and wrote down the opening hours.

Lily knew she couldn't delay. Her Monday with the boys felt covertly charged, even before she kissed them goodbye. On Tuesday morning she rose early for tea and plenty of porridge, then washed up and wiped every surface. She checked her Last Will and Testament once again, and left it on the kitchen table with the sealed letters. The fold-up chair and cushion were light enough. No water or sandwiches to weigh her down, but perhaps an umbrella would be prudent. Around her neck she hung her home-made sandwich boards: STOP ARMING SAUDI WAR CRIMES IN YEMEN on her front and GIVE PEACE A CHANCE on the back. She almost forgot the music she could plug into her ears thanks to Jon and Amy's Christmas present. Bach would be necessary, bless him. She hoped Susanna would remember the face paint.

The journey to the Embassy was smooth as Lily felt a new kind of calm numb everything. A couple of young people approved with thumbs up and encouraging comments; most of her fellow-passengers ignored her until, as she sat between her last two tube stops, a smart and scented City type standing over her with a gleaming post-Gym face surprised her with, "What's that about then? A demo on a Tuesday?"

Lily told herself not to assume or judge. There was truth to serve regardless.

"I'm beginning a long-term protest today," she said, her voice sounding thin, as if her throat was already dry. "To call attention to the death of innocents. They call war business. I call it a crime."

"I'll look for you on the News then?" His chirpiness left her unsure how to react. "Good on ya."

The tube slowed at Green Park; she squeezed past him with her boards. Outside the Embassy she unfolded her chair and sat, adjusting the cushion. It was mid-morning coffee break time and the street was quiet. Lily avoided eye contact with the armed police. It had just started to drizzle when Susanna arrived in a rush, expertly face-painted her forehead with NIL BY MOUTH and propped up beside her a very artistic board that read ON HUNGER STRIKE UNTIL WE #STOPARMING SAUDI, in black letters that seemed to drip blood. She handed her some leaflets about the UK arms trade, and posted her first film on Facebook Live: "I'm here at the Saudi Embassy in London where Lily Partridge, aged 71, also known as the #ReggaeGran, has just begun a hunger strike in protest..." Lily stood and reminded her followers of her own personal dance style, then sat and watched the street until Susanna paused in her commentary to zoom in with her phone and ask, "How long will you go without food and water, Lily?"

"As long as it takes," she said.

Susanna talked about the closeness of the last vote in Parliament. She turned the phone to capture the Embassy in all its elegance, and the policemen on the pavement opposite. Then she kissed Lily's cheek and was gone, almost running, promising to be back. Lily hadn't brought her phone. It would soon run out of battery anyway. And if nobody shared or retweeted she didn't want to know. The rain was nothing; it had almost stopped. Bach's violin concerto soared inside her.

She had no watch either, because she didn't want to know how slowly time passed. The policemen crossed the street to ask what she was up to and how long she'd be there. She just smiled as beatifically as she could before lifting her eyes silently to the sky. Soon they swaggered heavily away. Sometime in the afternoon a group of young peace activists, most of them familiar faces, arrived with a camera on a tripod and interviewed her. Lily wished her brain would retain statistics but explained that all she held on to was the horror they left behind.

"How is this personal, Lily? How come you feel strongly enough to starve yourself?" the young man asked, the one who might have family somewhere in the world that rained British bombs.

"I have grandchildren," she said. "Because they were born in the UK they can play without being terrorised by warplanes. Or killed by our

70

weapons. The Yemeni children are my family too. I want all children to grow up in a better world."

Her supporters stayed a while; others came after work. Some passers-by stopped and chatted. More than one tried to bring her water. When Susanna returned after her shift to tell her she was famous on social media already and all over again, the light was dimming and the air full of food as she filmed again, asking whether Lily was hungry or thirsty.

"Hungry for peace," she said.

Susanna went without supper too, staying until dark, singing the songs Lily had sung at Aldermaston and Greenham Common, and dancing with her until Lily thought it best to conserve energy. They took turns to use the café toilet before it closed. Susanna read her the tweets of support. Then Lily unfolded her silver foil blanket over her shoulders the way Susanna told her to before she left. Lily closed her eyes, picturing Jude and Jon and her babies. She had slept by Mick's bed in the hospital for four nights before he died and practice always helped.

Wednesday woke her with early sunshine. Or maybe it was the traffic; London started early. Lily always liked a cup of tea in the morning as soon as she'd been to the bathroom. She didn't suppose the café was open yet for a wee so she'd have to test her bladder capacity. In her dream Mick had come to drag her home and feed her on chips but that wasn't fair; he'd respected her in his own non-verbal way, never really explaining why he didn't join her but never holding her back either. Still, she wouldn't be here if he was alive.

No sign of any TV camera crew. They were probably too busy covering the Kardashians or a feud between football managers. No good expecting the three thousandth Nigel Farage interview to be set aside for Lily Partridge. She used some lip balm to moisten her lips: a last-minute addition to her kit. Susanna had promised to find somewhere nearby where she could shower when it became necessary.

That afternoon some Quaker women from Hampstead held a Meeting for Worship around her, most of them seated silently on the ground. There were visits from large groups of students and representatives of various peace organisations she supported with membership. Al Jazeera came to cover the story, along with some other journalists she greeted warily. That evening the Standard and Metro both carried a picture of her; Susanna's friend Baz brought them to show her, reading the less-than-accurate text that went with the images, including a quote she was quite sure hadn't passed her lips. Baz said it was "all good" and she

71

agreed, although she wasn't sure how much longer she'd feel like dancing on cue.

"Oh and Suze said you should have a phone to call your family and she'll bring you one tomorrow."

"Please tell her not to," Lily told him as he hurried off.

Thursday brought blue sky, sunshine and the taste of pollution – although she supposed that was probably cumulative and her lungs might be a greyer shade of pink by now. A crew arrived from a French TV station, and she found that she'd lost her A Level French when she wasn't looking for it. By the time lunch was served in the cafés and restaurants around her, hunger had begun to gape inside her, but it was water she longed for more. When a brief shower broke into the blue she caught a few drops in her open mouth and tried to feel joy in them. But her lips remained just as crisp and sore after they'd dried like the neat grass vivid around the Embassy: innocent grass that moved her. She knew she was changing. Her bodily self felt less substantial, her balance when she stood subject to wavering. More Quakers came and 'held her in the Light' as the temperature rose, and a Methodist minister came to sit with her and be as gentle, Lily supposed, as hospices and funerals required. Again and again she was asked whether she had done enough, made her point, was ready to resume her life.

"Not yet," she told them all.

On Friday men swung jackets over shoulders and women bared their legs. The young people who positioned themselves for selfies with her wore sunglasses and smelt of sunblock. One was eating an ice-cream as she approached Lily, and stood struck by shame as she finished it before taking a step further. There were, she guessed, more journalists than ever, and someone familiar, who came with a fast-moving young crew, said he was from Channel Four. Lily was tired and no longer tried to find different words. She just focused on children – her babies and the victims of war. Her forehead was tight and her headache nauseous.

"Will it achieve anything, for all your courage and commitment, if you're taken off to hospital?" asked the presenter she'd always trusted to care.

"Will you ask the Foreign Secretary to come and see me?" she asked, leaning in to the microphone because her throat made talking hurt.

It wasn't supposed to happen so fast.

Dozens of supporters came to find her on Saturday. They sang the song she'd danced to at the climate march and tried, in a line, to emulate her moves. It made her smile until she thought her mouth would crack in her face. Susanna spent most of the weekend beside her, some of it fasting. She rolled cigarettes and talked about her relationship with Baz, which was more sisterly than he understood, and the way her father tried to tell her how to live. At the end of a narrative through childhood and teens that Lily found hard to process in sequence, she added, "He doesn't want me to be an accessory, aiding and abetting a suicide."

"You're not," Lily told her, wishing she could find more voice. "It's a campaign."

"I wish you were my mum," Susanna told her, "but if you were I'd cry and beg you to stop."

"I'm begging THEM to stop," said Lily.

Susanna said she'd set up a PO Box address so that people could write actual letters, since Lily chose not to read online messages. She remembered the phone she'd promised to bring, an old cheap one she'd used at the Arms Fair, with no Contacts list.

"Call your family, Lily," she said.

Lily shook her head. "I can't. I love them too much."

"Why aren't they here?" cried Susanna. "I don't get it."

Lily didn't like to see her upset. She touched her hand. "I'm glad they're not."

On her second Sunday, as the heat soared, she felt herself surrounded at times by prayer from different faith groups who held hands, and sometimes laid those hands on her shoulder or her head. She joined in with the Buddhist chant and some of the hymns but the group from the Mosque stayed longest and answered her questions with animation. Water was on all their lips. Fasting was one thing, but she must drink. Some quoted biological science. Lily just squeezed their blessing hands and smiled. Then some women of her age or more turned up with shampoo, a towel and an eco water bottle, and she leaned her head back over the edge of the chair, closed her eyes and felt like a child again as the scent of lemon filled her cool, wet head.

It was in the afternoon that through the heat haze she recognised two shapes advancing with purpose, banner-less and holding no placards. Jon and Jude were rarely together, just the two of them, and it pleased her to see them that way, Jon with his new, academic-style beard, and Jude neat enough for a christening with her lipstick and little heels.

"Mum," she said. "Please."

"This is ridiculous," said Jon. "Fatuous. Pointless."

If she'd had the strength she would have teased him about swallowing a Thesaurus. She held out her arms and they stooped to kiss her cheek but she felt the tightness in them. Glad that Susanna wasn't there to accuse and denounce, Lily explained that she was finding it hard to talk – leaving a gap they filled, in turn and overlapping. After a while she told them that she knew: all of it, every word. She had thought it all.

"Please understand. There is so little I can do. So I have to make the most I can of it."

She started to tell them about the petition for another vote in Parliament and protests planned for the next weekend outside Downing Street. The words trailed wispy into the street sounds when she needed them to be full-bodied and tall.

Jon cut her short: "We're your family, Mum, not BBC News."

They'd brought pictures of the children, just as she hoped and dreaded. Min was in a helmet on her bike, racing with hair splayed behind, light as candyfloss. This was making her sentimental...

"What if I called her now?" threatened Jude.

"She doesn't know?"

Jude didn't answer, or get out her phone. "How could I explain this? Tell me!"

"I want to stop children dying ..." Lily began.

"She'd want you to eat. Look at you! You're grey."

Lily could have joked that she was never an oil painting. She needed Bach now. This was so hard for them, and she'd always tried not to hurt them, even when hurting her was their teenage MO. She was glad to think of them eating bread, drinking coffee, breaking the juice out of an apple at first bite.

"I love you," she told them.

"Fuck's sake!" cried Jude. "We love you too."

That was the point at which Susanna arrived with a birthday pile of mail, some of it international, and a dozen friends, most of whom Lily had last seen escorted into a police van for blocking the road to the Arms Fair after she gave way. Lily felt herself giving way now, deep inside where the hunger had stopped being rage and lay subdued like a victim.

Where her voice could hardly break through without water to plump it, put flesh on its bones.

Lily reached out to her tall, solid children who said they would go now, but she didn't quite make contact with their arms. Watching them walk in step, she willed them to turn their heads, but they just shrank away.

Some of her visitors were regular. There was Cedric, with a wispy wizard beard that might have been smoke blown free by wind, and nun-like Eloise, who reminded Lily of Julie Andrews except that her short bob was purple. She spoke so softly that her voice became harder each day to trace. Ty was doing a PhD in Politics and Philosophy; his rhetoric was as fiery as his thick hair, but like a student who'd partied too late the night before, Lily found it hard to hold focus. She wondered how bad she smelt, but could no longer imagine leaving, or finding the strength to stand under a shower. Then, on the hottest day of all, Susanna brought a bucket of water from the café to baptise her fully-clothed, rubbed her dry with a beach towel and let the sun bake her dry again.

During the third week she had more time to meditate on the tree by her side and the birds in its branches. Time to dance in her head, or with her hands, to the music that was becoming part of her. Time to remember: school, and the CND logo she embroidered on her satchel; being snogged against her will by a boy at Youth Club outside a church hall; meeting Mick at a wedding and thinking how little he had to say for himself before she realised how much she wanted to hear what he thought; whole days and nights watching Jude sealed into a plastic cocoon that breathed into her tiny lungs – then carrying her home weighing less than a picnic, and feeling so afraid that she would be no better with this life in her care than with the plants that one after one, browned, shrank and desiccated. Deaths, too many of them, ordinary and shocking.

Susanna said it didn't look as if the Foreign Secretary was going to take time out of his busy schedule to meet her. The tweets were fewer by the day. Individuals came, and small groups, but now they meant not to support but to call for surrender. Lily thought she heard crying but perhaps it was just part of the dream.

Someone brought a doctor on a morning when the shakiness clouded everything, especially her words. Lily heard him, ghost-like, as if he had no body. As if she had no body.

Then she felt water shock her lips. Like an electric current it stiffened and jumped her in her chair, eyes wide.

"No!" She meant to spit but her mouth welcomed it. She spluttered. It might have been poison now. "Not water," she said. "Make them stop. Parliament. Enough."

Twenty-six days – before the hospital admission, the tea and biscuits. Because Lily hardly believed in them, Susanna had the total printed on a T-shirt for her. She was feted all over social media by the groups she followed, with lots of coloured hearts. Channel 4 wanted to feature her in a documentary but she said it wasn't about her. She was nobody. And nothing had changed. The petition for another vote to stop arming Saudi had reached half a million but she had to look away unless the hope took hold. Lily was ashamed how quickly she resumed normality, albeit with a stomach disinclined to forgive. Food became a ritual that, like the Eucharist, her spirit rejected – yet beautiful, a mystery, a gift. She swallowed thankfully, dismissing shame.

It was a while before she was trusted with Mondays again. The boys were unchanged. Sometimes the twenty-six days might have been a film watched through a veil. But then it seemed to her like birth: pain and doubt, and certainty and desperate faith. Except for the abortion at the end.

"Bony Grandma," said Dom on her lap, and stroked where her stomach used to curve.

Jude kept Min away for almost two months, and when the car pulled up outside Lily cried, rubbing her eyes dry with her pinny. Min was her Christmas self. From the kitchen window Lily could almost see the current fizzing around her as she jumped out and ran, the dahlias in her hand facing earth and forgotten. She hoped Min still loved scones, and the way they made the kitchen smell. As she hurried into the hall she heard fast feet thud down the path.

"Grandma!"

Lily opened the door and stretched out her arms to receive.

L - #0848 - 010221 - CO - 210/148/4 - PB - DID3014071